The Doukhobors, Their History in Russia, Their Migration to Canada

THE DOUKHOBORS

Their History in Russia
Their Migration to Canada

BY
JOSEPH ELKINTON

ILLUSTRATED WITH NUMEROUS PHOTOGRAPHS OF THE DOUKHOBORS AND THEIR SURROUNDINGS, WITH PORTRAITS AND MAPS.

Philadelphia
FERRIS & LEACH, PUBLISHERS
29-31 North Seventh Street
1903

173

Dedicated

TO THE MEMORY OF MY BELOVED FRIEND

JOHN BELLOWS

AND TO MY FATHER

JOSEPH S. ELKINTON

IN ACKNOWLEDGMENT OF HIS INVALUABLE SERVICES ON BEHALF OF THE DOUKHOBORS

The Doukhobors

COMMISSIONER WM. F. MCCREARY AND HIS WINTER CONVEYANCE FOR TRAVELING OVER THE NORTHWEST TERRITORIES ARRANGING FOR THE SETTLEMENT OF THE DOUKHOBORS.

Winter 1898–1899.

"Grandmother" Verigin and the Patriarch Ivan Mahortov.

See page 53.

CONTENTS.

ILLUSTRATIONS.

ILLUSTRATIONS.

ILLUSTRATIONS.

Doukhobor costume, showing prayer sash and marriage scarf. See page 45.

INTRODUCTION.

In his admirable history of "The Dutch and Quaker Colonies in America," John Fiske reviews the migrations during the past three centuries of religious sects from the continent of Europe to America. Had his book been withheld until a year later it might have recorded the arrival upon our shores of another persecuted people, in some respects the most remarkable of them all. Their fearful sufferings in Russia and Transcaucasia remind us of those endured by the Huguenots and Waldenses in France during the Seventeenth Century.

Many dissenters from the Russian Orthodox Church have been exiled to the Caucasus and Siberia within the past century because of their religious views. Among these the Doukhobors, or Spirit-Wrestlers, claim the special interest and sympathy of all who believe in the principle of non-resistance.

In this connection the words of Fiske, in his introduction to the chapter on "Penn's Holy Experiment," apply most appropriately: "A careful study of religious persecution shows us that sometimes politics, and sometimes religion, have been most actively concerned in it. The persecution of the Christians by the Roman emperors was chiefly political, because Christianity asserted a dominion over men paramount to that of the Emperor; while 'Let us get rid of the unclean thing lest we be cursed for its sake' has been the feeling which has mostly sustained persecution."

"In Christianity the separation of the Church from the State took its rise; and while religion was made an affair of mankind, not of localities or tribes, the importance of the individual has greatly increased. The moment we cease to regard religious truth as a rigid body of formulas, imparted to mankind once for all and incapable of further interpretation or expansion; the moment we come to look upon religion as a part of the soul's development, under the immediate influence of the Spirit of God; the moment we concede to individual judgment some weight in determining what the individual form of religious expression shall be, that moment we have taken the first step toward the conclusion that a dead uniformity of opinion in religious questions is undesirable. In the presence of an Eternal Reality which confessedly transcends our human comprehension in many ways, we are not entitled to frown or to sneer at our neighbor's view, but if we give it due attention, we may find in it more or less that is helpful and uplifting which we have overlooked."

Primarily this history of the Doukhobors was undertaken as an appeal for the Christian principle of peace,—a principle universal in its application, and sorely needed by the world to-day. The Doukhobors at this moment stand forth to the public mind as representing this principle. Indeed, these patient sufferers have adopted for themselves the name of "The Christian Community of the Universal Brotherhood," based upon Christ's command to love *all* men. And this command cannot be set aside as "impracticable," when the whole Christian Church sustained it inviolate for more than two centuries. "To the physical violence of the Romans the Early Christians opposed a strength of trust in God, an indifference to their personal fate, a purity of life, a love for their persecutors, and a willingness to suffer always as Christians,—not as law-breakers,—which gave their martyr blood that propagating power which made it 'the seed of the Church.' Thus the Church, by means of the passive virtues, won the first great victory for peace over the world's greatest military empire, which remains an unexplained miracle, unless we admit that the powers on which she relied are actually greater than those which the empire employed."*

If the professing followers of Christ had only continued such a warfare as this during the intervening centuries, their history would not have been written in the blood of their enemies, neither would we have had to-day so incongruous a spectacle as that of Buddhist priests appealing to Christian missionaries to regard the teachings of the Prince of Peace, when He declared that His kingdom was not of this world, and that *His* servants did not fight.

---

* Elbert Russell.

The name Doukhobór (*k* almost silent, and accent on last syllable) has come to designate the distinguishing characteristic of the people to whom it was originally given in derision.

This name has followed these dissenters from the Orthodox Russian Church since 1785. It was intended at first to distinguish them from those dissenters who especially objected to the use and worship of *icons*, or images, and who became known as Iconobors.

A Doukhobor (Spirit-Wrestler) was looked upon as one who wrestled against the Holy Spirit, whereas the Doukhobors themselves turned it into another meaning, and said it conveyed equally well the idea of wrestling by *aid* of the Holy Spirit, and not with carnal weapons.

The reader may notice that not much space is given to the discussion of the possible origin of this interesting people, because nothing is known about it with sufficient certainty to justify a positive statement. Several writers have elaborated various theories of their origin, but none of these have a reliable historic basis; and one might as well give the credit to the immediate effect of the Holy Spirit upon these untutored peasants, as to suppose that this or the other human influence must necessarily be found to account for the rapid spread of their peculiar religious opinions in the latter half of the eighteenth century.

The same thing has occurred time and again during the history of the Christian Church. The sudden appearance of the Montanists* of the second century and the Pietists of the seventeenth century are only similar illustrations.

But wherever and whenever such a people arise they bring with them the refreshing breezes of a spiritual atmosphere, and protest with an unmistakable emphasis against the deadening effect of outward ceremonies. The deepest cry of our own and every age has been for spiritual freedom, and He who declared Himself to be "the way, and the truth, and the life" answered that cry when He said, "God is spirit, and they that worship Him must worship

---

* "The Montanists asserted the priestly dignity of all Christians, and consequently that the gifts of the Spirit are not confined to one order in the church, or even to one sex; and they would not allow that the gift of prophecy had been superseded by learning and an enlightened intellect.

"In opposition to the notion that the bishops were the sole successors of the Apostles they denied that any who have not received the spirit of prophecy from the Holy Ghost himself can be the successors of the Apostles or heirs to their spiritual power; and they repudiated the false idea that holiness of life is to be looked for in the clergy in another manner or in a higher degree than in the laity.

"They made a vigorous stand also against the spirit of accommodation to the world which was creeping over the Church, and notwithstanding the laws against private assemblies, in their meetings for fasting and prayer they disregarded such prudential measures as might avert the suspicion of the authorities. They even went so far as to condemn all usages of civil and social life which could in any way be traced to a heathen origin."—"Early Church History," Backhouse and Tyler, pages 97, 98.

Him *in spirit* and with *true spiritual insight*,"* as also, "If the *truth* shall make you free, *then* are you free indeed."

The Doukhobors are a peculiar people in many respects, possessed of high Christian ideals, but needing a certain education to correlate these ideals with those of their present surroundings. This education must proceed, however, on lines in harmony with their religious ideals, as will be discussed in the chapter on "The Problem of their Education and Training."

The Doukhobors have suffered so much for their faith during the past century and a half that they seem to have accepted persecution as the natural and historic condition of their lives, which they were destined always and everywhere to experience. They have even considered their sect to be an elect generation descended from the three lads who were cast into the burning furnace of Nebuchadnezzar, and surely they have survived the fires of State and Church vengeance remarkably well, whatever may have been their faults.

A century ago many of them were settled in a province of the Crimea, separated from the rest of Russia by desert steppes. But this settlement was ruthlessly broken up about 1842, and they were forcibly transported to the Caucasus, and eventually scattered among Georgians, Armenians, Circassians,

* Twentieth Century New Testament.

Tartars, etc., without, however, destroying their internal organization,—an individual theocratic community, living its own life and paying tribute only to the Czar. Thus surrounded, they formed themselves into a kingdom of peasants, while the weaknesses, corruptions and negligence of the Caucasian administration only strengthened the Doukhobors in their own opinions.

The loftiness of their moral opinions, the foundation of which is the negation of violence, their power to endure, their sober and laborious life, proved to them a veritable "shield of faith" and gave them the esteem of others.

At the close of the eighties two parties unhappily divided the ranks of their Brotherhood,—one willing to compromise with the government about military service, while the other grew still more severe in its regulations. The second was much in the majority (eight thousand out of a total of twelve thousand), and this larger party adopted three new principles, having, it is true, connection with their ancient doctrine, but which until then had not been completely formulated. These three principles are: Internationalism, communism and vegetarianism.

The new movement had been conducted largely by Peter Verigin, their youthful leader, and some other men who enjoyed the unlimited confidence of their party. In 1886 the Russian Government snatched these chiefs from the midst of their brethren and deported them to a place of exile within the Arctic circle. But the seed which they had sown could not be so easily removed, and the movement continued to go forward. In the course of ten years the Russian Government made a yet more determined effort to get rid of these persistent dissenters. But to destroy thousands of such stalwart men and women was not easier than to hide "a city set upon the mountain top." However, their condition was pitiable in the extreme when Count Tolstoi and the Society of Friends in England came to their relief by raising funds for their emigration to Canada, the story of which is told more at length in the second part of this volume.

The chapter on "Relations with the Civil Authorities" will probably reveal some difficulties with which the Dominion government has had to deal that were not generally known even to those who have been interested in the Doukhobors. That these difficulties have shown the Brotherhood in an unfavorable light may be frankly admitted, yet it was thought wiser bravely to face those truths which could not, in fairness to historical facts, be ignored.

The shortcomings revealed by the regrettable position which a portion of the Doukhobors have taken are manifestly mental rather than moral, and this knowledge should be an additional incentive to their friends to hasten the work for their education. It was very apparent to the writer that these long-persecuted peasants were going through a critical period of social and civil adjustment, and that their attitude toward the civil authorities, however illogical at present, gave evidence of a strength of purpose which promised good citizenship when once they became enlightened in regard to their privileges under that government.

It has been my desire to point out what these martyrs for a principle have stood for through a century of persecution, and what I am sure they still wish to stand for, however much their ignorance and fanaticism may have exposed them to misunderstanding. Acknowledging that we are all human and that the beam of self-complacency might well be removed from our own eye before we aspire to take the mote of ignorance from that of our brother, I would frankly confess to what these untutored men and women have taught me:

First, that no outward disadvantage can prevent the truest affection from revealing the universal Fatherhood of God, and from manifesting the meaning of that great commandment, "That ye love one another, even *as* I have loved you";

Second, that the essential things of life are very few and simple, and that just so far as we seek to minister to these fundamental necessities we secure both our own and our brother's happiness;

Last, but not least, that divine truth is frequently so associated with human error, even in the most devout minds, that we shall always need to separate and to cherish the spiritual purpose and ideal, apart from its expression, which is so often overlaid with useless forms and traditions.

ACKNOWLEDGMENTS.

P. Birukov, a Russian sympathizer, has studied the Doukhobors carefully, and added the latest valuable contribution to their history, "Tolstoi et les Doukhobors," translated by J. W. Bienstock into the French). I would express my obligation to him for much that is interesting and helpful in our common effort to educate this worthy, though peculiar, people, and to my friend Jane W. Bartlett for giving me access through the French to his compilation of facts and suggestions.

In like manner I am indebted to V. Tchertkov for his kindness in forwarding T. Abramov's translation of "Orést Novitsky's History of the Doukhobors,"—the most reliable work on the subject for over sixty years,—originally published in the Russian about 1832; as also for the use I have made of his "Christian Martyrdom in Russia" (1897). This book was written at the time of their most severe persecutions, and probably did much to arouse the interest of the English-speaking public to assist in the escape of the Doukhobors from their persecutors in the Caucasus.

To Aylmer Maude I would likewise express my obligation for the use of his chapter on "The Doukhobors" in "Tolstoi and His Problems," and to Joseph Barcroft for his admirable sketch of the Doukhobors in *The Friends' Quarterly Examiner*, Fourth month, 1900, as also to John Ashworth, of Manchester, England. My friend William Bellows kindly gave me the use of some of his photographs, taken when with the Doukhobors about the time they were first settling in America; and his late beloved father contributed much information which had been gathered from the State archives in St. Petersburg, and in many ways assisted me. It was his self-sacrificing and sympathetic efforts which first introduced me to the needs of the Doukhobors. The manuscripts and other collections of my father have also been helpfully placed at my disposal.

When this labor of love was begun, more than two years ago, without any literature or written records of the Doukhobors to guide me, it truly seemed like making "bricks without straw," but as these bricks have been twice "sun-burnt" by the rays of love and persistent effort, they are offered for what purpose they may serve.

It was my hope to meet or communicate with their leader, Peter Verigin, as I could not read his published letters, some two hundred and seventy-five in number, in the Russian. Thus I wrote to him in 1900, he being then in Siberian exile; but such is the censorship of the mail in that land that his reply had to come from Canada. I had hoped to hear directly from him since his arrival in America, and the publication of this volume has been delayed a few weeks in the hope that I might be able to share his opinions with my readers. His mother writes, after receiving information about his arrival in England, *en route* to America: "From such a joy I forgot about all my suffering and old age. I thank God for His mercy, and as after a long and stormy night, which burdened my soul for over fifteen years, now I am waiting for the bright and joyful sunrise, which will give warmth to my soul and heart-delight; the break of day has shown itself, and the light is not far. I am waiting with impatience for that day in which I shall see my son. Even now it is in my mind, as though I were realizing my meeting with him."

The historical chapters on the Russian nation were added to supply a background to the picture of the dissenting peasantry of that country—of which the Doukhobors are a small though important part.

The reader will have a better understanding of the recent fanatical outbreaks by taking this glimpse at the past. For instance, the present communal life of the Doukhobors is but an unconscious inheritance from the mediæval city guild, and the folkmote of later date. The Council of Florence once issued a manifesto expressing exactly the same spirit as that which the Doukhobors in Canada expressed to me repeatedly, viz.: "No work shall be done in the Commune but what is conceived in response to the grand heart of the Commune, made up of the hearts of all the citizens—*united in one common mind.*"

Such standard works as Wallace's "Russia" and Edmund Noble's "Russia and the Russians," with Kovalevsky's "Russian Political Institutions," have been consulted, as also "Russia in the Nineteenth Century," "Alexander I." and "Alexander III."

The influence of the Society of Friends with Alexander I. is told by Jane Benson in her pleasing narrative, "Quaker Pioneers in Russia," Headley Brothers, London.

All the profits from the sale of this volume will go toward supporting a school among the Doukhobors in Canada. If the reader can reap any part of the benefit which has come to me in the writing of these pages, it will be some compensation for the difficulties that have unavoidably delayed their publication.

J. E.

MEDIA, PENNSYLVANIA,
Second month, 1903.

The Doukhobors in Canada.

(1) (2) (3)

(1) Joseph Elkinton. (2) Eliza H. Varney.
(3) J. Obed Smith, Commissioner of Immigration.

CHAPTER I.

PERSONAL EXPERIENCES OF THE AUTHOR WHILE VISITING THEIR COMMUNITIES.

The untiring devotion of my father, Joseph S. Elkinton, to these Russian peasants, has stimulated my interest in them since their arrival in America. During the summer of 1902 I visited several of their villages in the Prince Albert and Yorkton colonies, and came to know the people and their surroundings quite intimately. One can scarcely imagine a more novel and interesting experience, or one more likely to expand the sympathies, than this trip afforded. The warm, personal interest in these people which has been awakened in me by actual contact with them I would be glad to communicate to others, and for this reason I make my narrative a closely personal one, hoping that my readers may feel, in some degree, as if they had traveled with me to the homes of these Doukhobors, had shared with me their truly oriental hospitality, and had felt, as I did, their truly Christian kindness of heart.

Much has been published of late that greatly misrepresents the majority of their communities. Several hundred of the Yorkton colonists, who number 5,500 in all, have been deluded by a religious fanatic, —not originally of their communion,—who has posed as a prophet, and has taught that the use of animals as beasts of burden is unscriptural, and that Jesus would soon come again in person.

As there were only 285 cows, 120 horses and 95 sheep liberated by the Doukhobors, and sold by government agents to prevent irresponsible persons from capturing them, it is evident that no considerable part of the forty-seven villages near Yorkton were involved in this craze. Each village has a hundred or more cattle; and the Doukhobors bought back all these liberated animals at the sale.

The pilgrimage was a more serious affair, and was happily brought to an end by the government officials before there were many fatalities from exposure. Several hundred men, women and children marched thirty or forty miles to Yorkton "in search of Jesus." The women and children were detained by the authorities at that place, being housed and fed by the English-speaking residents, while the men went on to Minnedosa, some 150 miles toward Winnipeg. Here they were put upon a special train by the Superintendent of Immigration, Frank Pedley, and Colonization Agent Charles Spiers, taken back to Yorkton, and so returned to their homes.

The sixteen hundred Saskatchewan Doukhobors have taken no part whatever in these foolish acts, and the large majority of those about Yorkton very much disapproved of them. The newspaper press has, by its exaggerated accounts of these matters and misleading comments thereon, done great injustice to the Universal Brotherhood. Probably one of the

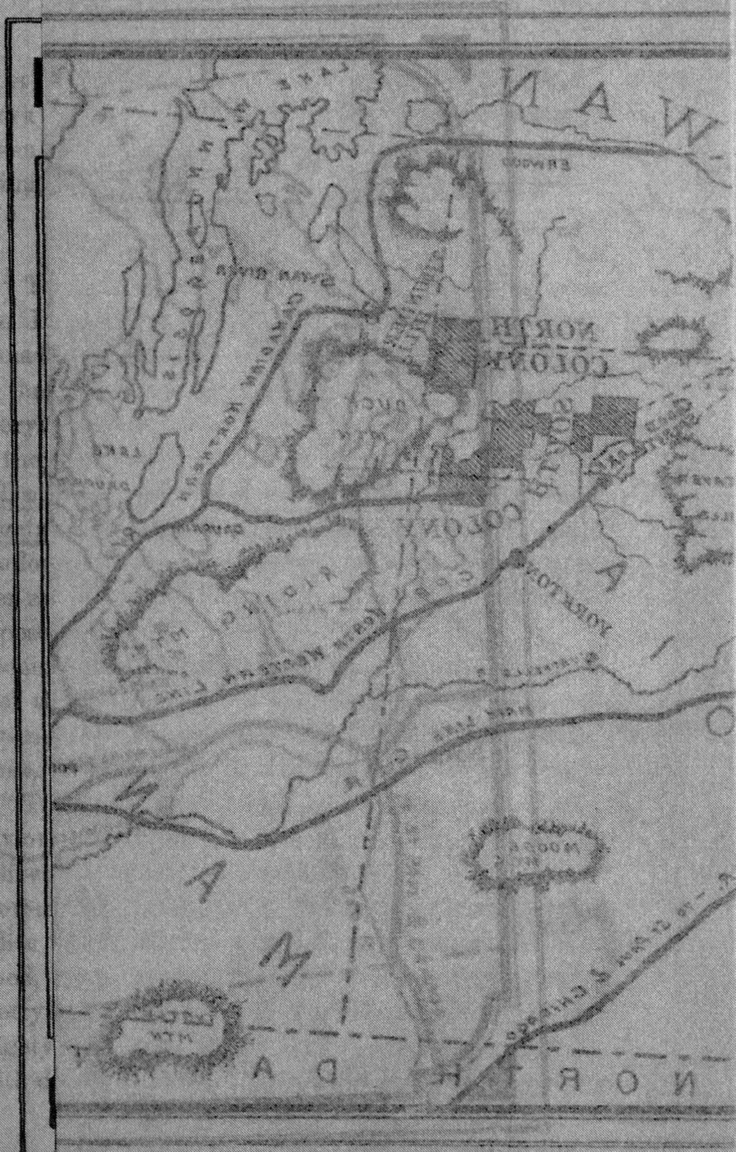

...r Settlements in the Northwest Territories.

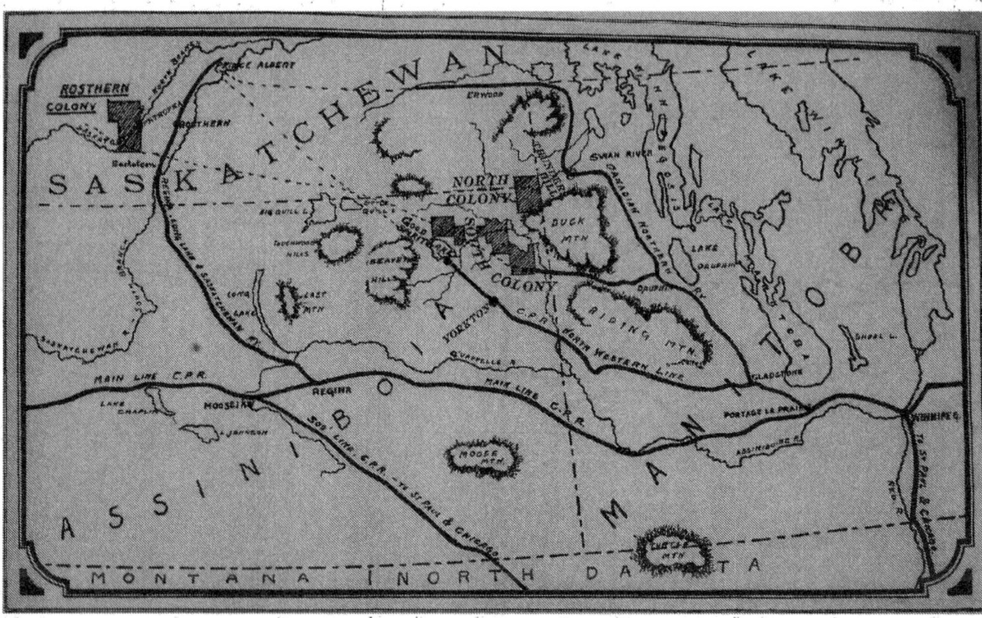

Doukhobor Settlements in the Northwest Territories.

most accurate of these reports appeared in *The* (New York) *World* of Eleventh month 9th, 1902, and is given in full as a fair statement of this unusual pilgrimage.

ON THE TRAMP WITH THE DOUKHOBORS.

"The strange outbreak of religious mania among the Doukhobors of the Northwest Territories of Canada has aroused widespread interest, not merely in the Dominion, but throughout America. People everywhere are talking of these 'Spirit-Wrestlers,' as they call themselves; these men who will not fight, will not work nor use horses nor cattle, who are strict vegetarians, and who follow to their farthest limit the logical conclusions of their beliefs. Six hundred men and boys have been marching through Manitoba, exposed to all the inclemency of the winter season, sleeping on the snow-covered prairie, with no other roof than the sky, with insufficient clothing, wholly dependent for their food on the charity of the residents.

"They were looking for the second coming of the Saviour. Jesus is to reveal Himself to them, they believe; is to be reincarnated, to meet them on the snow-mantled prairie and lead them forth to evangelize the world. He was to have met them at Millwood, according to their avowed expectation—a pretty little village, perched on the steep banks of the mighty Assiniboine—but though He came not, their faith did not falter. He simply tarried to try them.

Now they are sure He will appear in Winnipeg, the capital city of Manitoba, which they expected to reach by the 15th.

"The Doukhobors live in communities. They hold property in common. Tracts of land have been reserved for them by the Dominion Government. Some of these communities are located north of Yorkton, and others near Rosthern and Prince Albert, in the Northwest Territories. Smaller colonies are to be found in the vicinity of Swan River, in Manitoba. Three months ago a religious agitation broke out among the Yorkton and Swan River colonies. They refused to work their horses, or to milk their cows, turning them loose on the prairie. They refused to wear anything that had an animal origin; they discarded their leather boots and wore rubbers. They would not eat butter, eggs, or indeed any article of food connected however remotely with an animal.

"To the number of 1,700 (?) men, women and children they marched into Yorkton, bent on a pilgrimage to evangelize mankind. They were met by the Dominion immigration officials, and the women and children, after some little resistance, were compelled to accept shelter and food. The men, to the number of six hundred, marched away to the East, leaving comfortable homes, stocked with food for two or three years, and wives and children, to wander, they knew not where, till they should meet the Lord.

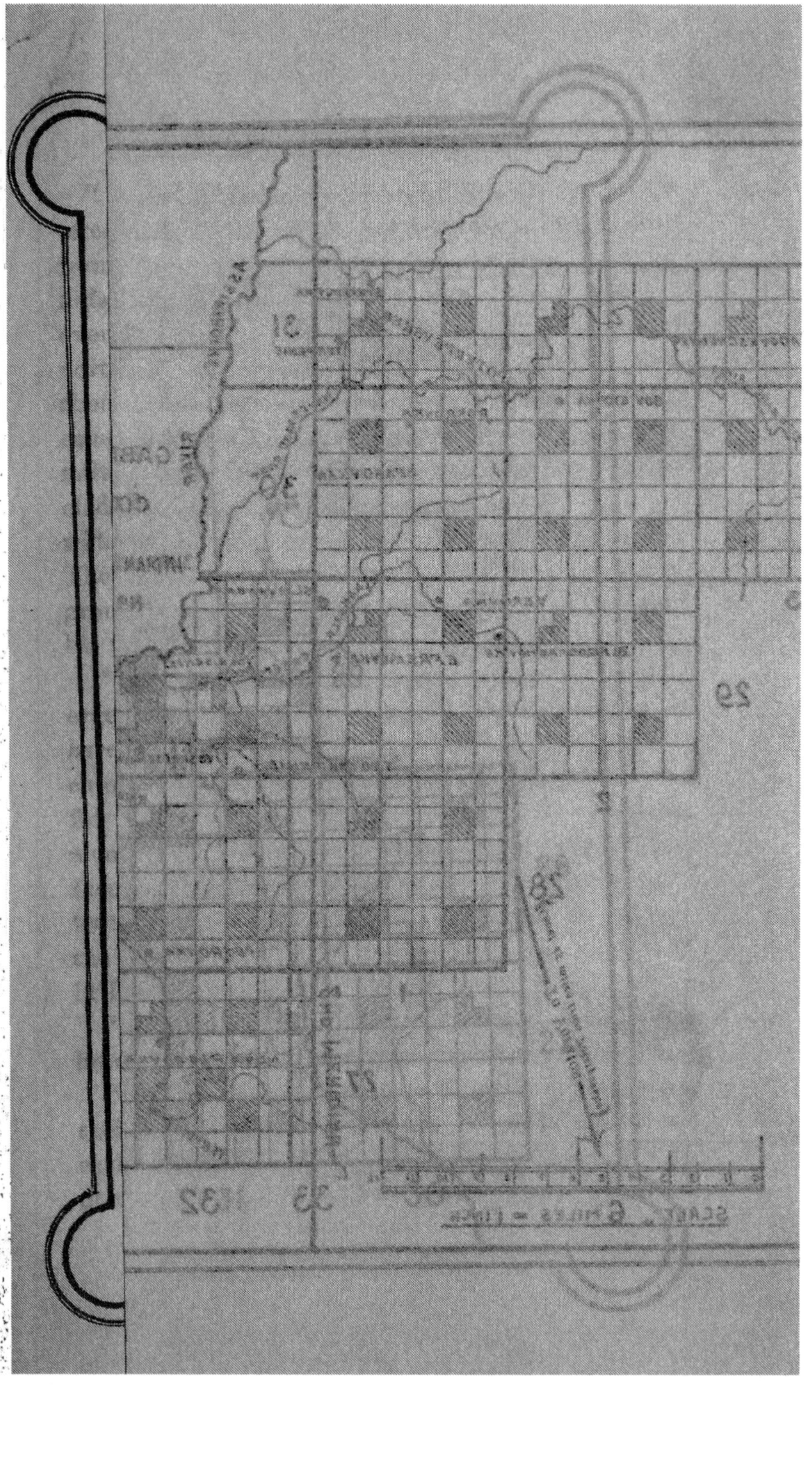

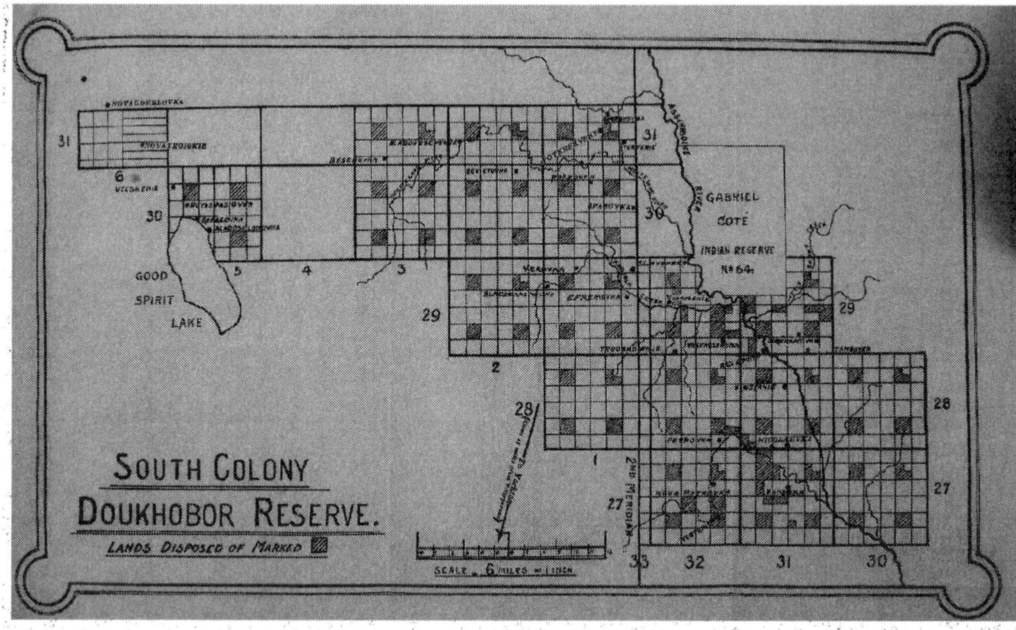
SOUTH COLONY
DOUKHOBOR RESERVE.
LANDS DISPOSED OF MARKED
GOOD
SPIRIT
LAKE
GABRIEL
COTÉ
INDIAN RESERVE
No 64
2ND MERIDIAN
SCALE 6 MILES = 1 INCH
31
6
30
5
4
3
2
1
29
28
27
33
32
30

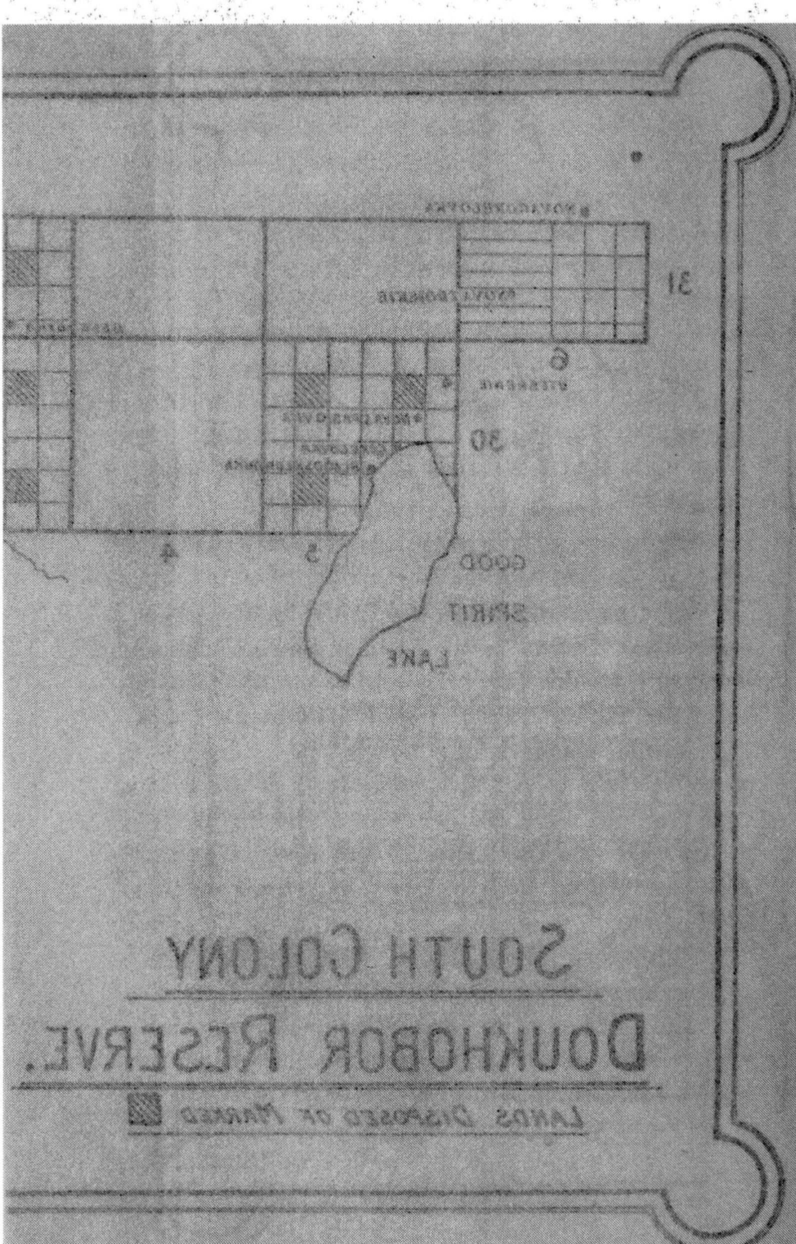
31
6
30
4
5
GOOD
SPIRIT
LAKE
SOUTH COLONY
DOUKHOBOR RESERVE.
LANDS DISPOSED OF MARKED

"This pilgrimage naturally evoked widespread interest in all classes of people, and, to gather some information regarding the motives, intentions and beliefs of the Doukhobors, I went up to meet them. I overtook them at Binscarth, a little village on the northwest branch of the Canadian Pacific Railway, about two hundred miles from Winnipeg. They came straggling into the town in a procession two miles long. Picturesque figures they were, mostly clad in blue, and with gaudily-colored scarfs. The wide, flaring skirts of their coats were kilted behind. Though the snow lay three inches deep on the ground, fully a score were barefoot. More than double that number were hatless.

"In front strode a majestic figure, black as Boanerges, and with a voice like a bull of Bashan. He was barefoot. On his head was a brilliant red handkerchief, and his body was clothed in a long, dusty white felt mantle, reaching almost to his feet. He strode along at the head of the procession. Suddenly his face began to work, his eyes to roll and his hands to twitch, and in a few moments he began to jump in the air, clutching with his hands and shrieking aloud in Russian:

"'I see him! I see Jesus! He is coming! He is here now, my brothers! You will see Him soon!'

"The long cortège stood stone still. Straining their eyes to catch the beatific vision, they talked to each other a while, during which their leader calmed down to a state of almost torpor, from which he, without a moment's warning, aroused himself to another religious frenzy.

"The Binscarth people gave them food—dry oatmeal, which they poured in little heaps on blankets, half a dozen pilgrims helping themselves from each heap. The meal was preceded by their favorite chant from the 8th chapter of Romans, and by the repetition in unison of prayer. Then the pilgrims sat in parallel lines and ate oatmeal dry from the sack. This, with bread, apples and the dried rose-buds picked from the prairie rosebushes, formed their menu.

"After the meal, which lasted about an hour, they repaired to the back yards of the residences, and for a quarter of an hour the pumps were worked without cessation to satisfy their thirst. An hour afterward the procession was formed, and the eastward journey resumed.

"I walked with them for the next eleven miles, conversing with different members of the pilgrim army. Knowing no Russian, I had perforce to talk only to those who could speak English. They do not themselves admit that they have any leaders. As we talked, a crowd pressed around us, eager to hear the discussion. My questions were translated into Russian for the benefit of the pilgrims not speaking English, and before Vassili Konkin, who acted the part of interpreter, replied, the answer was often the subject of some minutes' argument and deliberation.

"I introduced myself as one who desired to know

the reason of their wandering at this inclement season, in order that I might explain to all who read newspapers the motives prompting their pilgrimage. They all expressed their pleasure at seeing me, raising their hats, such of them as use them, with the courtesy innate to the Russians. They said they were glad to explain their beliefs to any one, much more to one 'who had many mouths'—indicating their appreciation, I supposed, of the power of the press.

"We walked along in silence for a while, until at last Konkin said:

"'We go to tell the peoples; is that not good, yes? What for Jesus come first time? To live good life, to teach peoples how to live. We try live like He lives—go to the peoples and teach them, and tell *them* He comes.'

"'But why did you start at the beginning of the winter? Why not wait till next spring? Then it will be warm and sunny. Now, if you go on and sleep on the snow, many of you must die.'

"'Jesus Christ, He say people must think of Jesus to-day. To-morrow God will see. He make cold warm. If not, He make us strong to bear cold. If we die, we see Him soon.'

"'But others of your people, Vassili, do not think as you do. They think you very foolish in this matter.'

"'Yes, that is so,' replied Konkin. 'But he see the light soon. In old days people think Jesus foolish. They laugh at Him, yes; they nailed Him to cross, and He die, and for long time men laugh and say, "How foolish! Him fool." Same way apostles. Peoples call them all fool, and none believe them. Some day, may be after we die, people say, "Doukhobor right," and they believe us. May be we no see Jesus yet; no, but we tell the peoples, and we see Him when we die. More soon we dies more soon we see Him.

"'God is necessary, but government—no. We wait till Jesus comes, then He take the bad people off the ground. When He come, then bad man trouble no more.

"'The Lord says, peoples not get rich—Jesus tell every one not get rich here, but to get rich in sky. If all poor, nobody would steal and be bad. If all poor, all good.

"'Peoples say, "You must come back and live on farms." God say, "Can't work for two boss." If live on farm and work for myself, me like me more than God and for God do nothing. If I like God for boss, I go out and walk and tell all the peoples.'

"I had told them that I had a two-year-old daughter, and Konkin was greatly interested.

"'What you teach your little girl?' he asked. 'What you give her to eat?'

"When I had told him he shook his head disappointedly.

"'Should no eat meat,' he said. 'The living should not live on the living.'

"'And you don't work your horses, either?' said I. 'Didn't God send them here for us to use?'

"'You like to work you?' he asked. 'How you like put in plough, wagon, beaten with stick, eh? No; God He say be kind to cattle, to all things; so we no work them.'

"'But, if the cattle are not to be used, why were they made?'

"'They made to look at, to make us glad when we see—like the grass, the flowers.'

"It was long past dusk. The sun had dipped behind dusky bars of orange and crimson, and gray, mysterious shadows crept across the prairie. Darkness closed down on the earth. Ahead could be seen the twinkling lights of the hamlet of Foxwarren, a score of dwellings and stores scattered around an elevator and the railway station. The snow began to fall in light flakes. The pilgrims halted and made their pitifully inadequate preparations for camping. With their hands they tore up some long grass to serve as beds. From their pouches each took a handful of dry oatmeal and munched it. Some scattered in the darkness to hunt for the dried fruit of the rosebush. With no shelter, under the open sky, they lay down on the snowy prairie, wearied with their twenty-mile tramp. Before flinging themselves down, they sang a psalm and quoted Scripture verses responsively, standing meanwhile with bare heads while the snow fell quietly over them.

"Then they gathered about me to say good-by. I must have shaken hands with two hundred of them.

"'You will tell the people what we say?' asked Konkin.

"I promised. Vassili looked at me sorrowfully, patted me affectionately on the shoulder and gave me a word of parting counsel.

"'We all of us wish,' he said, 'that you may see the light. We wish you not to smoke, not to work for money. Do not make it hell for self there'—pointing to my breast—'make it heaven. We love you much. We tell Jesus to come for you. Good-night!'

"As I turned to go several came up and asked me to read certain portions of Scripture. I noted down by the light of a match the following: Luke 12, Matthew 25, Romans 8 (their favorite chapter), Matthew 10, and Ephesians 6. Then, followed by many more 'good-nights' in Russian, I set out to walk to Foxwarren. As I neared the comfortable dwelling where I was to spend the night, I thought of those misguided pilgrims lying shelterless on the prairie, exposed to the rigors of a Manitoba winter. They have certainly forsaken all to follow their Lord, and, however their actions and beliefs may fail to harmonize with prevailing religious thought, none can deny the sincerity of these pilgrims."

start

How inexpressibly pathetic! Especially when one can recall their honest faces and many kindnesses. One is reminded of the Crusaders and of dancing dervishes in such an account, but it is only an exhibition of the character of the untutored Russian peasant, temporarily excited by religious enthusiasts. Dr. J. T. Reid, of Winnipeg, who is thoroughly acquainted with the Doukhobors, and was familiar with the facts of this migration, gave his opinion of these over-zealous pilgrims in *The Montreal Weekly Witness* of Tenth month 6th, 1902, as follows:

"We do not censure the Puritans as a class because there were many religious fanatics amongst them. To censure the Doukhobors just because a minority of them are religious enthusiasts is as unjust as the Doukhobors themselves are in judging all Canadians by the more uncivilized minority of our people whom they occasionally see on the frontiers of our civilization in the West. To censure them as a people on account of the fanaticism of their minority is as illogical as it were to class the whole American people with those who follow Dowie and Mrs. Eddy.

"In the West there are six classes of men who have at all times seemed to glory in the abuse of the Doukhobors:

"1. The politician of a certain school, whose political game is 'to get in,' and who makes political capital out of every opportunity 'to get the other fellow out.'

"2. The rancher, who wants the whole earth within the bounds of his own ranch.

"3. The class who cannot appreciate the high moral tone of the Doukhobors, and therefore look upon them as hypocrites.

"4. A fourth class who are so narrowly sectarian that they are unable to see any good outside the pale of their own particular creed.

"5. A fifth class whose grasping propensities in the West are being daily put to shame by the more Christian brotherly kindness of the Doukhobor, to whom Christianity is nothing if it do not include the love of neighbor.

"6. Some of the most unjust things said against them have been said by disappointed would-be missionaries, who thought the Doukhobors were spiritually benighted and were anxious to enlighten them. . . .

"Just as every Anglo-Saxon 'craze' runs its course, declines and disappears, so will it be with this fanatical exuberance of the Doukhobortsi."

Indeed, that the craze very rapidly passed its height, and began to decline, is shown by the following extract from the *Manitoba Free Press*, Eleventh month 21st, 1902:

"Mr. C. W. Spiers, colonization agent of the Dominion government, returned Wednesday from Yorkton, driving through the Doukhobor settlements as far as Fort Pelly, where he was met by Agent Harley, of the Swan River district. 'The Doukhobors,' said Mr. Speers, 'have returned to their re-

FRANK PEDLEY.
Supt. of Immigration, Ottawa.

C. W. SPIERS.
General Colonization Agent.

spective villages, and are again occupying their former homes. Their houses were in perfect readiness to receive them. Ample clothing was carefully piled up in the corner, and things set in order, previous to these people starting on their pilgrimage. The villages are well supplied with roots and vegetables, and these have been protected by the department from frost during the absence of the people. In fact, I had arranged some time ago for everything of a perishable nature to be protected. The villages are also well supplied with grain, consisting of wheat, oats and barley, and a quantity of flax. There is yet some threshing to do, and a number of grist mills that have been built by this community are in operation.

"'These people will require very little to support them for six months, and they are at present consuming their own products. There is a greater spirit of contentment than I expected to find, and a great majority of the returned pilgrims will again assume the duties of life along right lines.

"'I was informed that they purchased nine pairs of horses at Pelly on their return journey, which would go to prove that they are moving in the right direction. They met rather a cool reception from their brethren who remained and were not affected by the mania. This is having a good effect, because it must be remembered that only about twenty per cent. of these people were affected. I have been having officials take an inventory of all ascertainable property, and find the villages in a most satisfactory condition as far as supplies are concerned. The pilgrims feel that their missionary work was not a success, and I think I can safely say that eighty per cent. of the younger men are impressed with the necessity of commencing to work. I met a few who still want to preach, and there are a few leaders who will possibly keep up an agitation for a time, but it would be a difficult undertaking for any set of men to conduct such a movement again. I consider the situation highly satisfactory, and that the great majority of these people will be saved to the labor market of Canada, and make useful settlers.

"'The influence of the Doukhobors who remained at home is constantly working in the right direction. There has been considerable outside influence brought to bear upon these people, and some are remaining among them to advise them. As to how successful these influences may be, I cannot say. I am led to believe that these people should be let alone for a time, as they have had sufficient excitement. I have observed that in Saskatchewan, where we have sixteen hundred of these people, they are considered good settlers, are in a state of perfect contentment, and have had no one among them giving any special advice.'"

This excitement has brought the whole Brotherhood into discredit in the view of those who are not personally acquainted with their many sterling qual-

PHOTOGRAPHED BY JOSEPH ELKINTON.

COPYRIGHT, 1903, BY JOSEPH ELKINTON.

Group of Immigrants in Yard of Immigration Hall.

ities, but the Canadian Government has shown its liberal policy, and the humane action of its officials throughout these disturbing outbreaks has been most commendable.*

Indeed, it was one of the privileges of my late visit to the Northwest Territories to converse with these officers, who have had so many perplexing problems to solve in connection with the colonization work of the Dominion. This has embraced many nationalities within a few years.

All these immigrants come to Winnipeg, as the distributing center for Western Canada, to ascertain their ultimate location. Thus the Immigration Hall in that city was a place of peculiar interest to me, and a whole week was spent in studying the character of those who gathered in and about it.

The group near the front door are Swedes who had just arrived from their native land to try their fortunes in America. It was in this building that eight

---

* The Commissioner of Immigration, J. Obed. Smith, stated the position of the present administration since these disturbing actions on the part of the Doukhobors have claimed so much public attention, in "The Manitoba Morning Free Press" of Ninth month 23d, 1902, as follows: "The Doukhobors have been dealt with from the standpoint that they would and do form a most valuable acquisition to Canada, and are much-needed settlers of our vacant lands. To those who are disposed to criticise the presence of the Doukhobors I would say, that the sociological condition of these people (except the few who have imbibed strange notions) before coming to Canada, and now, must be taken into consideration, and results will prove from that standpoint alone the real value to the country of the Community of Christian Brotherhood, as the Doukhobors delight to call themselves."

hundred Doukhobors were temporarily housed and fed three years ago, and the testimony of their caretakers was very pleasing, as both the janitor and the matron told me they had never before had such a clean and orderly lot of people to provide for. The group in the yard is made up of four Galician women, two Germans from Russia (with bread under their arms), two Doukhobor men (with broad-brimmed hats), and a few Canadians. It was in this yard that I met forty or more Doukhobors who were seeking work in Winnipeg. An honest-faced youth of twenty at once attracted me, and it was pleasant to talk to him in English, and to learn that he bore the name of his uncle, Peter Verigin.

These Doukhobors assembled in the Immigration Hall on the first day of the week to recite their hymns and go through the Sunrise Service. This is always accompanied by the greatest seriousness of manner, and one can but be impressed with their sincerity and love one for another. A week later I witnessed this ceremony in their Saskatchewan settlement and photographed the scene in front of a granary. The men were mostly absent, working on the railroad, and this accounts for the greater number of women present at the "service." The boy is bowing to all the women in this group. Each man bows three times, kisses each of the other men once, and then bows once to all the women, to which they respond collectively by a bow. The women also bow and kiss each other as the men do. Finally, all the

"Sunrise Service."

men and all the women bow at the same time, bringing their foreheads to the ground in true oriental fashion. All this is accompanied by a united chanting of their sacred hymns, and is preceded by the recitation of portions of the scriptures, or of some prayer in ritualistic form.

This service began at four a.m. and continued until six o'clock. The early hour was originally chosen so as to escape persecution by their enemies in Russia, and they quite agreed with me in thinking that the meeting might now be held a little later in the day, as that necessity no longer exists. They always gave opportunity for remarks by the visitors, and listened most respectfully to what was said to them. Their patriarch, Ivan Mahortov, was present at the third sunrise service I witnessed, in which twelve men and thirty-six women took part, and he turned round at the conclusion and explained their belief with great dignity and clearness. My interpreter said he recited some Greek Church hymns dating back to 400 A.D., and even included the Virgin Mary in the summing up of their creed. Such is the force of early associations!

After the "service" in the Immigration Hall, we had a Molokan (a Russian sect in many respects similar to the Doukhobors), who entered heartily into sympathy with the occasion, to interpret for my father and myself; and we found that these Doukhobors had some wrong ideas about the Canadian Government, which we endeavored to correct. A bright little girl interpreted for the few Doukhobor women present.

From Winnipeg we went on to Rosthern, the nearest railway station to the Saskatchewan colony. This journey of five hundred and seventy-five miles was comfortably accomplished in twenty-four hours. To travel whole days with few human habitations in sight, and scarcely a fence or a tree, might have a depressing effect if it were not for the beautiful prairie flowers and occasional antelopes that can be seen from the train window. Yet there is endless entertainment in traveling on the Canadian Pacific Railway if one studies and sympathizes with the various classes of travelers. There are almost always four or five colonists' coaches on a train, in addition to the tourists' and Pullman cars.

At least half a dozen nationalities were represented on our train, and some of these representatives were going to their new homes on the prairie. On one journey of three hundred miles we had as fellow travelers a party of Welsh people who had just arrived from Patagonia, where they had lived twelve years. The children spoke Spanish, and had forgotten what English they had once known, which the parents regretted. The name of John Evans was evidence of their Welsh origin.

Upon our arrival at Rosthern we were met by Michael Sherbinin, and Nurse Boyle. The former is a Russian nobleman, who has cast in his lot among the Doukhobors, and is now teaching their children, while Nurse Boyle is ministering to their physical needs. Both of these useful workers were sent out under the auspices of the English Doukhobor Committee of London Yearly Meeting of Friends.

Next morning we started on Doukhobor wagons for the village of Petrofka, on the Saskatchewan River, twenty-five miles distant. On the way our Doukhobor driver gave us a soul-stirring narrative, told in Russian, of his experiences in the Caucasus. His sons had been imprisoned and so cruelly treated that one of them died in consequence. With tears running down his cheeks the father told us how he had nursed this young man, and how he had followed another son to his Siberian place of exile.

While we were still listening to the driver's story, a Mennonite overtook us. Seeing the over-loaded condition of our vehicle he very kindly invited Michael Sherbinin and myself to share his comfortable spring wagon, which we accepted. These Mennonites are particularly good neighbors to the Doukhobors. Our new friend told us that the Doukhobors had come to his house one evening three years before, as they were seeking their new home. There were several hundred in the company, and most of them were walking. They asked that a few of their women might be sheltered for the night. At first it seemed beyond his power to take any of them into his house, as it was small, but something in his heart bid him to do what he could; and he said it was always a great comfort to him that he had yielded to the impression, especially as he afterwards learned something of their experiences. He could not understand their language at the time he took them into his house, nor did he then know what brought them in such numbers to his door. We rode with our kind Mennonite friend to his home on the east side of the Saskatchewan River, and shared the evening meal with him before we rejoined our comrades.

To reach Petrofka we had to be ferried over the Saskatchewan. The approach to the ferry was quite perilous at this time, as the river was twenty feet higher than usual, and had overflowed its banks. The descent was very steep for several hundred feet, and, right at the river's brink, it became almost a sheer precipice. The following account from the pen of a traveler who had made the crossing the preceding winter will give a vivid idea of the difficulties to be overcome:

"Of trail there was scarce a semblance. For three hundred feet our path lay down a slope as steep and as smooth as a toboggan slide. At its foot were a few willow scrub, and then came a clear drop of fifty or sixty feet. If the team became unmanageable, and could not be stopped at the foot of the slide, the prospect of the drop beyond was not reassuring. . . . The interpreter said he would walk down, so as to lighten the load and pilot the way. He started slowly and cautiously, but soon the slope and his weight increased his speed. His feet twinkled faster and faster through the powdery snow that rose up and enveloped him waist high like a halo, above which his rotund body and gesticulating arms could be seen as he rushed to what seemed almost certain destruction. But Providence, in the shape of the aforementioned willow bushes, interposed, and he crashed into their interposing boughs, and fell, a portly, breathless heap of huddled humanity, among their protecting branches. Next it was my turn. I grasped the lines short, braced myself against the foot rail, and chirruped to the team. But neither of them exhibited the slightest inclination to proceed. The sorrel was particularly rebellious, and plunged and reared on the edge of the steep in a most nerve-racking fashion. Finally, with delicate little steps, and snorts of fear, they were persuaded to essay the descent. Until a little more than half way down, all went well. Then one of them slipped, and in a second, cutter and team were slithering down, the former on their haunches. Down below I could see my companion scramble with frantic haste out of our line of descent. His plump figure could be seen through the blinding snowmist raised by the horses, crashing through the underbrush with an agility out of all proportion to his weight. At the foot of the hill I partly succeeded in pulling the team to the left, thus avoiding the sheer drop ahead, and giving the horses an opportunity of catching their feet. The thin, limber willow twigs sang like whips as, bowing my head and straining on the lines, we dashed into the brush. There was a moment's wild rush, then a plunge and a bump, and the cutter was still—jammed against a tree stump whose top was covered with snow. The horses shook themselves, gave a snort or two, and then the brown proceeded nonchalantly to help himself to some outcropping tufts of slough grass. Neither of the team had a scratch, and no injury was apparent to the cutter. My companion 'lost his English' as he described the slide, and went off into German and Polish and Russian and Magyar in recounting its incidents."

The milder season of our own crossing reduced the peril of descending the banks, but increased those of the actual passage of the stream. The Doukhobor who managed the raft which was attached to a steel cable stretched across the river, felt very anxious about our passage, as there was a strong wind blowing us against the current. Once landed, we had a still more alarming experience, plunging through such mud as half buried our horses, and allowed the water to come into the wagon bed. The "snap" of our wagon shows it in such a hole or ditch, with the horses in water up to their breasts, and a woman nearly thrown out of the wagon. It was a very narrow escape, both for herself and child, for she was thrown violently over the side as the wagon dropped into this hole.

The mud was axle-deep in the roadway up which we struggled to the solid bank. When this was

PHOTOGRAPHED BY JOSEPH ELKINTON.

Crossing the Saskatchewan River—Petrofka Ferry.

PHOTOGRAPHED BY JOSEPH ELKINTON.

Prairie Trail and Slough, west bank of the Saskatchewan.

PHOTOGRAPHED BY JOSEPH ELKINTON.

Women waiting to extend a welcome to arriving guests.

PHOTOGRAPHED BY JOSEPH ELKINTON.

A typical house, with sod roof.

ascended we were greeted by some thirty Doukhobor girls, chanting their plaintive Russian hymns of welcome, while the men and matrons of the village stood on the brow of the bank. Thus surrounded by a hundred of these swarthy sons and daughters of the soil, and overlooking the tumultuous stream we had just crossed, one could but think of Miriam when she sang her song of deliverance on the banks of the Red Sea.

It was a sight not soon to be forgotten, as these very picturesquely-attired peasants stood on the top of that bank, with the sun setting at their backs, and the prairie stretching around us on either side of the river for thirty to forty miles in all the glory of its early summer verdure.

After photographing this group, before the evening shades had fallen—(one could see to read until 10 p.m.)—we proceeded to the hospitable home of Michael Sherbinin, upon the edge of the village, which we made our home while visiting the villages of this settlement of eleven communities.

When I called at one of the Doukhobor houses in Petrofka, the father, lifting his little boy in his arms, told me how the child had clung to him when he was forcibly taken from his family by the Caucasian authorities, and how, after three years' imprisonment, the lad did not know him. His argument with the military officer was written out at my request, and is substantially as follows:

"'The Lord Jesus commanded us not to fight, but to be kind and meek;—to love equally all who live on the earth, as Christ the Saviour of our souls loved us all, and gave his body to be crucified for us sinners, and has manifested his love before all nations. He said, "Resist not him that is evil."'

"'But why do you not want to serve the Imperial Power? We are going to fiercely persecute you and severely punish you in order to subdue you under the power of the Russian Emperor, and we will leave your wives and children fatherless.'

"'Dear Mr. Procureur, our Lord Jesus Christ said, "The time will come when they will persecute you for my name's sake; but be ye not afraid; for to the widows I will be a husband, and to the orphans I will be a father, and my eye beholdeth you all."'

"The procureur shouted to the Russian soldiers, 'Take him to prison!' Two of the soldiers ran up to me and put iron chains on my hands, and drove me rudely to the prison castle. My mother, father, wife and children followed me, and besought the soldiers to allow them to come and bid me farewell. The soldiers replied: 'Do not come near here, or we will run our bayonets through you.' The baby boy cried and stretched out his hands to me. The soldiers shouted at the little boy, 'Get away, far away!' and one of them ran with his gun after the boy and my wife. They got frightened and ran, and one of my boys fell down from fright. Then the soldier ran up to my wife and hit her with the butt end of his gun. I said to my parents and my wife: 'Farewell;' and I entered the jail in the town of Kars. There I was kept three months without being permitted to see any visitors. On the 15th of November they took me to the prison of Tiflis, a journey of three hundred and fifty miles. My parents, my wife and children followed me. They applied to the soldiers, asking to be allowed to bid me farewell. The soldiers answered: 'The commander of the fortress has ordered us not to admit you near. Go away from here, or we'll shoot at you.'

"Then I said from afar to my relatives, 'Live ye in the law of God and His hand will protect you!' My father Gregory said, 'Our dear child, we are very sorry to part with thee, but the Lord is our help. Let us go forth to suffer for His name's sake, and he will give us to meet where there is no parting!' Then the elder conveying soldier said, 'That will do for talking! Go on!' And then the children stretched out their little arms towards me and cried bitterly.

"After these events I sat in the prison of Tiflis three years. After these three years were over the procureur gave leave to my parents to come and visit me. On the 25th of May, 1898, my parents arrived to see me. They came to the yard of the prison, and I was admitted to meet them. I greeted them, and called to my little son, Nicolas, who was then eight years old; but the boy did not recognize me. He said, 'Let me go; I don't know thee at all!' With these words he escaped from my arms and ran to his mother. I wept bitterly and said: 'My God, my God, my children have forgotten me!'"

The view shows a Doukhobor wagon like that in which we had started to cross the prairie from Rosthern, standing at Michael Sherbinin's house, with Nurse Boyle wearing a white cap. This particular load of Doukhobor women and babies had come twenty miles for the purpose of having the children vaccinated. Michael Sherbinin took them all into his house and gave them a hearty meal. The school house, which Friends of Philadelphia are building, will occupy a site similar to this upon which Michael Sherbinin's house stands. The Mennonite Reserve is upon the other side of the river.

In traveling across the prairie to the surrounding villages we used the Bain Wagon, as shown in the picture. (See page 43.) The front seat is occupied by Vassili Vereschagin and his wife, who were helpful to us in many ways. They were about forty years of age, and were among the most progressive in adopting American ways of living. After Michael Sherbinin and his wife, who occupy the middle seat of the wagon, had interpreted my desires to them, Vassili would entreat his brethren to send their children to school. My mission was primarily an educational one, believing, as I do, that the education of their children is the

COPYRIGHT, 1903, BY JOSEPH ELKINTON.

Doukhobor team, with the Mennonite Reserve in the distance.

PHOTOGRAPHED BY JOSEPH ELKINTON.

The Sherbinin Homestead.

PHOTOGRAPHED BY JOSEPH ELKINTON.

Ready for the start, to visit the Saskatchewan villages.

effective way in which to reach their parents. Night after night we held conferences, and four out of five of their communities desired that a school should be started. I cannot forget the earnest faces of those strong men and women, standing three and four deep, in their clean, whitewashed homes, often until near midnight, eagerly drinking in the suggestions that were made regarding their educational needs. If those persons who have formed such unfavorable opinions of the Doukhobors because of the late outbreaks of fanaticism in the Yorkton district could visit these villages in the Saskatchewan settlement, their ideas would be greatly modified.

These Doukhobors have taken up their homesteads, and they have done marvels in the past three years towards improving their condition. The soil is very fertile, and being within the wheat belt, great crops of wheat and flax are harvested.

As we journeyed from village to village, separated sometimes by ten or fifteen miles, we saw badgers, coyotes, foxes and wild ducks, to say nothing of the innumerable prairie dogs. Upon our arrival at a village the men and women, and frequently the children, would be gathered at a house, selected by themselves, in which we were to be entertained.

As they were fond of being photographed, after the usual salutation of bowing was over, I would take snap-shots of the groups thus assembled. The women when at work always tuck up their skirts, which never trail upon the ground. (See page 39.)

An interesting street scene is at eventide, when the cows are coming in from the prairie. The large logs on the right in the picture were taken out of the Saskatchewan River by the Doukhobors to be used in building their houses.

As we passed through one village (Troitzkoye) we dined with Simeon Nicolayevitch Popov, a man of sixty-two years of age, who had built an entire flour mill, including the dressing of the mill-stones from rough stones which he found in the neighborhood. Three horses were turning these stones, and we found from personal experience that the flour was fine enough to make good bread, which we enjoyed eating.

The Doukhobors where I visited were vegetarians without exception, and they all seemed very robust in health. They need fruit, and it is a hardship that it cannot be grown in that climate.

Occasionally we would see evidences of considerable artistic ability. A certain house-yard fence attracted my attention, and I asked our driver who made it. He replied that he was the owner and had built it with his own hands. Everything about this house gave evidence of taste and skill. He is seen in the picture standing near the angle of his fence, while near at hand were several trees which he had planted.

The great oven is a characteristic feature of these Russian houses. The oven front stands six feet high and five feet wide. The interior baking space is ap-

PHOTOGRAPHED BY JOSEPH ELKINTON.

Village scene at eventide.

A model home.

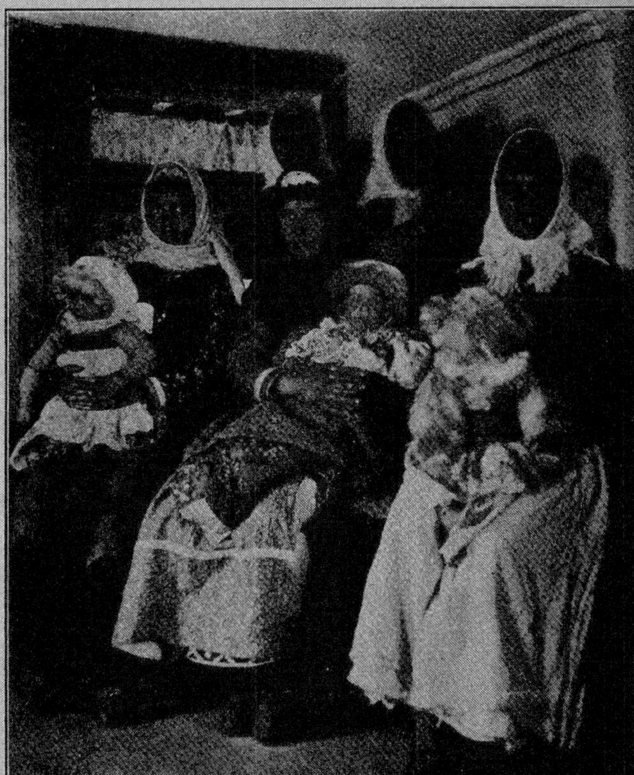

A baby show.

proximately three by four feet. On top of this oven several small children can be stowed away for the night.

I stood by this maiden of seventeen years who holds the long-handled lifter, as she deftly placed the copper pan near the glowing embers, and quickly withdrew it with a toothsome pancake. The batter cup and saucer, with the buttered cloth, are at the left, while the ashes were pushed to the right of the vestibule of the oven proper. (See page 47.)

At another time five young mothers were grouped in front of one of these ovens. The bonnets of these babies were quite elaborate, and their eyes very bright.

When we reached the village of Gorelofka, Savili Feodorevitch Choodyakov and his brothers, with their kind mother, were ready to give us a warm welcome, and we cannot omit to mention how all the good people of this village entertained us with royal hospitality. They also bestowed presents of clothes upon me. A widow of seventy years came to me with her marriage scarf, saying that she would presently die, and as her children were either dead or too far away to give them this sacred emblem of her marriage, she wished to bestow it upon me, as otherwise it would go into her coffin. The scarf is made of Russian crash, about two yards long, and has several bands of silk of various colors below a section of conventional design. Each woman is presented with one of these when she marries. They had shortly before given me a new coat and sacred sash, such as is worn during their Sunrise service. The cap (fedora) is made of a short, curly lambskin, and came from the Caucasus. (See first page of Introduction.)

The same style is seen on a little boy on the extreme right of a group of men, women and children. In this photograph it may also be observed how two layers of prairie sod make the roof. (See page 63.)

The women wear a very picturesque and comfortable hood, with a rosette of bright color on the front of it. The velvet band which encircles the head is invariably black; otherwise there is considerable variety in the color used, although the shape is always the same. In this group none of the chanting girls are wearing their white handkerchiefs or shawls over their hoods, as I requested them to take these off when being photographed. This white shawl is invariably worn by the women in the fields, and whenever they are working, the hood being reserved for special occasions. The young man on the right was about twenty years of age, and, being lame, was serving as shoemaker to the village.

The heavy winter sheepskin coat was quite comfortable when riding across the prairie, even in midsummer. The women in this group were sixteen and eighteen, and the boy about twelve years of age. The doll baby they had dressed especially for me.

When about to leave this colony I found that one or more of the Doukhobor girls could talk English quite well, and so we had some conversation about

Group of chanting girls.

Sheepskin coat and Doukhobor doll.

Baking pancakes.

"Sweet sixteen."

their coming home with me as domestic helpers. It was very interesting to see how the proposition was regarded by them. After thinking about it for some time the younger of the two thought she was willing to come, while the elder hesitated, for fear she "would not get back in time to get married." I asked her how old she was, and she replied that she was sixteen. The younger was thirteen. The men and women generally marry when about seventeen years of age.

After a week spent most pleasantly, barring the mosquitoes, in this colony on the Saskatchewan River, we returned to Winnipeg *via* Regina, in order to visit the Yorkton settlement, which consists of forty-seven villages, situated from thirty to ninety miles distant from that town (see map). The South Colony is on the Assiniboine and White Sand Rivers, while the North Colony is located near the Swan River, north of Fort Pelly, and there are six villages on Good Spirit Lake. The ride of two hundred and eighty-two miles from Winnipeg to Yorkton occupied a whole day by train, but it gave us another opportunity to appreciate the great work which the Canadian government is accomplishing in colonizing these vast stretches of prairie. We saw two trains of thirteen cars each, entirely occupied by Galicians. One of these trains unloaded before us. It was a sight that continually comes back to me as one of the most remarkable of this interesting journey. There were throngs of little children and larger boys and girls with packages of every conceivable shape upon their backs, while their parents were laboring under loads that almost eclipsed their picturesque costumes.

It was four days after our arrival at Yorkton before we could get a carriage to take us the fifty miles north to Poterpevshe, where "Grandmother" Verigin lives. The roads were so bad, on account of the constant rains for the two preceding months, that they were thought to be impassable. These days of waiting were improved by gathering together the Doukhobor men who had come to Yorkton to trade and to find employment on the railroad. One hundred and fifty Doukhobors had been called for by railroad contractors, and runners had been sent out to the various villages to bring them to Yorkton.

The picture shows such a group as we repeatedly conversed with, and they represent the class of men who went on the late pilgrimage. They could not appreciate the good will of the Canadian government in its homestead regulations, and they were afraid of signing their names to any document, as they had always gotten into trouble by doing so in Russia. Time and again we endeavored to enlighten them, but without the same success we had had with their Saskatchewan brethren. Notwithstanding this, they had traits of character we could admire.

Frederick Leonhardt and Michael Sherbinin were both invaluable interpreters, and the kindness of the former toward Michael Sherbinin and myself in shel-

Yorkton Doukhobors.

Blacksmith shop.

PHOTOGRAPHED BY T. V. SIMPSON, V.S.

Men serving as horses.

tering us under his most hospitable roof will always be a pleasant memory.

Robert Buchanan had come from Good Spirit Lake to Yorkton to see us. He and his wife have been very good friends of the Doukhobors, and can testify to their faithfulness as reliable servants. A Doukhobor and his wife have had entire charge of their home affairs for months at a time. He had influenced the Doukhobors near his home to take up their homesteads and not to go on the late pilgrimage, or release their horses and cows.

After this interview we started for Poterpevshe, and soon passed the Doukhobor blacksmith shop in Yorkton, where lived the largest woman I saw among them. Our team was one of the finest, but the driver dreaded the journey, as he declared he had not seen such trails during the past twelve years. We dined on the open prairie, and had it not been for the innumerable mosquitoes our camp-fire lunch of coffee and boned turkey would have been very much enjoyed.

The mosquito pest of this country is greatly against it. The air was literally full of them during the entire trip, and they would settle so close upon the coat of our driver as to change the color of it from black to yellow, as the wings of this variety of mosquito are straw-colored.

About this time we saw several men and boys drawing a loaded wagon, and as they drew near I asked one of them, through the interpreter, why they did not use horses. His reply was very candid, and in the words of Scripture (Rom. 8: 19, 22): "The whole creation waiteth and groaneth even until now for the manifestation of (mercy on the part of) the sons of God." I remonstrated that the Apostle was not writing about horses, but of a spiritual bondage which our unregenerate wills inflicted upon "the better part" in our own souls. He wished to include the animal creation as "sons of God."

The tenderness of this man's conscience was most apparent, and his honest face appealed to one strongly, so I knew not which to pity most, his body or his mind. They pulled that wagon through many sloughs that were dangerous for our horses to enter, and after a round trip of seventy miles I saw him again, and said I was very glad that they had survived their toils as horses. He looked earnestly into my face, and, with tears running down his cheeks, said: "If you would only think as we do God might make some use of you in your generation, for I see you have some ability." I assured him it would be some time before I thought as they did about using horses, and that their children would not hold such ideas.

About him stood a group of the most sincere and kind-hearted people I had ever met, showing every evidence of prosperity; and I felt that it was a psychological problem to eliminate this over-conscientious mental attitude from such a kind and true spirit. So it is with all the fanaticism that has appeared among this really worthy people. A people who will not fight, or steal, or drink anything intoxicating, or smoke, or use profane language, or lie, have a character which will bring forth the best qualities of Christian citizenship.

If we can but help and stimulate them to educate their children, in another generation these ignorant peasants will be transformed into intelligent farmers and tradesmen. It is greatly to their credit that they are very particular as to the teachers they admit among them, and no one need undertake that function who has not a sympathetic temperament.

About sunset, after six hours of plunging in and out of those dreadful sloughs, we came upon a group of twenty-five women who had been picking ginseng* root on the prairie. These Doukhobors were seated upon the grass, eating their evening meal, and apparently enjoying it greatly. They rose most courteously, but I requested them to be seated again while I photographed them.

That night was spent in the home of a German family with eight small children, and apparently several million mosquitoes. As it was a post-office, with a weekly mail service, we endeavored to divert our minds from these uncomfortable guests, by writing home, until the small hours of the morning.

Our experiences the next forenoon almost defy

* This medicinal root is to be found throughout the Northwest Territory, and the Doukhobor women and children have gathered several thousand dollars' worth each summer.

description, for these sloughs were such as Bunyan's Pilgrim never saw. Three times our horses came to a standstill in the midst of sloughs axle-deep in mud, and holding three feet of water above the clay which underlies the eighteen inches of rich black soil. The situation was novel, to say the least of it. One horse lay flat on his side, holding his head above the water, while the other sat like a dog upon his haunches.

The interesting part of the situation was to see how admirably the horses understood the difficulties of their position and responded to the driver's word. Instead of struggling, they rested until the driver got out in the mud and water and released the traces, when they sprang up and plunged forward on to more solid ground. A rope was made fast to the front axle, wound around the pole of the carriage, and extended some fifty feet beyond it. The horses were then attached to this rope, and with some encouragement from the driver they pulled us out. Twice after this we were compelled to get out of the carriage before it could be moved through the mud of the slough.

Sitting there surrounded by water, annoyed by mosquitoes, pretty well covered with mud, and in the midst of a thunder-storm, gave us ample opportunity to moralize upon the blessings of home. Never were mortals more thankful to get under a roof than we were that day when we reached a Doukhobor village and were taken into one of their comfortable houses, where we had our clothes dried. It is this wholehearted hospitality that impresses all who have visited these Doukhobors, and we cannot undervalue this trait, however defective they may seem in other respects.

This was the village in which my father had some three months before found a welcome, after he had traveled in a circle for eight hours at night. He was at that time on his fourth visit to these settlements, and had left this village to go on to the next about five o'clock in the evening. The driver lost the trail, and they wandered about in the dark, until the horse brought them back to the starting-place, about one o'clock in the morning.

A few hours brought us to the home of "Grandmother" Verigin, near the center of the village of Poterpevshe (meaning in Russian, "those who have patiently endured"), a veritable haven of rest, on the north side of the White Sand River. (See frontispiece.) This old lady of eighty-six is recognized by all the Doukhobors as a queen among them. They all pay their oriental respects to her by bowing most profoundly. These salutations were often quite impressive, and accompanied by much sincere feeling.

For three years I had desired to visit her, and to hear her history from her own lips. She told me, through my friend and faithful interpreter, Michael Sherbinin, how she had married when about seventeen years of age, in the Crimean Colony of the Milky Waters, and had lived there peaceably until 1842, when, by order of Nicholas I., she was taken to the Caucasus. The details of this journey were thrilling.

She had three little children, all under eight years of age, whom she cared for as best she could, while their party was driven along by the soldiers. When they came to the Caucasian mountains there were no good roads, as at present, over the mountain passes; and she remembered how the thirty men in their company could scarcely keep the wagons from going over the precipices. It was also dangerous for their horses and cattle to graze, and she would gather the grass for them with her own hands. The Circassians and other hillsmen would throw stones down on them from the heights above their heads, in more than one instance resulting fatally.

They were finally made to settle in the Wet Mountains, at an altitude of five thousand feet. Even here they prospered far beyond what was thought possible by their persecutors.

One night her husband was away from home, and her brother-in-law was also absent trading among some Tartars, who persuaded him, much against his preference, to remain with them over night. They then went to his house, and, as she opened the door, they killed the wife of the very man they had sheltered. They thought they had done as much to "Grandmother," for they struck her four death-dealing blows upon the head, one of which opened an artery, and then kicked her under the bed in a pool of her own blood. She rose up, however, and tried to open the window near her, but the robbers, supposing it was the effort of her little boys, broke the window-shutters in her face. She added: "Had they known I had gotten up, they would have come back and killed me."

When the men entered the house she had told her boys to keep very quiet on top of the oven, and they escaped being injured. They plainly saw the faces of the robbers who took ten thousand roubles out of a strong box, so that they were able to identify them at a later time. "Grandmother" told with much feeling how her dear little boys were asked to go among thirty criminals and point out those whom they thought to be the men who had entered their home and nearly killed their mother. They designated seven, and afterward "Grandmother" was told to say which they were, if she could. She said her eyes were so nearly closed by the swelling resulting from her wounds that she had to hold her eye-lids open to see any of them, and yet she selected the same seven that her boys had indicated, without knowing their choice. The ten thousand roubles were returned to the family.

"Grandmother" has had seven sons in Siberian exile at one time. Her son Peter Verigin has been their recognized leader for the last seventeen years. He and his brother Gregory are now liberated, and on their way to America.

As indicating the vigor of this old lady's mind the reader may be interested in a letter recently received from her.

"Village Poterpevshe, 11th mo. 25th, 1902.

"My Dear Friend, Joseph Elkinton:

"I beg pardon for the delay in answering your kindest letter which I received this autumn. Be assured that I had the greatest desire to answer you immediately, but it is only now that I availed myself of the opportunity to express to you the deepest gratitude and love for your extreme goodness, manifested by you towards us from our first meeting.

"God bless you for all your generosity, and I ask His favor to be worthy of it and to give me the possibility to see you again in my life. I pray to God for your health, and hope He will preserve you for the happiness of all our people.

"I am extremely sorry to confess that a part of us vex all our benefactors and friends by their foolish actions, but I hope that (our) Creator will enlighten their reason and help us to arrange our common life in the best way. The Lord had pity on me and sent me a great consolation—my son Gregory, who came recently from Siberia, and the joyful news that my other beloved son Peter * is on the way to Canada. I am sure you will partake of my hearty rejoicing and accept the humble compliment of your devoted [friend] truthfully,

"Baboshka (Grandmother)

"Anastasia Vassilinovna Verigina.

---

* See page 68 for account of the arrival of Peter Verigin.

"P.S.—This letter has been written by T. Dickericks, the brother-in-law of V. Tchertkov, who came from England to stay the winter with this (our) people, and help them in their needs, and he is very glad to have the opportunity to express to you, dear sir, his thankfulness for all the care and trouble that you and your venerable father took during the first time of settlement of his old friends, the Doukhobors."

"Grandmother's" household, in which I spent three happy days, was composed of "Grandmother," her daughter Anna Podovinnikov, and three daughters-in-law, with three grandchildren. This house was very comfortable, and attractively clean. It was built of logs, some thirty by fifteen feet, one-storied, and plastered inside and out. The inside was whitewashed so beautifully one always felt sure of absolute cleanliness, and this is characteristic of their houses in general. The beds were made of feathers. The chief room was eighteen by twelve feet, with the usual oven in the corner, near which I slept most comfortably. This room is back of the group on the porch. A vestibule six feet square allows the visitor either to enter this apartment, or, turning to the right through a similar door, to step into "Grandmother's" smaller room. Here she sat in the finely upholstered chair seen in the frontispiece, to receive her guests in queenly fashion.

The patriarch, Ivan Mahortov, met me here, having come thirty-five miles to see me. He is the most active man of ninety years I ever met, and I shall not easily forget his energetic manner when telling us of Stephen Grellet's and William Allen's visit to the Doukhobors in 1818. After hearing his description of the two Friends, I am quite disposed to think that it was William Allen rather than Stephen Grellet who prophesied concerning their coming to America.

It was certainly a very remarkable utterance for any one to prophesy so clearly, eighty years in advance, the future experience of a people, telling of their future persecutions, imprisonments, exile to a foreign country, prosperity and visits from Friends.

The Patriarch gave us some of his experiences during the twenty-eight years he served in the Russian Navy. From 1840 to 1853 he had no active service. Then the Crimean War opened, and he was stationed on the warship *Catharine II.*, then anchored off Sevastapol. The high officials of that town, with the officers of the Russian Army and Navy, were gathered in the Greek cathedral, hallowing the Easter service, when the English threw a cannon ball at the cupola, and shattered it over their heads—without, however, injuring the congregation. The Russian ship *Northern Star* was at once ordered to prepare for action by Commander-in-Chief Lazarev. A shot from the English man-of-war disabled her side-wheel, and it was proceeding to capture her, when two Russian frigates came upon the scene and tugged her out of danger. Thus two of the greatest "Christian" nations celebrated the resurrection of the Prince of Peace in the year of our Lord one thousand eight hundred and fifty-three!

When the old Slavonic inscription over the cathedral door in St. Petersburg: "My house shall be called a house of Prayer for all Nations," was mentioned, this veteran of ninety summers naïvely remarked, "Yes, and my countrymen have many a time fulfilled the rest of the text."

He was in the engagement when the Russian fleet sank nine out of ten of the Turkish men-of-war at Sinope, in the Black Sea.

The united fleets of England, France and Turkey then concentrated their attack on Sevastopol, anchoring at Eupatoria. As the Russians had no mounted artillery, the Russian sailors carried their guns and cannon on shore. Ivan Mahortov well remembers the difficulty of bearing a cannon thus strapped upon his back. Two Russian admirals, brothers, by the name of Estomin, planned a successful stratagem at this time, when they were likely to be overpowered. A courier was dispatched to the Emperor Nicholas stating there were sixty thousand Russian soldiers in reserve to meet the allied forces at Sevastopol, when in fact there were only twenty thousand. He was sent through the enemy's lines, duly captured and searched, and the Russians were allowed to withdraw their troops from Sevastopol without capture because of this misrepresentation.

Mahortov said: "At least three times during the siege of the city, when the batteries on either side were decimating the ranks of the other, and these were being immediately replaced, he heard repeatedly the appeals from the enemy in these words: 'Brethren, Russ (Russians) don't hit—fire aside'; and the Russians responded, 'Fire aside, brother.'" "After this," the old man told us, with tears in his eyes, "there was no more such carnage, and would to God that men and angels might never witness such hellish work again!"

He related another instance of that humanity which will ever assert itself while men are men, even when their rulers are compelling them to act as destroyers. The commander of his ship detailed him to visit a small detachment of the ship's crew, who had been stationed on the land to raise some vegetables in the Oushakova ravine. These Russian sailors had been captured by the English and their comrade took tremendous risks in stealing his way through three picket lines at night, especially as it was "in the very hottest times of the war." "One of my brethren found me secreted in the bush near their station and threw his arms around my neck. After enquiring for their health, I asked whether they had any food for themselves. 'Oh! yes, the English send us coffee, bread and butter in the morning, and the same food they have themselves twice a day beside this.' And then they tell us, 'Don't be afraid; we won't harm

"Grandmother" Verigin's home.

The patriarch teacher and his school.

you; it is only Victoria and Nicholas who are guilty in this business.' "

Mahortov was secreted during the day, and when night came he led his brethren back to the ship with remarkable success through the same dangers he had braved alone. He said: " I always served in arms under a silent protest, having a conviction that all war is wrong and I never aimed directly at the enemy." When asked how the higher officers regarded this sort of action, he exclaimed: " Oh! they had no time to take notice of that, but were only too glad to hide behind my back." Once, however, when master of a " top-sail " crew, who were somewhat noisy, the Captain's mate shouted, " Come down, Mahortov," and when he came down from the yard-arm he was ordered to take off his jacket and to receive one hundred lashes; this was repeated twice on his bare back, and thus he received three hundred lashes during an hour for no neglect of duty, of which he was consciously guilty.

This dear old man gathered the children of Poterpevshe around him and taught them the hymns which form so important a part of their education. As I approached this group I thought I had never seen just such animation on the part of an instructor as Ivan Mahortov displayed as he led, corrected and praised his pupils. The well at the rear is in " Grandmother's " yard, and serves the whole village. It was about fifty feet deep, and had a ring of ice in it fifteen feet below the top. One could but think of "the time that women go out to draw water" in the city of Nahor, as these Doukhobor women and maidens came each evening to fill their tin pails. Only the camels were lacking, and instead of the pitchers or jars balanced on their heads they carried the buckets on either end of a pole thrown over their shoulders.

Another group of children in front of a sawmill gives some idea of their faces. The logs are all sawn into slabs in this fashion. (See page 57.)

We soon went into conference with about one hundred delegates from the South Colony, and those of Swan River, to talk over their homestead interests. It was most interesting to see the delegates bow profoundly to the old lady.

As we went out of "Grandmother's" door, the patriarch said, in referring to the Doukhobors' hesitation about taking up their homesteads: "A scared hare is afraid of every stump," and it was very appropriate to the assembled delegates.

I addressed these delegates from the porch rail, where the old patriarch stands by the side of "Grandmother" (see page 60) and her noble daughter, Anna Podovinnikov, with the other members of her household on either side of him. After several conferences near "Grandmother's" house, during which it was difficult to get their signatures for any purpose, "Grandmother" said to me, through her daughter-in-law, she was sorry the delegates were so unresponsive, and she hoped I would overlook any-

Village children and "saw mill."

Saskatchewan Doukhobors.

thing that might have seemed discourteous, for she and all her household were thankful for my visit, and glad to learn what I told them of Canadian law.

The Commissioner of Immigration and ex-Commissioner William F. McCreary had requested us to interpret that law to them and to bring three representative men back to Winnipeg to talk over their interests, which we did.

If the women in these communities could have the deciding vote, many things would be better managed, and probably all the late fanaticism would not have been heard of.

The man in his shirt sleeves at the extreme right in the photograph of "Grandmother's" house is Ivan Podovinnikov, who lodged with Michael Sherbinin and myself during our stay in this village, and was most attentive and helpful. I cannot cease to thank him for putting me through a Russian bath—the most complete cure for a cold I ever tried.

The bath-house, some twelve feet square, was in "Grandmother's" yard. An ante-chamber, three feet wide and the width of the building, had clean straw nicely distributed on the floor. Entering the larger room one saw a neat pile of stones about two and a half feet high in the corner. These had been previously heated by a fire applied through the wall separating the two apartments, and there was no smoke. A slab three feet wide, extending the entire width of the building, was supported some five feet above the floor, as a shelf, upon which the bather was invited to lie down. Two or three cups of water were then thrown upon the hot stones, and the steam generated thereby was enough to smother or cleanse a dozen men. While immersed in this steam bath he received the best switching of his life from a bunch of birch leaves, applied so dexterously that the circulation was quickened to an incredible degree.

By taking a basin of cold water, and keeping the water constantly splashed in one's face, I found it possible to endure this operation for ten or fifteen minutes, during which time Ivan would repeatedly look most tenderly into my face, and anxiously inquire, "Enough? enough? more? little more?" After going out to cool down on the clean straw this process was repeated once or twice, and then, with alternate dashes of cold and hot water, the patient was dismissed, and wrapped up in a warm blanket, under which he remained the rest of the night.

All the Doukhobors bathe in these houses at least once a week, and they are very clean in their personal habits. I remember speaking to some of them because their faces were fairly shining with cleanliness and glowing with color, saying, "I suppose you have been picking strawberries on the prairie all day," and they replied, "Oh, no! we have just been in the bath."

Before leaving this village, so full of interesting people, I took some photographs of family groups. Three out of four wished to send these "snaps" to their loved ones in Siberian exile.

COPYRIGHT, 1903, BY JOSEPH ELKINTON.

COPYRIGHT, 1903, BY JOSEPH ELKINTON.

Families of exiles, showing Persian rugs brought by them from the Caucasus.

Wife and family of a Siberian exile.

A Doukhobor family of typical physique.

One of these includes an aged mother of the exiled husband and father. The wife stands in the rear and to the left of her five daughters, who range in age from twenty to ten years of age. One of the three wore an American straw hat, which she wished her father to see.

Another group shows the wife, whose husband is in exile, with her three married daughters. The Persian rugs under their feet were brought from the Caucasus.

A third has six children in it, and was solicited very earnestly by them for their father. This house is a half dug-out. The crop of weeds on the roof was very luxuriant. These dug-outs were very damp and dark within, somewhat reminding one of a cave. In one village I saw a cow walk up one of these roofs and look around with apparent satisfaction.

A fourth family group of a man and his wife with two married daughters is typical for size.

Ivan Mahortov sits in "Grandmother's" surrey on the front seat, while the old lady and her daughter occupy the rear seat. This carriage was given to her by the Doukhobors as a special token of affection, and she insisted upon my father using it last spring, when the frost was coming out of the ground, with the result that it was broken pretty much to pieces. But when I found it in the village shed, alongside of a Deering reaper and binder, it looked as if it had never been used. I put as many girls as I could on the two seats, and asked the boys of Poterpevshe to give them a ride, which they did with great glee, bringing the surrey to Grandmother's door. She was then willing to get into it to be photographed.

The last group of five women and four children is the household of Barbara Verigin (" Grandmother's " daughter-in-law), in the village of Bedesofka. She stands with hand upon the post. This was the last Doukhobor dwelling we lodged in, and the kindness of our hostess, as well as that of all of her family, will be remembered as long as memory lasts. She was a true disciple of the Lord Jesus Christ, and her loving spirit created the atmosphere of her household. Three of her daughters-in-law were under twenty-five years of age, while the fourth —the mother of the four children—is under forty. The husband of this daughter was killed on the railroad soon after coming to America. This was a terrible blow to the family, as his father died in Siberian exile about the same time.

Whatever may be the opinions of those who do not know the virtues of these Russians by actual acquaintance, we who have had the privilege of learning of their personal experience from their own lips, and have been witnesses of their self-sacrificing devotion to a high principle, and their affection one for another, must believe in them and their future.

About seventy-five years ago the "True Inspiration Society," a communistic society of Germans, came to America, and settled in Eastern Iowa, in five villages, numbering a few thousand souls. They have

Barbara Verigin and her household.

Grandmother's Surrey.

prospered wonderfully, and have become recognized as amongst the most successful and moral communities of that State. When I visited them twenty-five years ago their farming and manufacturing industries were carried on in the most approved way. We believe these Russians, who have escaped to this continent after a century of persecution, will, in another generation, prove no less prosperous.

Indeed, they have prospered remarkably already, as their comfortable homes and neat surroundings, full grain houses and numerous flocks, show. One cannot but admire their kindness to their less-favored neighbors. Time and again they have loaded up their wagons with food and clothing, and for whole days driven in search of the Galicians' homesteads, where they thought there was suffering for want of these things.

As we were passing one of these poverty-stricken households, the mother besought me to baptize her youngest child. I tried to explain the one saving baptism of spiritual life in her soul, as best I could through my friend Michael Sherbinin, when our Doukhobor driver, who could also speak the Galician dialect, turned to her, and with tears in his eyes besought her to find the Saviour in her own heart. His whole face was radiant with the love of God as he told her that the baptism the child needed, Christ alone could bestow.

It is a scene that continually comes back to my mind as one of the most impressive I witnessed while in the Northwest Territories. We were in a farm wagon, traveling across the prairie. This Galician family had just come to settle in a house scarcely fit for cattle to occupy. The roof was made of turf, and was partly fallen in. The mother was surrounded by six or eight little children, while her husband stood at her side, apparently much discouraged by their situation. It was raining, and the mosquitoes were terrible. We stopped to exchange a few words of sympathy with them, and to leave them some money. Then it was that this poor woman appealed to me in behalf of her baby. Her face was the picture of distress for fear the child might die before it was baptized. I suppose they mistook me for a Greek priest, as I had on a Circassian goatskin cloak.

Before we left her her expression was more comfortable, but such is the ignorance of these Galicians that we felt she only half comprehended our ideas of baptism.

As a pleasing finale to this chapter of my personal experiences, I insert an extract from the *Manitoba Free Press*, Twelfth month 23d, 1902, giving an account of the long-looked-for arrival of the Doukhobor leader, Peter Verigin, although as a matter of fact it occurred some months after I had returned to my home in Philadelphia:

" For hours before the train from the east pulled in yesterday afternoon, a woman promenaded the platform awaiting its arrival. She was awaiting her brother, whom she had not seen for fifteen years. When, at a little before three o'clock, the train drew in, there alighted from one of the front coaches a tall, quiet-looking man, carrying a black leather valise studded with nickel bosses arranged in curious design. A dark blue gaberdine reached half way to the knees; over his trousers were fastened close-fitting, dark-gray leggings, piped at the edges with black cloth. His headgear was a black fedora. Around his neck he wore a long cord, fastened to which were a heavy silver watch and a richly-chased gold pencil. Alongside the watch pocket was a fountain pen, secured by loops of the cloth.

"The traveler was Peter Verigin, newly come to Canada after fifteen years of Siberian exile. The woman awaiting him was his sister.

"In the crush of Christmas travel it was some time before those looking for the new arrival could find the object of their search. Accompanied by interpreter Harvey, who had gone east to meet Verigin, and by Ewan Ivan, Paul Planidin and Simeon Rieben, three Doukhobors who had been deputed by the communities to extend to the Doukhobor leader a welcome on his arrival, Verigin walked eastward along the platform.

"His sister saw him, standing half a head taller than the average, and ran towards him, followed by the other waiting Doukhobors, with joyful cries. Verigin dropped his valise, took off his hat, opened his arms, and cried, 'Anna!' He kissed his sister and the others, and quietly walked on toward the immigration buildings, being introduced on the way to

Mr. H. P. Archer, of Swan River; to Immigration Agent Crerar, of Yorkton—both of whom have been for days in the city awaiting his coming; to Mrs. Almanovsky, who acted as interpreter, and to the *Free Press* representative.

"On the party's arriving at the immigration buildings, Verigin was shown the room set apart for his use. Here he spent a little time chatting with his sister and friends, inquiring after his mother, who is eighty-six years of age, and who lives at Poterpevshe village with his sister, whose full name is Anna Vasilievna Podovinnikov. Then, after the baggage had been packed away and the foregoing domestic inquiries made, the party moved downstairs to Acting Commissioner Moffatt's office.

"Mr. Moffatt greeted Verigin warmly, welcoming him to the west in the name of the Dominion authorities. In answer to his inquiries as to his voyage, Verigin said it was a long journey—good, but rough. He had sailed from Liverpool, after crossing Europe from Moscow to Warsaw, and thence to England.

"'You'll be glad to be in a country,' said Mr. Moffatt, 'where there is religious and individual freedom.'

"'I haven't looked round yet,' answered Verigin, through the interpreter, 'so I cannot yet tell whether this is a free country or not.'

"'You know, however,' said Mr. Moffatt, 'that in Canada we do not put people in prison because of their political or religious views.'

"'Oh, yes,' answered Verigin, 'I know that.'

"'People have been looking for your coming for a long time,' said Agent Crerar. 'There are three hundred Doukhobors at Yorkton station, watching every train for you. And there is one person very anxious to see you,—your mother.'

"Verigin had up to that time been quietly courteous and dignified; but here his manner underwent a change, becoming alertly interested. 'Did you see my mother; yes?' he asked. 'When did you see her? Was she well?'

"Mr. Crerar satisfied him on these points, and then Verigin asked him when the train could take him there. 'I am in a hurry to see my mother,' he said. 'There is no train till to-morrow; yes? I would go to-day if I could; yes!'

"Then he realized that perhaps he might be taking up too much of the Commissioner's time. 'Shall I see you again, yes?' he asked. 'You are perhaps now too occupied.'

"Being assured on this point, Mr. Moffatt asked him concerning his visit to Ottawa.

"'I couldn't talk much business,' he said, 'for I have not seen the Doukhobors. Of myself I know nothing of their troubles—only of what I have heard. They tell me the people would not take up their homestead lands.'

"'Did you hear of the pilgrimage?' asked Mr. Crerar, 'and of the action taken by the government to prevent the pilgrims from being frozen to death?'

"'I have not heard any particulars,' answered Verigin. 'It was in print in the Russian papers. They said that two hundred people were frozen to death.'

"Mr. Crerar told him that this was entirely false. Pointing to the *Free Press* representative—who was the only newspaper man present at the interview—Mr. Crerar told Verigin that he had accompanied the pilgrims throughout their wanderings, and personally knew of all the facts in connection therewith. 'Is that so, yes?' said Verigin. 'I shall have much to ask him.'

"Throughout the interview Verigin said little, only speaking in reply to questions, and allowing the others to do the talking. His manner was marked with a natural courtesy and simple dignity that would single him out for notice anywhere. His voice is low, and of a singular sweetness. Physically, Verigin is a splendid type of his race. Tall and strongly built, and of erect and graceful carriage, he would attract attention among hundreds of good-looking men. His features are regular, and his skin of an olive pallor. His hair and beard—which is luxuriant—are black as jet. His eyes are dark and thoughtful, and his whole expression that of a man who has suffered much, and has triumphed over everything through the force of kingly courage and constancy.

"It was evident that he would make no statement as to his future actions, or the counsel he would give the Doukhobors, who for months have been anx-

Arrival of Peter Verigin at Terpenie.

Terpenie (White Sand River), the Model Village.
(Photographs by T. V. Simpson, V.S.)

Winter Scenes in the Doukhobor Villages.

(Photographs by T. V. Simpson, V.S.)

iously awaiting his coming, till he had personally familiarized himself with every phase of the situation. Mr. Moffatt, indeed, and wisely, did not attempt to draw from Verigin any statement. 'You will know all about the troubles the government has had with the Doukhobors,' he said, 'when you get among them. We all hope your coming may have a very good effect. We will do anything possible to help you. You must be tired after your long journey. And you must be hungry. So now I'll say good-bye to you, and wish you a safe journey to your mother to-morrow.'

"Verigin listened gravely, and when this was translated, rose and shook hands with the Commissioner. 'I thank you much,' said he; 'I hope my coming may be good. I hope so, indeed,' and so went upstairs to his room.

"In a few minutes a message was sent down to the *Free Press* man, asking him to join Verigin in the latter's room. The reporter found Planidin, Rieben and Verigin's sister busy in preparing a meal for the traveler. Verigin sat in an armchair, and, after welcoming the newspaper man, resumed his conversation with Mrs. Almanovsky, asking many questions as to the location of the different Doukhobor villages and communities. Before he had concluded, Agent Crerar came up to ascertain if Verigin would stay long in Yorkton. Representative Doukhobors from every village in Yorkton and Swan River colonies were there, and the government desired to have a list compiled of all the Doukhobors eligible for homesteads, the number of those willing to take up land, the number of those who had already made entry, and the reasons for not making entry on the part of those who refused. Verigin said he did not want to delay to hold any such conference at the present time,—he wanted to get to the village where his mother was.

"'Couldn't all these people see me to-morrow night?' he asked. But it was explained that the train did not arrive till late. 'Then let it be in two or three weeks,' he said.

"The conversation drifted to Russian topics. Mr. Crerar said that he had heard the Czar proposed releasing all Siberian exiles at the New Year. Verigin laughed heartily. 'You must have read that in a newspaper,' he said; 'what is said in newspapers is not always true. It is only the students that are going to be released.'

"He was asked to say something concerning his life in exile. 'That would be a long story,' he said. 'If I could talk English I should much like to tell you. But you cannot always trust interpreters. I was sent to exile from the Caucasus for five years; when that was passed I was sentenced for another five years, and when that, too, had gone, I was given yet another five years. When I was allowed to go free I wanted to go to the Caucasus to see my wife and son, but the government would not allow me, nor would they allow them to come to see me. They might have come to Canada with the Doukhobors four years ago, but they would not, because it would take them farther from me, and I do not know whether the government will give them passports to come to Canada, and perhaps I shall never see them.'

"As Verigin talked of his wife his voice broke several times. He sprang up from his chair, and paced up and down the room while speaking of them, and it was some minutes before he regained his composure.

"'What did you do while in exile?' next asked the reporter.

"'Do?' repeated Verigin, 'why, we ate and slept, of course. I used an axe, and carpentered, and built stores. We had all to earn our own living, for the Russian government allows nothing for the sustenance of its exiles. Many times I asked for a trial, but it was always refused. I was never condemned by a judge, or by due process of law, but by an "administrative order" of the government, which enables them to detain any person objectionable to it.'

"'Are the reports of cruelty and ill-usage of the exiles, of which we sometimes hear, true?'

"'In what way you mean, ill-use?' answered Verigin. 'The exiles are sent to a village. They have to walk all the way. If they are tired and fall behind, they are beaten. If they try to run away they are shot. If they go outside the village boundaries they are punished—maybe sent down the mines.'

"At Moscow, Verigin saw Count Tolstoi, who was rejoiced at his release. 'I wonder if the government hasn't made a mistake,' he said; 'you'd better get to Canada soon, for they may change their minds and give you another five years.'

"By this time Verigin's sister and the others had completed their preparations for the meal. The kettle was set on the white table cloth, woven by the Doukhobor women—(it was spotlessly clean and did not soil it in the least)—to use as a samovar. Bread and jam were the staples. Loaf sugar was poured out on a plate, and eaten as a relish. During the progress of the repast, Verigin chatted with perfect ease on general topics. He said he wanted to take a walk around the city that evening, as his Doukhobor friends had often written to him of its marvels. He looked with some surprise at the electric light when it was turned on, but merely remarked, 'I am seeing new things all the time.'"

CHAPTER II.

THE PROBLEM OF EDUCATION AND TRAINING.

To educate and develop into loyal citizens of a free State a people who have for a century suffered persecution and even martyrdom for conscience' sake at the hands of their rulers, requires the utmost tact and wisdom. Such is the frailty of the human mind, that custom and tradition are easily mistaken for the dictates of conscience. This was very noticeably the case among some of the communities of the Universal Brotherhood. The Saskatchewan Doukhobors were more disposed to accept the suggestions that were made to them about the schooling of their children than were their Yorkton brethren. The disinclination they all felt to accepting such instruction from the Government schools was the natural result of the cruel treatment they had previously received in Russia, creating a suspicion regarding all Government efforts to teach their children. When they were told that the Society of Friends had worked harmoniously for two centuries with the governments under which they lived, and yet had maintained its own schools, it seemed to open their minds to the desirability of literary instruction, if it could be obtained in that way.

About the time the Doukhobors were leaving Russia, Peter Verigin, their exiled leader, wrote to them: "People write to me that in America school teaching is obligatory. It is better to be so, because elementary teaching is necessary as a help in life; for instance, in order to be able to read or write something. One must not think that school teaching will completely enlighten a man, but I repeat, it can be a help, and a man by reading books can acquire knowledge, and also his mind will in general develop thereby.

"Briefly, I believe if God grants to our people to settle in America the elementary training will be necessary. It would be good if the children were so taught as to enable them to adapt the knowledge practically to the requirements of their daily home life."

With this clear recommendation of their chief, one would suppose that the rank and file of this brotherhood would adopt his wise suggestions on this subject, but unhappily other teachers, not originally of their sect, have been active in his absence, working upon their untutored minds. Their inheritance and former environment must also be considered if we would judge them fairly.

Time and again, when I talked with them, they would ask me if I could not look at these subjects of education and land tenure from their standpoint, and I may confess it required time and much effort to dispossess my mind of my Anglo-Saxon preconceptions. A most unjust seizure of a valuable horse by a school district trustee as a fine for the refusal to pay a school tax of $8.00, which the Doukhobors could scarcely understand as obligatory upon them to pay while their children were not admitted to the district school, had thoroughly outraged the whole community settled near Yorkton. By what warrant such an act was perpetrated no one could explain, but I endeavored to assure them that this instance was quite exceptional in the administration of the Canadian government.

While listening to one of their most intelligent and representative men, as he explained how unfavorably this action had impressed the Doukhobors throughout all their villages, their "standpoint" dawned upon me, so I could the better understand and the more sympathetically enter into their fears. In short, I realized

> "The heart must bleed before it feels;
> The pool be troubled before it heals."

Their ignorance and poverty and sufferings, with all the emphasis they put upon the spiritual verities, came crowding into my mind. Their inherited tendencies and limitations sadly limit their mental outlook, but in the midst of their crudeness and ignorance there is the promise of true character, for they have the foundation of strong minds.

Let us for a moment place ourselves in their position, step back two or three centuries in our educational advantages, and then endeavor to realize the isolation and oppression under which they have existed, ever and anon rallying to an ideal standard of brotherhood with a continual protest against the cruelty of an unchristian government. If, then, suddenly placed under the most enlightened and free government in the world, could we fully appreciate our new surroundings and opportunities at once? Would not the habit of suffering for a principle be so indelibly stamped upon our neglected minds as almost to compel us to think we were not doing our duty without experiencing some kind of torture? Thus they are, unconsciously, the victims of a mental habit formed under totally different conditions.

A people who think they have come, in spiritual descent at least, from the three children of Israel who came out of the fiery furnace without the smell of fire upon their garments, and who believe the mission of evangelizing the world has been committed to them, because they have the oracles of God in the form of the new and great Commandment of Jesus Christ;—such a people, exhibiting in no common degree the fruits of the spirit, should be led out of their mental darkness without offending their conscientious convictions. This is only possible through sympathy and love. The Apostle Paul dealt with such a state of mind and of faith when he wrote, "Let not him that eateth [meat] despise him that eateth [it] not; and let not him that eateth not judge him that eateth: for God hath received him. . . . Let us not therefore judge one another any more; but judge this rather, that no man put a stumbling block or an occasion to fall in his brother's way. . . . All things indeed are pure, but it is evil for that man who eateth with offense."

The truth has always been largely entrusted to poor, ignorant men. It was so in the first and in every subsequent century of our era. To be sure it was well-nigh buried by the Judaism and narrow-mindedness of the first disciples of our Lord, and it is still struggling for recognition in the professing Church of Christ.

"But these very limitations may become a blessing. Not to supplant others in the strife after earthly position or possessions, but to gain the spiritual power to turn the limitations which defeat into the instruments of heavenly blessing, makes one a prince with God. Limitations are often the conditions of the birth of character." *

The more I talked with these honest-hearted men and women the more fully and deeply impressed became the conviction that they possessed the very germ of moral, civil and spiritual reform, and that within a few years their children will acquire such knowledge of American life and customs as to correct the misunderstandings of their parents. One of the very pleasant scenes that I recall was the evident satisfaction which the older members of a certain family in the Saskatchewan colony showed when a little boy of ten years read to me out of an English primer; and this method of reaching the elders is the key to the whole educational situation. As soon as the parents have confidence in those who teach

* George A. Barton, "The Roots of Christian Teaching as Found in the Old Testament."

their children,—that they will not undermine any of their religious tenets, and are working in a truly disinterested way,—they extend their hearty co-operation.

The educational service which Nellie Baker, of Toronto, rendered to the Doukhobors is one of the brightest spots in the history of the settlement. It is graphically described in *The Christian Herald* of Eleventh month 7th, 1900:

"The Doukhobors are anxious to become Canadians and to be able to communicate with the Anglo-Saxon settlers around them. Knowing this, two ladies of Kingston, Ontario, Mrs. Eliza H. Varney, a Quaker, and her young cousin, Miss Nellie Baker, determined to establish a little summer school at one of the Doukhobor villages on Good Spirit Lake. Mrs. Varney had already passed the summer of 1899 there, conducting a dispensary for the Doukhobors, who have no physicians among them. They pitched their tents near three of the Doukhobor villages: a small tent for their residence, another for the dispensary (which was under Mrs. Varney's charge), and a third, 20 by 20 feet, for the school, over which Miss Baker presided, and for which work her studies at Queen University (together with a natural aptitude and Christian sympathy) had fitted her. Mrs. Varney had won the affections of the villagers the previous year, and they were not slow to send their

Eliza H. Varney.

Nellie Baker.

children to the new school, some of them arriving before the ladies had unpacked their luggage.

"Miss Baker's report of her experiment, which has just been made to the Canadian Commissioner of Immigration, shows what difficulties she encountered. She found herself confronted by a tentful of boys and girls, with none of whom did she have a single known word in common. 'By signs and motions,' she says, 'I got them seated in rows on the prairie grass of the tent floor, and holding up a pencil said "One." I could not detect any apparent comprehension. Then taking up another pencil, I said, "Two," and then another, and said, "Three." Still no response, and my heart sank somewhat. However, I decided to repeat the method, and as I said "One," I noticed a look on a boy's face that told me he knew I was counting, and I saw him turn and speak to the others. Almost instantly they understood, and soon, repeating after me, they counted up to ten.'

"From this beginning the course of teaching proceeded. Some of the pupils walked five miles to school and five miles back every day. The children were never tired. The favorite method was object teaching. 'They learned the divisions of time from a watch, to count money from coins, and so on. The children had a natural taste for figures, and at the end of the two months the older children had succeeded in getting through one-half of the multiplication table, and some of the more advanced pupils were in the second (Canadian) reader.' In writing, she declares that some of them equaled or surpassed the teacher.

"The children were anxious to have tasks assigned to them to prepare at home, and never were satisfied with the amount of such tasks; they always wanted more. At first the Doukhobors did not know that Miss Baker's work was, like Mrs. Varney's, entirely voluntary and unremunerated. When they found it out, they sent a committee to her to offer her some compensation, although they were in need themselves. When she declined it they told her that they thanked her 'all the day and all the night.' Some of the older boys, who did not know a word of any language but Russian at the beginning of July, can now, after barely two months' teaching, correspond with Miss Baker in 'fairly understandable English!'"

"Lally Bernard" says in *The* (Toronto) *Globe*, Twelfth month 1st, 1900:

"The greatest care should be exercised in the choice of the teachers sent to the Doukhobor colonies. The men and women who undertake to teach these people will have an immense responsibility resting upon their shoulders, and immature teachers, or those who go mainly from a sordid motive, may do irreparable harm. Miss Baker's work was a labor of love, and was accomplished under great difficulties, but her interest and sympathy were so keen, and her intelligence of so high an order, that the work she did was unusually successful."

PHOTOGRAPHED BY NELLIE BAKER.

Nellie Baker's classes.

PHOTOGRAPHED BY NELLIE BAKER.

Some of Nellie Baker's pupils.

Helen Morland, of London, has been conducting a school at Good Spirit Lake for three months, under the auspices of English Friends, and Hannah Bellows, daughter of John Bellows, expects to join her in the spring of 1903. As stated elsewhere, Friends of Philadelphia are providing a school for the Prince Albert colony, on the banks of the Saskatchewan River.

I have just received a letter from one of their leaders, in which he asks that this new Saskatchewan River school-house be built in his village. This man went from village to village with us entreating his brethren to put aside their fears that an English education might lead their children away from their religious doctrines, and I assured them that it was my desire in no wise to interfere with these. He is one of those of whom it can be said, in the words of Aylmer Maude, "Neither oaths of allegiance nor the stupefying effect of [military] discipline can be depended on permanently to shut out from men's hearts and minds the ideals of the prophets and the aspirations of the saints; [for] when the test came events showed that among these common, illiterate Doukhobors, along with obvious faults and limitations of their own, there dwelt a large measure of the spirit of martyrs and the courage of heroes; and so wonderful are the workings of the Holy Spirit that those, whose faults and limitations in ordinary life may be patent to all candid observers, may yet be found faithful unto death in the day of trial."

To educate such a people is indeed a profound problem, and we will need to undertake the task after a careful study of the conditions from which they have escaped, in order to appreciate the difficulties they had labored under for a century.

M. Ponomarev, Inspector of Primary Schools in Russia, recently summed up his observations when inspecting the rural district schools as follows.

"In Russian villages the shepherd is happier than the male teacher, and the latter happier than the female teacher."

"The moujik considers the teacher a man who lives at his expense, and he pays him less than the shepherd. When snow has fallen and the boys are without anything to do, being unable on account of the winter to be of help to their parents, the latter think of their education. An 'outchitel,' or schoolmaster, is hired by the villagers, who agree to feed and to pay him. The price varies from 10 to 50 roubles ($9 to $40) for the whole winter, which is very long in Russia. As to the food, it is not so good as that of the shepherd; each family whose children frequent the school feeds in its turn the schoolmaster. The school building is a miserable hut, often contiguous to the house of the moujik, where pigs, hens and cows are fed twice a day. It is the business of the teacher to keep his school clean. There is no ventilation; at the approach of the cold weather all windows are hermetically closed with clay or glazier's putty. The moujik cannot understand that anything should be opened in winter time. In regard to the heating, it is quite primitive. Each scholar is bound to bring some pieces of wood to heat the school. When it is freezing too hard the pupils do not come, and the teacher, being compelled to remain until the evening, envelopes himself in his touloupe, or sheepskin, and stays motionless in a corner of the 'khata,' or school hut.

"Such is the custom in poor villages. In the rich villages the schoolmaster, instead of being a martyr, becomes a tyrant. He strikes the pupils brutally, tears off their ears, pulls their hair and breaks their teeth, for he is almost continually drunk. The official report instances many cases in which the children were violently thrown on the ground and bruised by the teacher's feet to such a point that the blood gushed out from their noses and mouths. But what is most extraordinary is that those queer schoolmasters intrust the task of teaching to the best scholars. These are called 'the first group,' or 'the professors,' and they are not above eight or ten years of age. While they try to teach their little comrades the schoolmaster sits down to drink in the next 'kabako.'"

The Doukhobors were denied even such instruction as this account represents, and it is not to be wondered at that they should look with contempt upon such instructors.

On the other hand they would do well to appreciate that education in its proper and true methods is essential to them if they would develop all their faculties, and detect how intimately the intellectual and religious processes are blended. The Bible, even as an intellectual corrective of religious ideas, would be invaluable to them, and this, under enforced illiteracy, they have not had the opportunity to read. But they are not the first people who have been made the victims of false teaching through their ignorance of the Bible.

As these children of the soil are very observant of natural phenomena and appreciative of the beauties of the physical world, it seems very fitting to approach them through this channel, and I found them more easily convinced by the parables of Christ's teaching along this line than in any other way.

It is one of the most simple and effective methods that can be employed, and is also a happy way of teaching the Bible to them. This also appeals strongly to those who have been blessed with an intimate knowledge of the Holy Scriptures from their infancy, and who have had the advantage of seeing the practical illustration of the truths contained in them applied to daily living, as many of the Doukhobors have endeavored to do.

The number of Scripture quotations that I heard while among them made me marvel at the diligence of the Doukhobors in instructing their children in the Scriptures, especially considering how few can read. Yet I could clearly see that many important passages had been omitted, and some misconstrued, the context being disregarded. Naturally, they do not wish strangers to indoctrinate them with new interpretations, as they have suffered so much to maintain their own; and yet by playing upon their natural mental bias they can be easily led into the acceptance of new ideas. We have seen how some of them were willing to accept such literal and foolish interpretations of familiar texts as started them on a pilgrimage in search of Jesus, and to discard the proper use of animals. Yet their very proneness to error indicates how readily they may respond to right teaching, and this was illustrated by the fact that no Doukhobors near Good Spirit Lake, where Robert and Elizabeth Buchanan have taken so much interest in them, would join their deluded brethren of the Yorkton colony.

As I studied the unique combination of spiritual ideals with undeveloped mental powers which some of the men of the Yorkton colonies exhibited in the conferences I had with them, I saw that endless patience and a sympathetic appreciation of their convictions were absolutely essential to lead them out of their mistaken conclusions. Yet, granted patience and sympathetic treatment, their enlightenment is not a hopeless undertaking by any means. The high moral standard they maintain, and their thrift, bear ample evidence of a right development of the mind in many respects, and yet their inability to see that their spiritual interests do not necessarily conflict with such sane institutions as the homestead and registration laws and the public school system, reveals a crudeness of mind which cannot be overcome at once.

The most speedy solution of these difficulties would be to give the *women* of their communities their rightful place. They are greatly in the majority, many of the men having been killed and banished. One finds three times as many women as there are men in their villages. These women have often had to carry all the burdens of making and keeping up the home, with the training of their children.

Repeatedly I urged the Doukhobor men to give their women an opportunity to speak in their conferences, but the oriental idea obtains so positively and persistently it was very difficult to get any expression from them at such times. Once out of the Assembly, however, they would frequently give their opinions, sometimes far from complimentary to their brethren, including ourselves in one instance. On this occasion my interpreter overheard a typical debate between the women of a certain household on one side, and the men on the other.

We had talked for some time, and I proposed that the fourteenth chapter of John might be read in Russian, when one of the Doukhobor women said, in an undertone, "Those men are no good, or rather they are helpless, unless they have the Bible or some book under their arms; while we have the truths they speak of in our hearts, and are living them out daily." The man standing opposite to her across the room replied, "I advise you to hold your peace and listen, for you may learn some things you don't know."

We were highly amused with this bit of independence on the part of our critic, for she expressed her honest opinion, and there was a truth in her thought worthy of our consideration, while the supplementary suggestion of the man also had its place.

"With reference to their children," says Aylmer Maude, "I think any one who has seen how obedient, considerate, and quick to be of use, the Doukhobor children usually are, will be inclined to admit that most of us have much to learn from these people on the subject of education. Even regarding instruction (as apart from education proper), their knowledge of agriculture and of useful handicraft, coupled with a serious attention to religion as a guide to daily life, are more likely to help them to live useful and happy lives than any knowledge of vulgar fractions or of the eccentricities of English orthography."

The self-control which they instill into their children may well put to shame most American families. Soon after their arrival on this continent a group of Doukhobor children were playing with some Canadian children, when one of the latter was accidentally hurt and ran home crying. The father of this boy was so enraged that he rushed at the only Doukhobor child who remained on the playground, and kicked this little fellow, who had not been playing at all, but innocently sitting near the scene of the trouble, so that he died shortly after from the injuries received.

The parents of the lad and all the Doukhobors forthwith signed a memorial expressing their sorrow for the boy's death, but asking that the man who killed him should not be punished. Such an attitude of mind and heart was reflected throughout their communities in the children. Indeed, it was one of the very pleasant features of my visit among their villages to observe the gentleness of their manners. I do not recall a single instance of quarreling among all the groups of children I saw at play, and when I gathered them together they invariably showed a courtesy toward the smaller members of the group.

These bright-eyed boys and girls would stand by the hour to hear some story of how houses were made in America, or how steamships were propelled across the ocean, etc. Several of them, not over twelve years of age, had picked up enough English to understand without an interpreter. If their daughters between twelve and sixteen years of age were permitted to go to school they would within four years acquire sufficient knowledge of English to be competent to teach their younger brothers and sisters.

But here is one of the practical difficulties to overcome, and it was on this very point that I had the warmest contention with their elders. There were frequently twenty-five to thirty robust girls of fourteen to sixteen in each village who ought to have had the privileges of a primary education. To send a girl to school, however, seemed never to have dawned upon them, and it was only after the most earnest assurances that they were just as worthy and capable of receiving instruction as their boys were that I obtained a promise of permission for these girls to go to the boarding school now about being erected in the Duck Lake colony.

One might hunt the world over and not find a more promising or more inspiring mission field,—such a physically vigorous and highly moral people, with such alert minds. Surely, with all their ignorance, and even fanaticism, such a people is worthy of our help.

It was Annie Besant who said, in her autobiography: "Plenty of people wish well to any good cause, but very few care to exert themselves to help it, and still fewer will risk anything in its support. 'Some one ought to do it, but why should I?' is the ever-reëchoed phrase of weak-kneed amiability. 'Some one ought to do it, so why not I?' is the cry of some earnest servant of man, eagerly springing forward to face some perilous duty; and between these two lie whole centuries of moral evolution."

Much may be accomplished if those who feel a right prompting to engage in so good a work will go among these Doukhobors with a sincere desire to learn from them;—for in some things, especially touching their religious opinions, they consider themselves quite as much enlightened as their instructors; and this trait cannot, by the way, be said to be altogether peculiar to the Doukhobors. In this connection, for their religion is inseparably bound up with their education, one must always have regard to the superior claims of their faith, and be able to appreciate the strength of their convictions; while on the other hand we should, in the language of Aylmer Maude, " be on our guard against confounding the sect with the truths on which they have built their polity." The sect has erred in the past, and has even split in pieces, as some larger and more favored bodies of Christians have done, and there are many possibilities of disintegration for the future, but the correctness of certain principles to which they have testified, and for which they have suffered, " will remain as long as the conscience of man continues to influence his actions."

These long-persecuted peasants need to be shown how the mind enters into all human beliefs, and thereby introduces an element of human fallibility which has to be allowed for to an extent which few suspect.

Another phase of the educational work which should not be overlooked results from the Russian custom of sending every peasant to learn some handicraft during half the year. In this way we can account for the readiness of the Doukhobors to make almost anything with their hands. To utilize this quality, and not allow it to lapse, a manual labor department should be attached to every school started among them. It was particularly pleasing to see just such provision made by themselves in the basement of a school house which the Doukhobors had built in one of their villages.

This, it seems to me, is the best way to go about getting into close touch with them. Of course the teaching of the English language is important, and may be carried on simultaneously. The greatest need on the part of their would-be helpers is an honest heart with a practical head.

If such practical, sympathetic instructors can be found, who will enter heartily into their customs, and make use of them to lead the people to a larger appreciation of the privileges of the free and enlightened government under which they now live, great progress in their development will appear. If, on the other hand, there is an undue insistence upon Anglo-Saxon ways and thoughts, it will only tend to drive them further into the false ideas about "liberty" which they so often express, confusing spiritual freedom with social or industrial independence. If I were to express briefly my idea of the best plan to help them it would be: First, to get their confidence by a hearty appreciation of their opinions and customs,—which have, in general, much about them that one can admire,—and to lead them by easy steps to distinguish between their conscience and their customs, and thus eventually to recognize their own educational needs.

In attempting to educate those who have such strong convictions and inherited customs as the Doukhobors have, it certainly is wise to work along the line of least resistance.

Their strongest principle is that of love to their fellow men, and the affection they show for their families is proverbial. The reflection of this affection was strikingly apparent among the children themselves, for, being drilled in the school of self-sacrifice, they instinctively responded to any appeal made in a loving spirit, at least when the subject was within their mental grasp. As soon as a Doukhobor realizes that you are genuinely in sympathy with him, his services are at your disposal, but without this sympathy one will labor in vain. It would, therfore, be well to appreciate at once that one must recognize their merits.

Even the most advanced among them are sometimes crude in their ideas, but possess a certain innate honesty and simplicity of thought that is quite refreshing. An interesting instance of this has recently come to hand in connection with the building of the school-house in the Prince Albert colony. My correspondent is one of their most earnest and progressive men, about forty-four years of age. He says: "As the Terpenie and Oospenie people showed the warmest interest in the school, our brethren ask that one-half of the building be built in Terpenie village, as we are told that the proposed school-house is to be one of two stories."

In the language of one * who visited the Doukhobors at the time of their first settlement in Canada, we still think while "these people may not have the book-learning of Americans, and we may be able to teach them many useful things, *the benefit is not all one-sided.*

"The gentleness of manners that springs from kindliness of heart has a great charm, and the contrast between the casual greetings of the modern civilized world and the deferential salutation of the Doukhobor men and women leaves one something to think about.

"Our modern acceptation of the word 'education' is a strange one, and the definition of the term 'culture' as a condition of the intellect rather than amassed knowledge is a definition which is not sufficiently appreciated on this continent."

* "Lally Bernard," in "The Canadian Doukhobor Settlements," a series of letters to "The (Toronto) Globe."

CHAPTER III.

THE DOUKHOBORS AS HOMEMAKERS.

When the vanguard of the Doukhobor emigration reached this side of the Atlantic there were not wanting critics who could see in the movement only an influx of paupers. In truth, the Doukhobors arrived in Canada almost utterly destitute of material wealth. Their transportation from Russia had absorbed whatever slight resources they had previously possessed, and even then had only been made possible by the help they had received from the Society of Friends. The Canadian Government was forced to help them in securing transportation to their new prairie homes, and in providing the necessaries of life after they got there; and many times since its watchful officials have stood between their wards and absolute starvation. Large sums of money have been spent by the Friends of Philadelphia and of London Yearly Meetings to stock their farms and to provide them with implements of husbandry and other necessaries of agriculture. Perhaps no other people ever received so much help from the charitably-disposed in so short a time. Yet one thing on which their best friends and their harshest critics could now absolutely agree is the statement that they are not now, never have been, and show no signs of becoming, paupers. Their pitiable poverty was their misfortune, not their fault; and every lift which helping hands have since given them they have utilized as aids to them in the task of helping themselves.

Their initial task of making habitable shelters for themselves was one which would have strained the resources of the hardiest pioneers. They were located on the bare prairie, almost without tools or building materials, distant from sources of supplies, without money, harassed by sickness, subject to the rigor of a strange climate, with winter fast approaching. The energy, resource, ingenuity and fortitude which they displayed under these circumstances are well described by May Fitz-Gibbon ("Lally Bernard"), who visited them during the summer and fall of 1899, soon after their arrival:

"The men of each community were called upon to hire themselves out as farm laborers and railway navvies. The distances in the West are enormous, and it meant simply the exodus of the men from the villages, and an absence that was to be counted by weeks or months. Then, too, in a village of perhaps a hundred and twenty souls they might have a yoke of oxen or one pair of horses, and these were to plough, and carry lumber for the frames of houses, and, more than all, transport flour from a great distance to feed the community. The question was a grave one; winter comes quickly in these latitudes. But the question was answered by the women, who turned to, helped the few men left in the village to build the houses, and not only trod the mortar and used their hands as trowels, but carted the logs, drawing them for miles with the aid of two simple little wooden wheels, which were no bigger than those of a child's go-cart. The earth for the mortar was carried on their backs in baskets woven of willow or in huge platters hewn out of logs; the water was carried at times for half a mile in two buckets hewn like platters out of trunks of trees and hung at the end of a long sapling. A deep trench was dug, and by the edge sat a score of women less strong than their Spartan sisters, chopping with a rude hatchet hay or grass to mix with the water in the trench or pit. Bucket after bucket of water was poured in from the primitive wooden pails, while six women with skirts kilted up nearly to their waists trod the mortar until it was as smooth as paste. Another gang of women carried it in the wooden troughs to the houses, where six or eight others plastered the logs both inside and out with the cold clay paste.

"The neatness of the work was astonishing, for while in some cases logs large enough to build a log house were to be found, in others they had to be woven out of coarse willow branches, the upright posts alone being of sufficient strength to support the roofs of sod (two layers) laid on with a neatness and precision that is seldom seen in this country; and the walls of the houses themselves were not only stuffed with clay, but presented, both inside and out, as smooth a surface as if the trowel of a first-rate plasterer had been at work. In many cases these people

PHOTOGRAPHED BY WILLIAM BELLOWS.

Women working in the fields, preparing for wheat-sowing.

had neither tools nor nails, and the carpentering work of the interior of the houses is a marvel of ingenuity."

It was under difficulties fully as great, and met with courage and resource equally surprising, that the beginnings were made in the work of cultivating the soil. So few draft animals were available, and the needs for them were so pressing and multifarious, that much earth was broken by the women harnessing themselves to the plough. The pictures of this novel scene were widely disseminated, and elicited much unfair comment from the uninformed on the supposed cruelty of the Doukhobor men. The real significance of the operation is thus explained by May Fitz-Gibbon in one of her letters from the Doukhobor Settlements:

"The women of the Doukhobors are not in the habit of drawing ploughs or of building houses, but, like many others of their sex, they are capable of rising to the occasion; and this was one of the occasions when they distinguished themselves, as many of our pioneer ancestresses have done in days gone by. The summer season in that part of the world is short, and the supply of horses and oxen very meagre. The men of the village had been obliged to bring logs for the houses from a great distance, and many of them were working on distant farms. Flour ran short; the distance to Yorkton meant a tramp of at least thirty-nine miles, and the return meant the carrying of large sacks of flour on the women's shoulders. A woman's council was held, and it was decided that the only cattle available were to be sent to Yorkton, and the women declared that they would pull the plough. There was not an hour to be lost! they knew that the lives of their children and husbands depended on the effort they were willing to make, and a splendid effort it was. In days to come one of the Russian artists in their midst will paint a picture which will be a source of pride to the descendants of these women who shouldered this burden with the same steadfast courage with which they have borne many others. **(See picture, page 216.)**

"The fact that there are so many more women than men must be borne in mind, as it will explain how willing these women of the Doukhobors are to lessen the burden that as a matter of necessity the men are called upon to bear."

Indeed, the part which the women play in the industrial life of the community is very important, apart from the exceptional duties which have devolved upon them in these troublous times of pioneering. The household management falls to them, as it does to their sisters everywhere; but amongst the Doukhobors this includes a whole department which has grown obsolete in American homes. They are spinners, weavers, dyers, embroiderers, tailoresses, and even milliners, so far as the art is practiced in their communities. Their work in the making and decorating of house, table and ceremonial linen is often exquisitely fine, and is the wonder and delight of all observant visitors. One of these who visited Terpenie (Saskatchewan) a few months before me thus expresses himself:

"During the meal I had admired the beautiful decorative work done by the needle on the garments of the daughter-in-law, and at its conclusion the women of the house displayed specimens of their weaving, dyeing and embroidery. The articles they exhibited were both useful and ornamental in character. Some of the weaving was particularly fine, the texture of some of the table linen being equal to that produced by the best looms of Belfast. Nearly all the linen was woven with a simple check or diaper pattern in red at the side and ends, and much taste and skill were shown in the arrangement of these. The dark woolen cloth, of which the women's skirts were made, much resembled Irish frieze. The clothes of the men were made of similar material, but generally lighter in color. Some of the kerchiefs worn by the women were beautifully embroidered in fine wools, work being as well executed as the most captious critic of art needlework could desire, the design being usually regular or geometric, and almost ecclesiastic in simplicity and harmony. The knitting shown me by the daughter-in-law was as fine as that of the famous Shetland shawls, and of the same gossamery quality. The staple colors for the woven fabrics seemed to be browns, fawns and grays, but in knitted work, and in the more decorative portions of the goods intended for personal wear, brilliant coloring is general. The dyeing, the spinning and the weaving are all done by the community. The yarn is spun on the old-fashioned distaff. For the dyeing, aniline dyes are coming into general use, and I saw the communal loom, in sections, for it was not yet put together, and had not been used since the village was founded. It was a primitive wooden arrangement, that would look curiously archaic beside the modern mechanical marvels that fabricate the textiles in general use, but its effectiveness when operated skilfully was beyond question."

It would be tedious to enumerate the ways in which the women of the communities have stepped beyond the ordinary bounds of household duties to help the settlements through their troublous infancy. One seemingly insignificant source of revenue, the sale of medicinal roots, which they dig from the prairie sod, has been so industriously pursued by them that it has brought many thousands of dollars into the communal treasuries. Then it must not be forgotten that in many families there are no men at all to help bear the burdens. "Siberia swallows up the flower of the Doukhobor manhood." Even in the following summer the visitors from Philadelphia Yearly Meeting,—Joseph S. Elkinton and Jonathan E. Rhoads,—found women engaged in the roughest tasks of the field and doing the work of both men and horses.

"The women were digging out sand and loading it upon a wagon for building purposes, and they used their shovels dexterously. The wagon thus filled was drawn by eighteen women—six abreast, three on either side of sticks or cross pieces, connected with the wagon by a chain. The movement of the load, with a woman on top of it, indicated much muscular strength, accompanied with concert and grace of action. Horses were scarce, and the men being employed in working on the railroad, were the reasons the women were thus engaged. Twenty women, ten abreast, holding up new rakes and pitchforks as they came in from the field, was a pretty sight here, as elsewhere."

Bravely as the difficulties of that terrible first winter were met and overcome, they left sad reminders behind them. The Philadelphia Friends found a great deal of sickness almost everywhere. Much of it was due to exposure to the bitter weather, and much more to overcrowding and living in ill-ventilated rooms; while the Doukhobors who had sojourned in Cyprus had brought many cases of fever away with them. Scurvy was widespread and was "spoken of in this community as indicating a shortage of food last winter." There were no physicians and no medicines in most of the communities, and in one case a wagon-load of four women was met, three of whom were ill, and were being driven to Yorkton, fifty miles distant, to secure medical attention. To one who has had experience of these prairie trails the thought of the ride of those poor sick women must cause an involuntary shudder.

But not to dwell too long on this side of the story, it may be said that the visitor of the past summer (1902) has found things in a very different condition. They are still isolated, and especially in case of sickness or sudden need of any kind their isolation is a great hardship, but their thrift and perseverance have begun to bear rich fruit, and they have already made great steps toward conquering their circumstances. Perhaps it was because the main motive for my visit was educational rather than material relief, but I find that my impression of their needs related mainly to their mental shortcomings. Few cases of serious suffering from lack of food, clothing or shelter came to my attention. Good harvests, full granaries, flourishing gardens, were, not universal, but quite frequently met with. Many communities had the latest improved farm machinery, and farm live stock was often found in the pink of condition. The anonymous writer who visited their settlements but a few months before me gives quite a rosy account of their material welfare, and while it was taken from one of their more progressive settlements, it agrees with my own observation respecting the situation in these:

"In Terpenie there were between one hundred and sixty and one hundred and seventy inhabitants, forty-seven families in all. Between them they had twenty horses, a hundred and thirty cattle, and forty sheep. In the village of Hierolofka, ten miles away, there were five hundred cattle and a hundred horses. Last fall the Terpenie people had plowed with nine ox or horse teams, in three weeks, three hundred and twenty-five acres of land, and, with the amount of breaking done, they would have this year a thousand acres under cultivation. Their principal crop would be wheat, but much barley and flax would be grown. Last year the crops were good, he said, but they had sold none of the grain yet. The present price was too low. They would wait, he said, until they got a railroad, and then they could get a better price for their grain. They did not know when they would get the road built, but they believed Mr. Sifton would see that they had proper shipping facilities. They had ten grist mills, operated by waterpower at Terpenie and Hierolofka. To get the necessary water supply, the Terpenie people had built a canal two miles long—all of it by the spade, and all of it done by the women of the village while the men were working in the fields or on the railroad. It was completed last fall, and would be in operation this spring. The stones used were those formerly in the old Hudson's Bay fort at Prince Albert, and were teamed nearly a hundred miles. The flour is, of course, ground 'forthright,' and would make the same dark bread in general use among the Doukhobors.

"The residents of Terpenie have forty-seven homesteads. This year the Hierolofka people will have four thousand acres cropped. As an instance of the extensive nature of their farming operations, they purchased last year forty binders, seventy mowers, and a hundred and twenty plows. Nearly all this was bought on credit, and no better comment on their commercial reliability need be adduced than the fact that on January 1st of this year, though hardly a bushel of grain had been sold, less than fifteen per cent. was unpaid, and this is regarded as being as good as the bank. They make use of everything—like Autolycus, they are 'snappers up of unconsidered trifles,' picking up nails, old horseshoes, or such things, and carrying them home and putting them to use. They buy only absolute necessities, having learned in the hard school of Muscovite tyranny that economy is wealth. At the towns in which they deal, the merchants are anxious that more of the same class of settlers should come into the country. They say that much opposition was at first manifested at the Doukhobor immigration, but that those who know them best have nothing but praise for them, either as farmers or citizens. In a very few years the Doukhobors will be in an enviable financial position, in fact wealthy. They are peaceable, law-abiding, industrious and thrifty, are anxious to learn English speech and desirous of following Canadian customs."

This same writer pays a tribute to their politeness of speech, demeanor and action which is typical. No observer that I know of has failed to bear substantially the same testimony:

"We met a party of five Doukhobors—grave, deliberate men, large of stature, slow of speech, with an unaffected, natural courtesy both simple and dignified. We reined up that my companion might speak to them, and one of them, with whom he was acquainted, introduced us to the other four. Each, as his name was mentioned, lifted his heavy black fur cap and bowed. They told us the village was half a mile from the top of the ravine. They lifted their hats again and bowed as we drove on. 'Talk about French politeness,' said my companion, 'it's not in it with the courtesy of these people. They raise their hats whenever they meet each other, and differ from Frenchmen in that they are quite as polite to their own people as they are to strangers. I've traveled a great deal, and I never saw such genuine simplicity and courtesy. Wait till you get to the village, and you'll see that all I've said is true.'"

In conclusion, we may fitly quote the testimony of Nellie Baker, whose educational work among them has been already mentioned. She says:

"The dignified courtesy and hospitality extended to us in more than a score of their villages, the manly bearing of the men, the delightful sympathy and affection with which they regard everything connected with their homes,—an estimation of the home that has little to learn from, and possibly something to teach to, even Anglo-Saxons—their dwellings, that already surpass in comfort and cleanliness those of any other class of settlers excepting those from older

Canada and Great Britain, all testify to the desirability of the Doukhobors as settlers, who will, I believe, soon make good Canadian citizens. It does not require very keen perception on the part of one having had a welcome into hundreds of their homes to be assured that this is a community living up to high moral standards and holding tenaciously to the simple tenets of Christian faith."

CHAPTER IV.

RELATIONS WITH THE CIVIL AUTHORITIES.

No phase of the Doukhobor problem has done more to perplex the government which extended them hospitality, and to embarrass their friends and well-wishers, than the attitude which the Doukhobors have maintained toward the civil government. This has in many cases amounted to a complete denial of the authority and righteousness of any governmental control over the individual, and a persistent distrust of the kindest and most well-intentioned efforts of the Canadian government to help them.

When I called the representatives of forty villages, composing the Yorkton and Swan River colonies, together at Poterpevshe, it was for the purpose of explaining the position which the Canadian government took in the registering of homesteads, marriages and births, and I was impressed with the inability of these men to comprehend that purpose, or rather to free their minds from the suspicion that any compliance with the governmental regulations might involve some ulterior and unpleasant obligation—conflicting with what they understood to be "the law of God." When the patriarch, Ivan Mahortov, quoted the Russian proverb, "A scared hare is afraid of every stump," just as we entered upon a discussion as to the wisdom of the homestead law, I felt distinctly, and told the delegates, that this was a most critical juncture in their history. They acknowledged the truth of this, but they could not agree among themselves that it was necessary to apply in *severalty* for their homesteads, even though the Canadian government would permit them to hold their farms in common after the entry had been made; and as to registering marriages and births, they thought it need be no concern of the government to know who was married or born.

There is one central feature of their communal life that we shall do well to consider carefully,—a feature which helps us to realize how far back their present community instinct goes, all unknown to themselves. For generations and centuries the peasant institution of the *Mir* has existed, and one cannot but see how advantageous it has been under the conditions which surrounded the average peasant in Russia. Indeed, except for the mutual support they were enabled to give one another by their communal system, it would scarcely have been possible for them to survive all the persecutions to which they were subjected. So all who would help them should appreciate the hold this brotherhood idea has upon them, and not press them unduly to break away prematurely from their communal customs. It was noticeable that in those villages where all was held in common, as at Poterpevshe, for instance, the comfort and harmony apparent were greater than in some other villages where the individualistic system had been adopted.

While we believe the Canadian government affords every opportunity to its settlers to prosper under its homestead laws, yet no great harm could result from granting to the Doukhobors the privilege of possessing their lands in common; and this has practically been granted to them until such time as they can see the benefit of applying for it in severalty. It is not to be wondered at that they should dread to divide up their allotments when fully one-third of the peasants in Middle Russia have been brought to utter ruin by such division, and excessive taxation after total failures of crops.

P. Kropotkin says: "For the last twenty years a strong wind of opposition to the individual appropriation of the land has been stirring again through the middle Russian villages, and strenuous efforts are being made by the bulk of those peasants who stand between the rich and the very poor to uphold the village community." He further adds, after a careful study of an immense mass of material collected during the colossal house-to-house inquest conducted recently by several *zemstvos* (county councils), embracing a population of twenty millions in different parts of Russia, that "wherever the Russian peasants, owing to a concurrence of favorable circumstances, are less miserable than they are on the average, and wherever they find men of knowledge and initiative among their neighbors, the village community becomes the very means for introducing various improvements in agriculture and village life.

Here, as elsewhere, mutual aid is a better leader to progress than the war of each against all, as may be seen from the following facts. In South Russia the use of perfected ploughs rapidly spread. A village community, after purchasing a plough, experimented upon a portion of the communal land, and indicated the necessary improvements to the makers, whom the communes often aided in starting the manufacture of cheap ploughs as a village industry. In the district of Moscow, where fifteen hundred and sixty ploughs were lately bought by the peasants during five years, the impulse came from those communes which rented lands *as a body* for the special purpose of improved culture."

While passing through the Doukhobor villages one could readily observe the latest and best reaping and other agricultural implements in those villages where the common purse was available for their purchase.

(Communal)

In the Third month, 1901, a statement was issued by a number of Doukhobors claiming to act as delegates from and as representing "the Society of the Universal Brotherhood, in Canada." Underneath the names of the delegates appears the further signature: "Address for letters, A. Bodyansky, Yorkton, Assa., Canada." The statement rehearses at some length the questions at issue between the Canadian government and the Doukhobors (or a certain party among them), beginning with the petition presented Sixth month 22d, 1900, which was in substance as follows:

"Petition to the Canadian government from the delegates of the Society of Universal Brotherhood, near Yorkton, Assa.:

"Before everything else, we must extend to you, from the communities which delegated us, their sincere and heartfelt thanks for opening the country which is governed by you to us, for your endeavors to help us to settle and for your interest in our welfare. We feel and express to you our great gratitude. But now, after becoming acquainted with the laws of your country, we are obliged to make another request, that you take into consideration our beliefs, which we consider to be the laws of God, and grant us the possibility to settle and live in your country without breaking those laws. You doubtless understand that we cannot break these laws, as we believe them to embody the Truth of God, but we have found out that you have in force laws the fulfillment of which will be a direct breaking of such Truth. Enumerating below what points in your laws do not correspond with our understanding of the Divine Truth, we ask you not to enforce against us such of your laws as contradict our beliefs, and thus give us the possibility of living in your country without breaking, openly or tacitly, directly or indirectly, our conception of the Truth.

"(1) The laws of your country require that every

male emigrant 18 years of age, who wants to settle on vacant government land, has to record it in his name, and, after a certain term, such land becomes his property. But we cannot accept such a law, cannot record homesteads in our individual names, cannot make them our private property, for we believe that in so doing we would break directly God's Truth. Who knows this Truth knows also that it opposes the acquisition of property. But if, through human weakness, a man may be forgiven for considering as his own anything which he has acquired by his labor, and which is necessary for his daily use, like clothing, food, or household goods and utensils, there is no excuse for a man who, knowing the law of God, still appropriates as his own something that is not the fruit of his labor, but was created by God for the use of everybody. Is not the division, the ownership and the recording of land the main cause of wars and strife among men, and is it not the cause of there being masters and serfs? The law of God commands men to live like brothers, without divisions, but in union for mutual help; but if a man cuts out and appropriates land for himself,—land which he did not work to create,—how is he going to divide with others the results of his own labor? And as every breaking of Divine Truth brings evil, so did evil creep among us when we thoughtlessly accepted land under your homestead laws. Already the division of land between our various settlements has caused quarrels about that land among us, quarrels unknown to us heretofore. And what will be the result if each one of us becomes the owner of a separate piece, and the land under our settlements becomes private property? It will prove a great temptation to the strong, and fatal to the weak. Taking all the above into consideration, we petition you to let us have the land for settlement and agricultural purposes, not upon your general conditions for emigrants, but upon the conditions given to your Indians—that is, the land to be held by the community, and not by individual members. It matters not to us whether that land be considered our community property, or the property of your country; but we would like it to be considered as given to us for an indefinite period of time, and if you wish us to pay rent we are willing to do so, provided we shall be able.

"(2) You have also a law in your country that everybody who wants to contract marriage, in order to make it legal, shall obtain a license, and pay two dollars for the same; and that a divorce can be obtained only in the courts; and if a person should remarry without a divorce so obtained he is liable to imprisonment for many years.

"We cannot accept such a law, for we believe that it also breaks the law of God. We cannot believe that a marriage can become legal because it is recorded in a police register and a fee of two dollars paid for it; on the contrary, we believe that such recording and payment annuls marriage and breaks up its real legality. We believe that the real legalization of a marriage union is when it is brought about freely as a result of a pure feeling, of a mutual moral affection between man and woman. Only such a pure feeling of love, born of the mutual recognition of moral traits of character, creates a real legality of a marriage according to the law of God,—not a record of the same in a police register and a money fee. Every marriage which has its source in this pure feeling of mutual love will be legal before God, although it were not registered, and other people would not recognize its legality; and every marriage not the result of free will and pure love, but contracted unwillingly, or for lust, or money, or any other consideration, will be always illegal before God, although it should be registered in all the police records and considered legal by everybody. Therefore we believe that legalization of the marriage bond belongs solely to God; and we cannot consent to transfer the legalization of our marriages from God to the police. As to divorce, we believe that every man who has divorced his wife is an adulterer, and forces her to become an adulteress; and that every remarriage, or marrying a divorced man or woman, is also adultery. But we believe also that the law of God is the law of freedom, that an open sin is lighter than a secret one, and that if a marriage union is contracted otherwise than through a pure feeling of love, such a union is illegal from its beginning, and constitutes the sin of adultery; and that therefore when persons living in such an illegal union come to such a conclusion, and conceive the impossibility of making such a union legal, out of two evils the lesser for them will be to divorce and to separate. And in such a case a divorce may become legal, if the heavenly Father will forgive the sin of the divorced parties, and so allow them to remarry with free consciences. As the forgiveness of God can be known only to the two people concerned, no one, nor any human institution, can make a divorce either legal or illegal, for they cannot be competent to know whether God forgave the sin of divorce or not. That can be known only to the consciences of the divorced themselves.

"In consideration of the above, we cannot recognize as correct, and cannot accept any human laws as to the marriage union, being sure that all pertaining to it is in the province of God's will and human conscience.

"(3) There is another law in your country, which requires that every inhabitant shall give notice to the police of every birth and death in his family.

"We cannot accept that law, for we see no need of it in the order of things prescribed by God. Our heavenly Father knows, without a police register, whom He sends into the world and whom He calls back. Only the will of God is important to humanity, for upon it depends our life and death, and not upon a police register. A man will live until he is called by his Creator, although he should not be recorded in a police register, and can die immediately after having been registered as living.

"We do not refuse to answer, if called upon, about the number of births and deaths in our communities. If anybody wants to know it, let him ask; but we will not, of ourselves, report it to any one.

"Having explained what in the laws of your country is irreconcilable with what we consider the Divine Truth, and which we cannot break, we once more petition the government of Canada to grant us exceptions concerning the use of lands, legality of marriage unions, and registration, in order that we may live in Canada without breaking the Divine Truth as we understand it."

To this petition no formal reply was made by the government officials until nearly six months had elapsed, but quiet measures were taken to have the known friends and benefactors of the Doukhobors attempt to dissuade them from their refractory and dangerous course. Aylmer Maude, who had taken a prominent part in the direction of the exodus from Russia, wrote a letter, which was widely circulated by government agents in the Doukhobor settlements, pointing out the weakness and the necessary futility of the petition. A committee of Philadelphia Yearly Meeting also drafted and forwarded to the villages the following communication:

TO THE CHRISTIANS OF THE UNIVERSAL BROTHERHOOD IN CANADA.

"The Friends of Philadelphia Send Greeting.

"From the time your trials through persecution became known to us our hearts have gone out to you, and our minds have been affected by the griefs you were made to bear.

"We still greatly desire your welfare, both in the things which increase your comfort in this world, and in that spiritual knowledge and holy obedience to the laws of God which come to us through faith in Him; and in the possession and practice of which we are saved with an everlasting salvation through Jesus Christ.

"We desire to be closely united with you in seeking after this hope of eternal life which our Father in heaven has revealed to the children of men by the sending of the Lord Jesus Christ into the world. He is indeed our King and Law-giver, and it is He whom we must obey, as He makes known to us His holy will. This we believe He does, both by the Light of His Holy Spirit in the secret of our hearts, and by the teachings of the Holy Scriptures, which holy men of old wrote as they were moved by the spirit of truth.

"Ancient Israel acknowledged God to be their ruler and guide, but at the same time were given written laws to regulate their actions and dealings, which were administered by men who were appointed for this purpose; and to these good laws and human rulers the people submitted themselves.

"After the coming of the Lord Jesus Christ into the world, His apostles enjoined obedience to outward rulers, as being those who in the providence of God are set over the nations and peoples to preserve order amongst them.

"The Apostle Paul wrote, 'These are God's ministers attending to these very things'; and again, 'Rulers are His ministers to us for good, and to them we must be obedient, not only for wrath, but also for conscience' sake.' He commands that we should pray for kings and for all who are in authority, that we may lead a quiet and peaceable life in all godliness and honesty. Now, we are aware you have lived under a government which has required you to do some things which are directly contrary to the laws of Christ,—to fight and destroy men's lives, and to offer to God a worship which is not in spirit and in truth. These are matters in which the rule of Christ, as it is plainly laid down in His teaching, is denied and set at naught. And in these matters Christians ought to obey *Him* rather than *men*.

"There are, however, many laws enacted by men which contribute to peace and good order among them, by securing to all their just rights and privileges, and give to every one an opportunity to seek his own welfare without at the same time depriving others of the like opportunity.

"Among these laws which we approve as being

agreeable to the Divine law is the holding of land in individual ownership, by which the legal occupant may improve, cultivate and use it for his own maintenance and for the general advantage of the community in which he lives.

"It is easily perceived that such laws help to preserve the peace, by preventing unjust and covetous persons appropriating to themselves the fruits of the labor of those who are industrious and quiet in their lives.

"There are persons in almost all countries who disregard justice and honesty, and it is to restrain and correct these that laws are made: as the Apostle Paul has written, 'the law is not made for a righteous man, but for the lawless and disobedient, for the ungodly and for sinners.' Righteous people intend to live holy and innocent lives, but are willing to be put to whatever inconvenience may come to them in complying with laws made for the general good, in order to give the influence of their example in favor of good government, that it may not be weakened in its dealings with those who practice injustice and crime.

"While we speak of ownership in land and other property, as Christians we know that ourselves and all that we possess belong to God, and that we are only stewards to use that which has been honestly acquired for His glory and for the good of our neighbors who need help. Therefore, in this sense none of us can say that what he possesses is his own; but as a steward to whom has been entrusted a charge he should manage and use it for the benefit of his fellow-creatures as well as for himself. We will remember and observe the golden rule, 'Whatsoever ye desire that men should do to you do ye likewise even so to them.'

"In the covenant of marriage our Saviour has laid down a rule which his followers are bound to observe. It is this: 'Whom God has joined together let not man put asunder,' 'Whosoever puts away his wife saving for the cause of fornication, and marries another, commits adultery; and he that marries her when she is put away commits adultery.'

"It is the duty of human government to prevent vice and immorality in this matter, and to make regulations by which children should be cared for by their parents, which would not be the case if parents loosely lived together, and separated when they are tempted to cohabit with another person.

"Much scandal and reproach would result to the Christian name if those who claim it adopt a practice sometimes called free love; or allow a man to have at the same time more than one wife, or a woman more than one husband. Death of a wife or husband can alone dissolve the marriage tie; after which the survivor is free to marry again, if done in the liberty of the spirit.

"The laws of Christian nations rightly forbid such libertine practices, and the laws of Canada requiring the registration of marriages are designed to prevent bigamy by making it plain who are joined in marriage, while the registration of births shows who are the children of married parents, and who are responsible for their care.

"We thus address you, our Christian brothers, in the desire to help you to accept the experience of many who are and have been the faithful servants of God, and yet have, in these things to which we herein refer, been able with a good conscience in the sight of their Maker and Saviour to be governed by the laws of the countries in which they live. Among the members of our (Friends) Society we have known no instance of any one refusing to comply with the laws of their country regarding the registry of land titles, marriages, births, and deaths; although many of them have suffered much for their conscientious objections to war, oaths, tithes to the clergy, and other matters relating to religion.

"While human government is so often enforced by the use of deadly weapons and the punishment of death, and in those respects is opposed to the law of love and mercy enjoined by the teaching and spirit of Jesus Christ, yet Christians have safe precepts and examples for submitting to and actively complying with those requirements which are intended to promote the general welfare of a nation, without involving any acts which are injurious to their fellowmen, or are contrary to the worship and service due to Almighty God, whose we are and whom we wish to glorify.

"We therefore would persuade you to humbly look up to Him, and ask that He will give you light and grace to see and believe that He will justify you in complying with the laws of Canada which are now referred to, and enable you to enjoy with thankful hearts the fruits of His goodness, in making a way for settlement in a country where peace and liberty of conscience are so largely found.

"We heve been instructed and encouraged by your faithfulness to religious convictions, in refusing to take any part in preparation for war, and by learning of the dreadful persecution you suffered for the possession of a good conscience. Our desire now is that we may be closely united together in the bonds of Christian love and fellowship, and that we may continue to be helpers of each other towards the heavenly kingdom.

"Jos. S. Elkinton.
"George M. Comfort.
"Ephraim Smith.
"Jonathan E. Rhoads.
"Samuel Morris.
"William L. Bailey.
"William Evans."

The extreme solicitude expressed in this communication for the maintenance of pure morals among the Doukhobors shows very forcibly the alarm which the incident created. Even the best friends of the Brotherhood, not without reason, took the argument against the licensing and registration of marriages to be a plea for loose family relations. Fortunately, it has been shown beyond a doubt that such laxity is almost utterly unknown amongst the Doukhobors, and the sinister meaning which it was feared lay in this demand is seen to be nothing worse than perversity or infirmity of mind and temper. It is against this perversity, obstinacy and density that the further efforts of the Dominion government and other friends of the Doukhobors have been directed. In First month, 1901, the following reply to the petition of the Doukhobors was sent from the Canadian Department of the Interior:

"Ottawa, 7th January, 1901.

"Semen Semenov, Vassili Popov and others, village Blagodarofra.

"Dear Sirs:—In further reference to your petition to the government of Canada, of the 22d of June last, I beg to say, that since my interview with your head men in the month of November, I have discussed the subject-matter of the said petition with the authorities here, and in reply can only state what has already been written you, namely, that in reference to the question of taking up land it can only be done in the ordinary way. We have only one system of granting free homesteads to settlers, and the same rules apply to every settler coming into the province of Manitoba or the Northwest Territories, irrespective of his nationality or religious belief. These rules and regulations are the result of many years' experience, and have been found to be the best, both in the interests of the settler and of the country in general.

"I might point out to you that it would be impossible for the government to retain lands for your people unless they have entered each man for his own homestead, as the lands would appear vacant in our books, and other parties would go and settle on them and apply for entry, and we would have no grounds for refusing to grant the same.

"I might further say, however, that after your individual settlers have completed their homestead duties a patent will issue to each homesteader, giving him the full and absolute ownership of the land, after which it is his own to dispose of as he thinks best, and if your people should then decide to appoint trustees to hold the land in common for the use and benefit of all the people, that is a matter about which you can do as they wish, and one in which the government will not interfere in any way. You will notice that all your own friends (both Mr. Maude and the Quaker Society of England) take exactly the same view which we do on this question, and I therefore trust that you will at once set about having your entries made for this land.

"As before stated, if it is not convenient for your people to pay an entry fee at the present time, the entry may still be made, and we will charge the entry fee as a lien against the land, to be paid off with interest at six per cent. per annum before the patent can issue.

"The government is quite willing that your people should reside in villages, the cultivation of course to be done on the individual homesteads.

"In reference to that portion of your petition concerning the giving of information for the preparation of vital statistics, relating to births, deaths and marriages, I might say that this matter comes under the jurisdiction of the local government at Regina. There is, however, no possibility that your wishes in this matter can be met. On this subject there is one law for all the people of Canada, from the Atlantic to the Pacific, and it applies to everyone, and the question of making any changes in respect to the Doukhobors will not be considered for a moment. A complete public record must be kept of every person married, with names and dates, and of every child born, and of every person who dies. This is the usual system, as you are aware, and has never been objected to by anybody, and good, law-abiding people have no reason to fear compliance with this part of the Canadian law.

"In conclusion, I may state that the people of Canada were pleased to have you come to their country. They are prepared to treat you liberally and well; to put you on an exact equality with themselves; to give you the benefit and protection of their laws; but, as I stated to you at our interview, no special laws will be made for your people, nor will they be treated in a different manner from any other class of settlers in the country, or who may come into the country.

"As soon as you have been three years in Canada you may become full citizens, and have the same voice in the making of our laws as we have ourselves.

"On this point there will be no object in continuing the discussion, as the laws of the country must prevail absolutely, and you will find as you become better acquainted with the laws of Canada that it is only the wicked and vicious who have any reason to fear them. Therefore I trust that in all these matters you will see that it is to your own interest to give a ready and cheerful compliance to our laws, in accordance with the advice of your own friends.

"Yours truly,

"J. G. SURRIFF,

"Commissioner Dominion Lands."

To this letter, as to that of Aylmer Maude, the committee of delegates made reply, adhering to the ground taken in the original petition, and repeating their previous arguments, with very little sign of comprehension of the case against them, or of the admirable patience and restraint shown by the authorities. In fact, they went a step beyond their previous position to make direct charges of falsehood and bad faith against their friends because these did not approve the petition.

Here, substantially, the case has stood ever since, and still stands. The Dominion authorities have naturally been unwilling to proceed to harsh measures to enforce their authority, and the matter has largely been allowed to drift, in the hope that the logic of events would finally penetrate the reasoning faculties of the recalcitrants. In this hope they have been partially justified. In certain localities, and under the influence of certain persons, much progress has been made,—homesteads have been duly entered, the registration laws have been complied with, and whole settlements have made substantial progress in enlightenment. On the other hand, many localities have made no sensible progress whatever, and new vagaries, such as the Pilgrimage described in a preceding chapter, have arisen to vex the officials.

The recent arrival of Peter Verigin in Canada, after his release from his long exile in Russia, may prove the needed solvent to this vexed situation. According to the *Manitoba Free Press*, of Winnipeg, it is confidently expected that "his counsel will solve the Doukhobor problem, probably for all time, one way or the other. If he recommends the communities to enter for their lands, and in other respects obey the regulations of Canadian law, they will certainly loyally comply. If, on the other hand, he endorses the stand of agitators and ex-pilgrims, all hopes of the Doukhobors' submission may be abandoned. In either case the course of the government will be simplified. In the latter alternative the land at present occupied by the Doukhobors will probably be thrown open for settlement. The authorities hope, however, that Verigin's coming may lead to a complete and speedy pacification of all the communities." In this hope all the friends of the Doukhobors will fervently join.

One of the puzzles of the situation is to know the real attitude of the great body of the Brotherhood in these matters, and the extent to which the petition and the subsequent writings in the controversy represent the real sentiments of the communities. It will be noticed that these communications emanate from Yorkton, the least progressive of the settlements; and that the person who seems to have drawn up the instruments is one A. Bodyansky. After investigating the matter the Dominion officials reached the conclusion that Bodyansky was little better than a professional agitator, and he was finally forced to leave the country. It is yet too early to know the result of this move, and there seems good ground for hoping that the situation has been improved thereby, but this is by no means certain. It seems likely that while Bodyansky was directly responsible for fomenting much of the disturbance, he had the material ready to his hand in the shape of widespread discontent and unrest. As has been before stated, only a very small proportion of the

Doukhobors can read and write, and they are therefore necessarily dependent on some lettered person for the statement of their case in writing. Of course under such circumstances no one would expect a document like the petition to state accurately the views of the uneducated majority, but it is probable that it did represent, though crudely and indefinitely, the existing mass of discontent and unrest, the most prominent characteristic of which was simply an instinctive and inbred attitude of antagonism to all government.

Unreasonable and childish as this attitude appears to the citizen of a free government, it can be largely explained by the experience of the Doukhobors under the Russian despotism. When government is essentially tyranny there is small wonder if its victims come to look on all government as unrighteous. Yet there is room and need, and we believe there is capacity, on their part, for a better understanding of the essential functions of all right government, and in particular of the enlightened and benevolent free government under whose care they now find themselves. We appreciate how their conception of Christ's kingdom of peace and brotherhood cannot be reconciled with the militarism which is so inseparably connected with most of the governments of the civilized world, but there is a wide difference between this belated method of settling disputes and those governmental regulations which are necessary for the common welfare of all citizens of a free republic or limited monarchy. To educate the Doukhobors to a sense of these differences, and to an openness to receive and appreciate new ideas, is undoubtedly the crying need of the situation.

To honor one's conscience is a duty, but to discredit another's is far from admirable. While we share the Brotherhood idea of equality in all spiritual privileges, we think those privileges ought to be conceded to mankind at large, and not so interpreted as to mean that *we* are the only people who have the oracles of God.

The liberty to follow the dictates of their conscience can in no wise release them from their obligation to support a government so liberal as that under which, in the good providence of God, they now live,—a government whose chief purpose is to secure "the blessings of life, liberty and the pursuit of happiness," and one that has released them from any necessity to violate their conscience by military service.

By their peaceful but firm refusal to obey the un-Christian demands of any law they did not believe to be consistent with that of God, they have been driven into a false position toward *all* government, and the writings of Count Tolstoi and his followers have emphasized this disposition. The habit of passive submission to any punishment inflicted by the civil or military authorities has become so fixed as to continue after the original cause has been removed, and we may well remember how frequently this tendency has appeared in the religious history of all ages and sects!

As this volume was passing through the press my attention was directed to a consideration of these questions in a work by P. Birukov.* The author was one of three Russian gentlemen who went to the Caucasus about the time the Doukhobors were most severely persecuted (1897), in order to investigate their troubles and report the facts to the Czar. His interest in suffering humanity was rewarded by being permanently exiled from his native land. As he has given much thought to their needs, I gladly give space to his suggestions for a solution of the present difficulties.

He says: "Their [the Doukhobors'] failure to yield obedience is shown in many ways, from the refusal to give military service, to the refusal to uncover their heads before the state officials, and even the Czar.

"But such is the power of a religious idea that the swords of their persecutors were dulled, and the oppressed sect increased and their devotions spread.

"The Doukhobors who emigrated to Canada, while welcoming their happy removal from a land of persecution to one of liberty, do not wish the government of Canada to interfere with their affairs.

---

* "Tolstoi et les Doukhobors," translated from the Russian into the French by J. W. Bienstock, Paris, 1902.

They consent to pay tribute to Edward VII., as they did to Alexander, and to Nicholas, but they are not disposed to submit to the civil law." *

"Two issues can end this conflict: first, under the influence of their new surroundings, and, by recognition of Canadian life, the removal of their objection to individualism could be brought about, and the Doukhobors would submit to all the demands of the Canadian government; secondly, if their protest against individualism becomes strengthened, the Doukhobors will submit to persecution, but nevertheless the government of Canada will be forced to recognize their independence, and they will be settled in a country apart, which will be given to them. The government of Canada hesitates to take one or the other of these courses, and in putting off the decisive step shows its true wisdom. But all this affair is complicated by the interference of a foreign element. One of the friends of the Doukhobors who lived with them in the Caucasus, full of sympathy for their exalted Christian ideals, for which the Doukhobors were persecuted, left Russia and became literary interpreter of the Doukhobor protestations against the government of Canada.

* I found this to be the case to considerable extent in all their colonies, with this difference, however, between the Prince Albert and the Yorkton settlements,—that in the former the taking up of homesteads was not considered a violation of their desire to be free from all connection with the government.

"He gave, according to the expression of one of the emigrants,—an intellectual man living among the Doukhobors in Canada,—'the Christian phraseology' to the request of the Doukhobors.

"But the motive for the protestation he raised to a higher Christian and anarchistical view than was shared in by all the Doukhobors. But as these are illiterate, they accept this literary expression of the protest more on account of confidence in the author than by their absolute acquaintance with its contents. To our question as to what they thought of the contents of the request, one of the signers answered: 'As to that which Bodyansky has written, you know that we have not enough mind to understand each word, and there are certain words which do not suit us at all, but Bodyansky is a tenacious old man, and interprets always according to his own way.' Yet in letters of the Doukhobors who have signed the request is expressed the firm resolution not to yield to the government of Canada upon three points which form the object of the request: individual property-holding, civil marriage, and civil registration.

"The protest against the formality of the acts of individual sale does not bear upon landed property in general,—it is directed against the interference of the state in the division of land.

"The protest against the interference with their marriage customs is not against marriage in general, but against the interference of the government in the institution of civil marriage.

"So their protest against registration is not against registration in general, but against the obligation to communicate to government information about their interior life.

"In addition to the written declaration of this kind by the Doukhobors themselves, that which confirms our remarks is that the most Christian part of the protestations,—that against landed proprietaries,—is shared by only a small minority of the Doukhobors; while the protest against the civil registration, which touches least the Christian doctrine, is shared in by almost all the Doukhobors of the three colonies, even by those who have not submitted to the intellectual influence above mentioned.

"The situation being thus set forth, we are going to try to solve the very difficult question: What should the two adverse parties do? That is to say, the Doukhobors, who do not wish to submit to the demands of the government of Canada, and the government of Canada, which does not wish to give up to these demands.

"We are far from desiring to take to ourselves the rôle of master and guide in this affair, but we believe it our duty to explain our opinion, since the Doukhobors themselves have asked counsel from us.

"As to the Doukhobors, we believe above all that they ought to be enlightened concerning all that is being done around them, and this is why they ought to cease to call their opposition ‘the most Christian act’ of the Universal Fraternity, and to simply call it the obligation for the Doukhobors to recognize their autonomy.

“It is then in this sense that it is necessary to engage in discussion with the government of Canada, since under all circumstances pecuniary relations will be maintained between them. The Doukhobors should elect among themselves representatives who will be charged with the necessary relations with the government of Canada. And as probably the government of Canada could adapt its regulations to their conscience, these same attorneys should hold these registries in the most convenient way for the Doukhobors to comply with the law.

“This would not in any way prevent the Doukhobors from continuing their advance in moral development and their aspirations to attain ideals of pure Christianity. In the same way this will not prevent the development among them of the principles of communism or of the abolition of property in severalty.

“What should the government of Canada do?

“First, continue the policy of waiting that it has wisely adopted, and not be in haste to take a decisive step; second, if it is possible, do everything available to yield to the demands of the Doukhobors. Such a policy will be most advantageous for it and for them, considering how, during the fifty years of life of the Doukhobors in the Caucasus, they were the most exact in paying taxes, and that during this period no one was arrested for civil or criminal misdemeanor.

"Since for their individualism the Doukhobors do not demand any right, but only the possession, without obstacles, of the land which will be assigned to them, it seems to us possible to satisfy their demand."

While thus advising the policy of Christian forbearance to our good neighbors of the Dominion, we have a word also for our dear friends, the Doukhobors, who have received abundant evidence of sympathy from the present administration.

We would ask them seriously to consider what Christian good will was manifested upon their arrival on these shores; how thoroughly welcome they were, and what efforts their best friends, among all denominations, made, together with the officials upon whom devolved so heavily the labor of settling them. We ask how they can possibly regard such evidences of disinterested kindness otherwise than as proceeding from hearts like their own, which are ever ready to supply the needs of the suffering?

We would, after having enjoyed their confidence and their hospitality, express the fullest appreciation of their conscientious convictions, but would ask in return that they will consider the Canadian government has only one purpose in its requirements, and that is to give all who come to live under it the greatest opportunity to enjoy the blessings of freedom, both material and religious.

Nothing could be more natural than a suspicion that some advantage is likely to be taken of us when for a century we have suffered from every point of contact with a cruel government, but why should we so misjudge the character and actions of one which has shown so much consideration for us?

The Exodus from Russia.

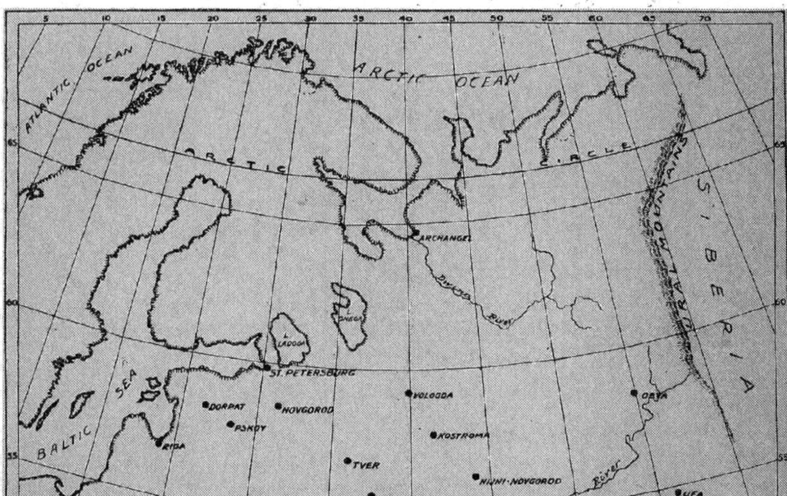

Doukhobor Settlements in the Russian Empire.

The Milky Waters colony was just north of Sevastopol and bordering on the Sea of Azov. The settlements in the Caucasus were in the three provinces of Tiflis, Kars, and Elizabetpol, between the Caucasian Mountains and the Persian frontier, as indicated by dotted lines. The Doukhobors first appeared in the territory between the Black Sea and the dotted line to the north of it.

CHAPTER I.

RECENT PERSECUTIONS.

The story of the rise, progress and persecutions of the Doukhobors is a long and bitter one, running back into the dim light of the middle of the eighteenth century. Those events which directly brought about their emigration to Canada are, however, comparatively recent, and to understand these we need only glance at their history during the last generation.

A period of comparative ease and prosperity intervened between the last Turkish war, in 1877, and 1887, when universal conscription was introduced into the Caucasus. The strict observance of the religious practices of the Doukhobors lapsed to some extent, and considerable money was accumulated by their several communities. In some of these an Orphan House was established, and the presiding officer came to have almost unlimited influence over the brotherhood—now settled in three Governments of Transcaucasia, Elizavetpol, Tiflis and Kars.

Their numbers had increased to twenty thousand, and while they had great difficulty in raising grain of any kind at an elevation of five thousand feet on the Wet Mountains of Georgia, they devoted themselves so successfully to breeding cattle as to become well-to-do in many instances.

The leaders of this sect have been strong characters since the beginning of their settlement on the Milky Waters, but how they are chosen is difficult to ascertain. Pôbiróhin, Kapoustin, Kalmykov, his wife, Loukerya Vasilyevna Kalmykova, and now Peter Verigin, have successively occupied this important position during the past century. These leaders endeavored to govern wisely "under the immediate control and with the co-operation of the Deity Himself, by means of inward universal inspiration and revelation from above." (Novitsky.) So that, as A. Maude says: "With all their limitations and deficiencies, with their history for nearly a century before us, one may fairly say of the Doukhobors that (except in times of external persecution), without any government founded on force, they have managed their affairs better than their neighbors have done; with no army or police, they have suffered little from crimes of violence; and without priests or ministers, they have had more practical religion, and more intelligible guidance for their spiritual life. Without doctors or medicine or bacteriologists (though ignorant even of the first principles of ventilation), they have been, on the average, healthier and stronger than most other races. Without political economists, wealth among them has been better distributed, and they have (apart from the effects of persecution) suffered far less from extremes of wealth and poverty. Without lawyers or written laws, they have settled their disputes. Without books, they have educated their children to be industrious, useful, peaceable and God-fearing men and women; have instructed them in the tenets of their religion, and taught them to produce the food, clothing and shelter needed for themselves and for others.

"As a community they are to-day abstainers from alcohol, non-smokers, and for the most part, vegetarians. It would be difficult to find a class of people equally numerous among whom there is less immorality, or among whom the family bond is more regarded."

Communism, which the Russian peasants generally favor, has become with the Doukhobors a religious principle. In the face of this we have the same individualistic ambition occasionally asserting itself which has rent asunder other religious sects of similar high ideals. We would gladly pass over a division of this character, but the facts remain. A contention arose among the Doukhobors about the year 1886, when Peter Verigin was banished to Archangel. He had been trained under Loukerya Vasilyevna Kalmykova for five years, with the express intention of succeeding her as chief administrator and "Prophet" of the Doukhobors, but upon the death of this rather remarkable woman, quite a faction, known as the "Small Party," insisted upon her brother being recognized as the leader. Recourse was had to the Russian law—the first time for fifty years—and several of the "Large Party" were sent to Northeast Siberia. This was finally accomplished by the Small Party's bribing the Government officials with a gift of ten thousand roubles.

A long and detailed account of these events (introduced to the reader by a letter from Leo Tolstoi) appeared in *The* (London) *Times* for Tenth month 23d, 1895. It was written by a friend of the Doukhobors who had visited the Caucasus, in order to gain his information on the spot. From this article we give extracts:

"Such obvious acts of injustice (as those described above) agitated the whole community; and coming to the conclusion that there is no justice to be had from Government, the Larger Party resolved to act independently.

"They collected a new fund of one hundred thousand roubles, making all the private property of the richer members equal with that of the poorer, and they handed over the management of this fund to Peter Verigin, about whom they drew more closely than before."

A widespread religious awakening took place among them; they ceased to smoke, drink wine and eat flesh; they practised communism, and resolved no longer to bear arms, even in self-defense. In their time of laxity some of them had fallen in with the practice of their neighbors, not only to defend themselves from brigands, but also from wild beasts. While this awakening was taking place, Peter Verigin and a few others of the leading men were banished first to Archangel and then to Siberia, in consequence of the intrigues of the Smaller Party, who accused them of rebellion.

During his transportation from Archangel to a remote place in Siberia in the winter of 1894-5, Verigin was "visited in Moscow by some of his spiritual brethren from the Caucasus, and they returned home with a proposal from him, which was accepted by the whole Larger Party, to abstain from oath-taking, from military duty, and from every participation in the violent acts of the Government, and to destroy all their arms. From that time the Doukhobortsi began to refuse to serve in the army. The first man who refused was Matthew Lebedeov, who served in Elisavetpol in the reserve battalion. For special service, honesty and intelligence, he had been made a non-commissioned officer. Ten of his brethren were in the same battalion, and together they agreed to announce their refusal to bear arms by absenting themselves from the parade on the first day of Easter. When the sergeant-major discovered the cause of their absence, "he fell upon Lebedeov, threatening and insulting him." Lebedeov at first quietly told him the facts, and then "took out his gun from the pile and handed it over to the sergeant-major. Then the latter changed his manner, began to beg pardon for his abusive language, and to entreat Lebedeov to alter his decision. But Lebedeov remained inflexible."

After many ineffectual entreaties from fellow

officers, "the commanding officer ordered Lebedeov's arrest. He was escorted to a dark, underground cell called 'the pit,' where he was kept in strict confinement, receiving only bread and water in very small quantities." His ten companions followed his example, and were imprisoned separately, that they might not encourage one another; but communication went on continually between them by means of the soldiers, who were all in sympathy with the prisoners. The case took its judicial course. They were tried in Tiflis Seventh month 14th, and the court sentenced them to the disciplinary battalion—a place of cruel torture—Lebedeov for three years, and the rest for two. Most of these men, as well as many others, are now in Siberia.

After this, case after case began to occur of refusals of Doukhobor soldiers to serve. A few soldiers of the Orthodox Greek Church followed their example. When a Doukhobor refuses to serve, he shortly explains his reasons for so doing.

"Q. Why do you not wish to serve the Emperor?"

"A. I should like to obey his will, but he trains us to kill men, and my conscience refuses that."

"Q. Why does it refuse?"

"A. Because the Saviour has forbidden us to kill men, and I believe Him, and follow God's will."

"Q. What are you?"

"A. I am a Christian."

"Q. Why do you call yourself a Christian?"

"A. Because I know Christ's teachings. A Christian's living spirit will not and cannot do such deeds as yours." "From this point the authorities are unable to turn to us," added the Doukhobor who gave me this information.

When the Governor of Tiflis was going to visit the villages of the Doukhobortsi, the chief of the district ordered thirteen men from these villages to guard the road from brigands. They ought to have appeared with arms, but they came without them. On the chief of the district questioning them as to why they had come without arms, they answered that they had no need of arms, because, in case of meeting brigands, they were not going to shoot or to beat them, but only persuade them. And at the same time they declared that they refused all service in the government. They were arrested and imprisoned.

Those who refused to take out militia certificates were also imprisoned and afterwards sent to Siberia.

The Doukhobors continued to act in this way on various other occasions of collision with the Government. But all this was only a beginning; there was as yet wanting a general solemn expression of their renunciation of violence. This expression was found in the resolution to burn their arms—such arms as almost every one around them was accustomed to carry and keep in their houses.

The night between Sixth month 28 and 29, 1896, was chosen for this purpose, the eve of Peter and

Paul's Day. (The Doukhobors observe the feasts of the Greek Church, giving to them a symbolic meaning.) This burning of arms took place simultaneously in the province of Kars, in the government of Elisavetpol, and in the Akhalkalaki district of the Tiflis government.

In the province of Kars the officials found out the place of meeting, and many arrests were the result.

In the government of Elisavetpol the burning of arms passed off without trouble, but in the Akhalkalaki district a collision with the officials occurred, the story of which I shall relate in the words of those who took part in it:

"We resolved," said an old Doukhobor, "to serve no longer, and not to obey either the Tsar or any other authority, but to serve God only, to walk in His path, and to do good. We also resolved not to do hurt or use violence to any one; and, above all, to refrain from killing, not only men, but also all living creatures, even the least little bird. That left no need for us to keep arms, and we resolved to destroy them, so as to prevent them from being used by other men for evil purposes. We chose the day of Peter and Paul, and made an announcement in all our villages. We left only knives, but every weapon made to kill men we collected and brought together to a place previously arranged. This place was long ago chosen by us for our great prayer meetings, and is called 'The Cave.' It is really an excavation in the rock. The place is about three versts from the village of Orlovka, and a little further from our other villages. We met at this place, made a pile of all the arms, covered it with wood and coal, poured kerosene over all these, and set the whole on fire. There were present about two thousand people.

"We were anxious lest the authorities should prevent our action, and, therefore, we did not tell every one about our intention; in fact, we met with no hindrance. The inhabitants of other neighboring villages, Armenians, came. They saw how we burnt the arms, but nobody revealed the night's business; and in the morning the pile was burnt out, and we began to pray, and to sing, and to read psalms. After the prayer we returned each to his home, and awaited what punishment might be prepared for us by the Government. But the day passed quietly. In the evening we went again to the same place, and began to burn over again what had escaped the fire, to prevent anybody from using it. We brought some more coal and bellows to blow up the flames, in order to melt the metallic parts into one. That night passed quietly also. At the dawn of day we again began to pray. The people assembled in greater numbers. There were women and children. The inhabitants of different villages came in vans.

"As I said before, we kept secret our intention to burn the arms, being afraid we should be hindered; but our neighbors, the Doukhobortsi who were in disagreement with us, had a suspicion that we were doing something with our arms. Not knowing accurately what, however, and hearing that we were collecting arms, they decided that we were going to rob the Orphan House, about which our quarrel with them arose. As we expected that the authorities would drive us away, or exile us for refusing to serve the Government, some of us made preparations for traveling. All these preparations were taken by our enemies as preparations for a rising or a robbery. They were so afraid of an attack that they denounced us to the authorities. There were stationed at this time in the village of Gorelovka, inhabited by the Doukhobors of the Small Party, two battalions of infantry and two hundred Cossacks.

"Thus the soldiery were already here, and the Governor came to the place of the supposed rising. . . . A messenger came to us, ordering us all to go to the village of Bogdanovka. The old men answered, 'We are at present praying, and till we have finished we shall go nowhere; if the Governor wants to see us let him come to us: we are thousands, and he is one.' The messenger went away, and we continued to pray and sing psalms, intending after prayer to go to the Governor and learn what he wanted with us.

"The prayers were not yet finished when our men who were stationed as watchers informed us that Cossacks were to be seen. We closed together and waited for them. In front of them rode the commanding officer, who, as soon as he approached us, shouted, 'Hurrah!' and with all his hundred men made a rush upon us. The Cossacks began to beat us without restraint, and to ride us down. The men who stood in front were the most badly beaten, and those who were in the middle of the crowd were almost suffocated by the pressure. . . . Some of the Cossacks were ashamed to strike. . . .

"At last they discontinued the beating, and we, bruised and covered with blood, gathered in a crowd and went to the Governor. The women walked with us, but the Cossacks began to cut them off from us, crying that there was no need of women. But the latter said they would follow their spiritual brethren everywhere. The officer ordered them to be beaten with the whips, but they cried that though they should be cut in pieces they would still go; and they went, the Cossacks withdrawing from them.

"After marching a little we stopped, remembering that we had left our carts behind us, and there was nobody to look after them. Then the Cossacks began to beat us, ordering the women to go for the carts, but the women refused; then we were allowed to send from our number one man for each cart to drive the horses, and we continued our route to Bogdanovka, where we were to meet the Governor.

"As we continued to walk, we began to sing a psalm, but the officers stopped our singing, and ordered the Cossacks to sing obscene songs, such as we were ashamed to listen to."

The interview with the Governor resulted in another beating, and then after a list of their families had been made out they were allowed to return home. The account in *The Times* continues:

"After this began the so-called 'execution,' i.e., the quartering of the Cossacks upon the villages of the Doukhobors. This measure is applied as a punishment in various kinds of risings of the people. The soldiers thus quartered are given the right to use the property of the inhabitants, and to behave in their houses just as in a conquered country. The cruelty of this punishment depends on how far the authorities allow the soldiers to go. One certainly could not expect a light 'execution' from that officer who had previously cruelly beaten quite innocent men. And so it proved to be."

"Two hundred Cossacks," said the Doukhobor, "were quartered in our villages, in each of which they stopped three days. They made camps in the streets, and took from our houses anything they liked; and if displeased, they beat us with the lash. They demanded that we should show them respect, and if we did not salute them they beat us. They ate all our poultry, of which we had plenty. We were not allowed to go outside our village, so that we knew nothing of what was going on in other places, but we heard that in Bogdanovka, where the Cossacks had behaved most outrageously, many violations of women had occurred, which acts the authorities approved.

"In Orlovka the Cossacks entered a house where a woman, Marya Cherkenovka, sat at work, sewing.

start

They asked her, 'Where is the master?' She answered, 'I do not know.' 'How is it you do not know?' 'I should not know even if you had not come.' And she continued to sit and work. Then she was dragged outside and beaten with the lash. In the same village, an old man of sixty, Kiril Konkin, was beaten with the lash so cruelly that he died on the road after being exiled. . . . [Many more such accounts are on record].

"After the 'execution,' they began to expel the Doukhobors from their villages, first by five families from every village, then by ten, and in a few days the remaining part were sent after the others. After the order to clear them out was given, three days were allowed them to make arrangements to pack and to sell their whole property. The things sold for a trifle. What cost fifty dollars was sold for five; what there was no time to sell was thrown away, and the whole population was absolutely ruined. The cattle were left abroad and the corn in the fields.

"Altogether there were expelled from the Akhalkalaki district four hundred and sixty-four families. These were scattered over four districts in the Governments of Tiflis, Dushet, Jori, Trouet and Siguakh, among the villages with Georgian population, as if with the purpose of starving them out. They were settled by two, three or five families in a village, without grant of land, and prohibited from any communication among themselves. They gradually sold all their belongings, and became laborers to the

Georgians; but, in spite of their complete ruin, those who can do so continue to help others who are poorer than themselves."

While the Doukhobors were thus being scattered among strangers, many of whom were deeply touched by their patient sufferings, we have accounts of many heart-rending scenes. Their chief men, both old and young, were seized and transported to the most remote districts of the Empire, and the grief which is still so pathetically expressed by the bereaved families, is strong evidence of their domestic fidelity and affection.

By the above letter to *The* (London) *Times*, and by accounts of their terrible sufferings published by friends of Tolstoi in Russia, the case of the Spirit-Wrestlers became known to a considerable circle of readers, both in England and Russia, and many inquiries were made concerning them.

It may be of interest to the general reader to notice the spirit in which these faithful followers of the Prince of Peace define their situation and principles when in prison and exile for conscience' sake. A letter from the Doukhobors, in Elisavetpol prison, dated Sixth month 8th, 1896, reads thus:

"Dear Friend and Brother in Jesus Christ:

"We inform thee that, according to the mercy and grace of our God and Lord Jesus Christ, we are all in peace and welfare. We heartily greet thee and thy brethren, and wish you welfare in your lives. May God sustain thee, dear brother.

"Though we are strictly watched in order that we may not be in communication with you and the other brethren, yet we cannot be silent.

"When we turned away from the ways of the world, when we began to fulfil the law of God, the commandments of Jesus Christ and of our conscience, then we became hated, slandered, and put into prison, on the pretext that we do not accept the power of the Emperor.

"Are we not all children of the same Father? A true Christian cannot make war and shed the blood of his brother, but, on the contrary, he loves him more than himself. For this our brethren are dispersed in painful and distant exile, in order to prevent the spreading of the knowledge of the truth, and of the teaching of Jesus Christ. . . .

"Let us ask God to give us patience in meekness to endure these persecutions, calumnies, insults, blows, humiliations, sufferings and illnesses, for this will obtain the love of God.

"Dear friend, they know not what they do. They think that by such unreasonable, self-willed, unmerciful tortures they please God. Forgive us, Lord! us sinners and our persecutors! Turn them away, Lord, from the ways of iniquity, and teach them the way of truth! May the Lord God hear the groans, wailing and cries, the voice of prayer of His servants; may He liberate from servitude His people, and save them from the nets thrown over them!"

A similar letter was sent by them in response to a greeting from some members of the Society of Friends.

After a time sufficient interest was evoked in England and in Russia for a considerable collection to be made for these people, many of whom were dying from hardships and starvation. This, along with letters and messages, was conveyed to them personally in the winter of 1897-'98, by an English and a Russian sympathizer. The latter thus describes a meeting of the Doukhobors, which occurred just as they arrived at a Doukhobor village:

"All those who had come over for the meeting assembled in one hut; altogether there were about one hundred and fifty persons. It was so crowded that all had to stand. The door was open, and the passage also was crowded. St. John and myself and a friend from Tiflis were seated around the table. Notwithstanding the crowd there reigned complete silence. Altogether I must say that not in any cultivated society, or any circle of either young or old people, have I ever met with such good behaviour at large gatherings, with such tact and tolerance during debate, as I noticed among these people. One at a time speaks calmly, not hurrying, knowing beforehand that nobody will interfere until he has finished what he has to say. If it happens that several persons begin to talk at once, precedence is given, without unnecessary persuasion or displeasure, to one of them. When anyone leaves off speaking, the next one, before beginning, generally asks: 'Well, Vanya, have you finished?' There is in all this much respect for the personality of one another, and much love. From this results an order such as it is impossible to keep in an ordinary company by any number of chairman's bells.

"First of all, I gave them the greetings of all their friends, Russians as well as foreigners,—also from Leo Tolstoi. I told them I had to hand over some money and some letters. The letters I proposed to read aloud. In a few words I related where and how the money had been collected; then it was counted and handed over. One of the Doukhobors then said that all who were present wished to express their thanks in their own way, and the whole crowd began to move, and made a low—a very low —bow. A general sigh, stifled with emotion, was uttered, and one could hear sobbing. Seeing before me the backs and heads of the bowing people,—people whom I respect so highly, and who have suffered so much for the truth,—expressing this murmur of gratitude, and seeing also their deeply-moved faces, I was touched to the soul.

"After this, I read the letter from V. Tchertkov [containing messages from English sympathizers]; it made a deep impression. All the time one could hear sighs, and words of gratitude:—'Save them, O Lord!'—'Grant them eternal life!'—'Help them on their righteous path!'—and so forth. After the reading was over one of them said, 'We thanked you for the charity you bestowed upon us for the body, and although it is very dear to us, *this* charity, being spiritual, which nourishes the soul, is much dearer to us; how are we to thank you for *it?*' And again all made a low bow, and again, like a wave, arose a murmur of gratitude and love."

The same writer further describes how he found these people:

"When I was about to visit them last year, I expected to see either fanatics, or a people particularly inclined to mysticism. I expected that they would be sad and dejected, and that it must be more agreeable to hear about them than to live among them. I know, too, that the majority of those who have heard of the Doukhobors, and sympathize with them, have the same notion.

"In reality it turned out to be quite different. In spite of the fact that last year (as in this) they were in extremely bad circumstances, suffering from fevers, eye diseases, etc., their food so insufficient that it was a wonder how their large, strong bodies could be sustained, in spite of the great mortality, and the unnaturalness of their life of idleness, owing to scarcity of work, and in spite of the fact that almost every family had some of its members exiled or languishing in prisons and penal battalions,* I no-

* "In these battalions, according to the regulations, the prisoners were expected every day to comply with the de-

ticed among them, from the first day, and the first words, such vitality and animation, such abundance of hearty energy, and such soberness, as I had previously had no idea of whilst living among people who cannot decide as to the life they want to lead, whether for God or Mammon, and who consequently are wearied out, suffering and discontented.

"Contrary to my expectations, I saw that they do not subject themselves to any oppressive principles which limit the freedom of their individuality. Each one, when considering any question, is guided by his own spiritual understanding. That is why they are so energetic, joyful and free. And all their actions, which to us seem extraordinary, are to them quite usual. This results from the fact that their conduct is looked upon by them only as the outward manifestation of continued inward, spiritual force. And out of this conception arises the fact that there is no need for people to carry out this act or that, prompted by any other motive than the impossibility to act otherwise.

"Therefore there are no vain actions, as nobody will praise them; there are no actions from fear of

mands of military discipline. As the Doukhobors could not conscientiously do this, they were subject to an incessant series of punishments,—flogging, confinement in a cold, dark cell, diet of bread and water, prolongation of sentence, and so on. But in the autumn of 1896 an order was issued from the government that those who refused military service on religious grounds were not to be imprisoned in military places of detention."—"Christian Martyrdom in Russia," page 51.

censure on the part of the brethren, as no one will blame them; there are no actions out of blind submission to the majority, as no one either expects or demands anything from another. Moreover, if there be any one whose inner consciousness does not strongly exhort him to live this life, he always has the possibility of joining the Small Party.

"In my presence the news came that one of the Doukhobors, who was kept in a penal battalion, not having strength to bear the tortures, consented to serve. All who were present in the hut had only just heard about it, and I was able to observe their immediate attitude towards this matter. Nearly all of them spoke with sorrow about him and pitied him: 'Dear lad, he had to bear much pain; and now it will be still harder for him, poor fellow.' All spoke of him with such affection, such grief; they feared that he would find it still harder to live after his consent to serve in the army. They spoke of his youthfulness, of the sensitiveness of his nature, and of his severe sufferings.

"The feeling is just as tolerant and tender when it happens that one of the exiled goes over to the Small Party, not having strength to bear the hardships of persecution. Generally he comes, bows to all, and asks forgiveness for leaving them. On their part, those who remain give him their best wishes: 'May God grant you to live there as well as possible. One can serve God everywhere.' They ask forgiveness for not having been able to make his life among them more easy. They give him two horses, a van, and food for his journey.

"Their relations to their neighbors who have never shared their faith is equally kind. Soon after the settlement of the Doukhobors in the government of Tiflis, a Georgian in one of the villages fell ill. It happened to be in autumn, and the corn gathered in by him was not yet removed, but was lying in sheaves in the yard. As the rain was pouring down the corn would have spoiled. The Doukhobors came to know of this, went to his place, threshed the corn, put it in its place, and went away, almost without seeing the owner.

"In another village one of the Doukhobors once heard, during the night, some noise going on near the horses. He went out to see what was the matter, and saw that a Georgian had led his horse out, and was mounting on it, and was about to gallop away. The Doukhobor began to shout: 'Stop! stop!' so persistently that the Georgian—though he was already some distance away—stood still. The Doukhobor said: 'I only wanted to tell you that you need not be afraid, and that you should not consider this horse as a stolen one; if you want it, take it.' The Georgian stood still for awhile, reflected, came back and returned the horse."

The same writer had some discussion with them on the use or disuse of ceremonies, pointing out to them that those of the Small Party go through the same ceremonies, but that this fact has not prevented them from declining in the spirit. He asked them whether such a view of ceremonies as he had expressed separated him from them or not? They all, without exception, replied that as soon as we acknowledge the command to love God and our neighbor, nothing could ever disunite us. Some of the younger ones showed a tendency to apologize for their ceremonies; the older ones thought that their sympathizers, if they lived among them, would probably by and by understand them, and join with them in their form of worship.

The English visitor, A. St. John, spent some time moving about among the sufferers, and after this he went to Cyprus for the purpose of discovering whether that island would be a suitable home for the Doukhobors in case they should be allowed to emigrate. He remained there long enough to receive the first party of emigrants, to help them in their difficulties in that unsuitable climate, and finally to accompany them to Canada,—as will be more fully related further on.

The exiled leader, Peter Verigin, was kept informed as far as possible of what was happening to his brethren. The following letter, written from his place of exile, was on two occasions placed in the hands of Court ladies who have near access to the Empress, but it is not known whether it ever reached the Empress Alexandra or not:

"May the Lord God preserve thy soul in this life, as well as in the future age, Sister Alexandra.

"I, a servant of our Lord Jesus Christ, am living in the testimony and glad tidings of His truth. I am in exile since the year 1886, from the 'Spirit-Wrestlers' [Doukhobor] Community of Transcaucasia. The word 'Spirit-Wrestler' should be understood thus: that we in the spirit and with our soul profess God (see, in the Gospel, the meeting of Christ with the Samaritan woman at the well).

"I implore thee, sister in Christ the Lord, Alexandra, pray thy husband Nicholas to spare the Spirit-Wrestlers in the Caucasus from persecution. It is to thee that I address myself, because I think thy heart is more turned towards the Lord God. And there are at this moment more women and children suffering: husbands and parents are confined in prisons, and families are dispersed in the native villages, where the authorities incite the population to behave coarsely with them. This falls especially heavily upon the Christian women! Lately they have been putting women and children into prisons.

"The fault on our part is that we, as far as it is possible to us, endeavor to become Christians. In regard to some of our actions, their understandings may not be sufficiently enlightened.

"Thou art probably acquainted with the teaching of vegetarianism; we are sharers in these humanitarian views. Lately we have ceased to use flesh as food,* and to drink wine, and have forsaken much of

* "The Doukhobors were vegetarians at least as far back as the beginning of last century, but towards the middle of

that which leads to a dissipated life, and darkens the light of the human soul. Refusing to kill animals, we in no case regard it as possible to deprive men of life. If we were to kill an ordinary man, or even a robber, it would seem to us that we had decided to kill Christ.

"The State demands that our brethren should learn the use of the gun, in order to know well how to kill. The Christians do not agree to this; they are put into prisons, beaten and starved; the sisters and mothers are coarsely defiled as women, very often with railing exclamations, 'Where is your God?' 'Why does He not help you?' (Our God is in heaven and on earth, and fulfils all His will.)

"This is sad, especially because it is all taking place in a Christian country. But our community in the Caucasus consists of about twenty thousand men.* Is it possible that such a small number could injure the organism of the State, if soldiers were not recruited from among them? At the present moment they *are* recruited, but uselessly. Thirty men are in the Ekaterinograd penal battalion, where the authorities are only tormenting themselves by torturing them.

"Man we regard as the temple of the living God,

---

the century they had relaxed in this respect, as well as in regard to their other principles."—"Christian Martyrdom," page 102.

* This is a large estimate, and included the "Small Party," who had betrayed their principles.

and we can in no case prepare ourselves to kill him, though for this we were to be threatened by death.

"The most convenient manner of dealing with us would be to establish us in one place where we might live and labor in peace. All State obligations in the form of taxes we would pay, only we cannot be soldiers.

"If the Government were to find it impossible to consent to this, then let it give us the right of emigration into one of the foreign countries. We would willingly go to England or (which is most convenient) to America, where we have a great number of brothers in the Lord Jesus Christ.

"From the fulness of my soul, I pray the Lord for the welfare of thy family.

"The servant of Christ, PETER,
"(living in exile in the Government of Tobolsk.)"

Another epistle, showing his Christ-like spirit, was addressed by the same writer to his suffering brethren, under date of First month 2d, 1896:

"The concern of most importance to me, when thinking of my fellows, is that they might as far as possible try to become humble and meek, which is indispensable for entering the kingdom of God.

"I think that when they have begun to be worried, and their material state to be ruined, they must be very careful not to be tempted. I hold that anxiety of material well-being constitutes already a great stumbling-block and injury to the soul. I ask that you will advise all who know me not to be angry, not to grumble at the Government because it oppresses them. But let them bear, with God's help, any trial which befalls them. Let them only remember what Christ, and afterwards the Apostles, had to suffer for the Truth. It is important to bear, without complaint, scorn for the Truth, but it is still more important, when suffering for Truth's sake, to bear that patiently.

"PETER VERIGIN."

CHAPTER II.

THE EMIGRATION.

In Third month, 1898, news was received in England by V. Tchertkov that permission had been granted to the Doukhobors to emigrate. The immediate cause of this permission was a visit from the Dowager Empress to her son in the Caucasus. During this visit the Doukhobors succeeded in presenting to her a petition, asking permission to be settled all together in some remote place, or to be allowed to emigrate. The Empress handed over this petition to the superior authorities, and the leave to emigrate was granted.

This welcome news resulted in great activity among the friends of the Doukhobors in England. A committee of the Society of Friends co-operated with V. Tchertkov and his coadjutors in raising a fund for their help, in making arrangements for the emigration, and in selecting a suitable place for a new settlement. They were in constant communication with Leo Tolstoi and other sympathizers in Russia.

After a long time of negotiation and inquiry, two pioneer families of Doukhobors went to England, as delegates, for conference with their friends. The two Doukhobor men left their families behind them in Essex while they went with Prince Hilkov to Cyprus. Their report was not favorable, but it came too late to stop the first emigration to that island. In the meantime there had been active preparations going on in the Caucasus, and a ship was chartered and ready to leave Batoum. The experience was very unusual, and the whole situation most difficult to deal with. America had been thought of, but the idea of removing so many settlers to that great distance seemed at first an impossible dream. The cost, to say nothing of other obstacles, was more than could be faced. Where else, then, should they go? No other land seemed to welcome them, and the urgency to get away quickly from Russia was very great. The Cyprus venture was made, as we know now, with disastrous results.

In the meantime, the Doukhobor pioneers returned to England, all eager for America, the land of their desire. Autumn was at hand, and they wished to view the land before the crops were all gathered. Correspondence with people likely to be interested, both in the States and in Canada, had been going forward from the center of operations in England, and the best judgment favored Western Canada as the most likely place for a settlement. It had also been discovered that between the different communities of Doukhobors (those of Kars and other districts being better off than the banished ones) there were funds sufficient to pay for the ocean voyage, if help were given for railway transit and the expense of settlement. So possibilities for this great exodus began to appear.

Aylmer Maude, a man well fitted for his work,

agreed to undertake negotiations with the Canadian government. He and Prince Hilkov accompanied the first two Doukhobor families to Canada. Prince D. A. Hilkov is a man of striking personality, and has had a very interesting life history. "He is a nephew of the present Russian Minister of Railways, and was an officer in the Russian army at the time of the Turkish war in 1878, serving in the Caucasus, and during his military life there met many of the Doukhobors then living in that hill country. One day he killed a Turk in battle, and captured his horse; but another horse, an extremely fine animal, escaped him after a long chase. The Prince returned to camp much discontented and dissatisfied, thinking at first that the failure to get the horse was at the bottom of his disquietude. It gradually dawned upon him, however, that his unrest came from having killed a man. The more he thought upon it, the more he realized the bad use to which he was devoting his strength and energy, killing people whom he did not dislike, and whom he had never met before, and he determined to leave the Russian army. This he could not do at once, but he abstained from the further taking of human life, though often in positions of great personal danger.

"At a later period Prince Hilkov left the military service, and settled on his mother's estate in Southern Russia. There he occupied himself with agriculture, and came into closer touch with the peasantry. He saw how miserable they were and how hard their life was, in consequence of heavy taxation and enforced military service. Moreover, the quantity of land allotted to them at the emancipation of the serfs was insufficient for their needs. Ultimately the Prince came into possession of his mother's estate, and immediately divided it up among his peasants, he himself living by his own toil, and dwelling on a small section of land which had been allotted to him by the peasants themselves. By this act Prince Hilkov acquired great influence among the peasants, and was consulted by them in all their troubles, more particularly with regard to the extortions of the priests of the Russian Church for performing the burial and marriage services. The Prince finally advised the peasants to do as the Stundists and other Protestant sects in Russia were doing,—to get along without the priests altogether;—advice which was at once adopted. This proceeding caused a serious shrinkage in the church income, and he was denounced by the priest as the founder of a new sect."

The free bestowal of his patrimony upon the peasants of his estate brought down upon the Prince the wrath of Alexander III., and that of his court. "He was remonstrated with to no purpose, so firm a hold had the altruistic impulse taken on him. The late Czar sent for him, and informed him that his estate was the pesthouse of the Empire; exhorted him to return to the faith and customs of his ancestors, and warned him that persistence in his doctrine would lead to serious trouble. The prophecy proved true, as the predictions of those who have the power to verify them are apt to do. Shortly afterwards, while the Prince was living quietly at home on his estate, officers, commissioned by the Czar, entered it with the cruel news that they had come to take his children from him. His eldest son was snatched from the frantic mother's embrace, and his little daughter borne away by the rude Cossacks. . . .

"The broken-hearted father had resolution enough to demand an explanation from the Czar. His Imperial Majesty condescended to assign as a reason, that no Prince of the Russian Empire should ever be brought up in the pernicious faith espoused by Prince Hilkov, if he could prevent it. The decree proved absolute. . . .

"Prince Hilkov's two children were handed over to his mother, at her request, to be brought up in the Orthodox faith. The Prince was banished to the Caucasus, where he lived among the Doukhobors. A few years later the Russian Government banished the leaders and prominent men of the Doukhobors to Siberia. The Prince was then sent to the Baltic provinces, and placed among the Lettish-speaking people. There he lived for two years, after which he received permission to leave Russia altogether." Subsequently he was very useful both as a negotiator and an interpreter in helping the Doukhobors to settle in Canada.

In different parts of America, helpers were raised

up who rendered valuable assistance. The Society of Friends in Philadelphia, Pennsylvania, and in other places, formed committees for the raising of funds, and for the collecting and spreading of information, and they have given practical brotherly aid in many ways during and since the emigration.

The government and railway officials in Canada proved sympathetic, and did all they could to help forward the preparations. Count Tolstoi, with his usual clearness and energy, stated the situation at this critical juncture in the following appeal, which was widely circulated:

"I happen to know the details of the persecutions and sufferings of these people; I am in communication with them, and they ask me to help them. Therefore I consider it my duty to address myself to all good people, whether Russian or not Russian, asking them to help the Doukhobortsi out of the terrible position in which they now are. I have attempted to address myself, through the medium of a Russian newspaper, to the Russian public, but do not know yet whether my appeal will be published or not; and I now address myself once more to all sympathizers, asking for their assistance, (1) in the form of money, of which much will be needed for the removal of ten thousand * people to a distant place; and (2), in the form of advice and guidance in the

* Two thousand of these died before the emigration was effected. Count Tolstoi contributed $17,000 for the relief of the Doukhobors by the sale of some of his publications.

difficulties of the coming emigration of people who do not understand any foreign language, and have never been out of Russia before.

"I trust that the leading authorities of the Russian government will not prevent such assistance being rendered, and that they will check the excessive zeal of the Caucasian administration, which is, at the present moment, not admitting any communication whatever with the Doukhobortsi.

"In the meantime, I offer to act as intermediary to all those who are anxious to help the Doukhobortsi, and who wish to enter into communication with them, for until the present my communications with them have not been interrupted. My address is Moscow, Hamovnichesky, Pereoulok, 21.

"Communications upon this subject may, for greater safety, be sent to me through the medium of my friend, Vladimir Tchertkov, now living in England, who will be glad to furnish further details, and the latest information on the subject, in answer to any inquiries addressed to him at Purleigh, Essex.

"LEO TOLSTOI.

"April 1st, 1898."

English Friends then came to the rescue with the following appeal, which also had a wide circulation:

"APPEAL FROM THE SOCIETY OF FRIENDS.

"Minute of London Yearly Meeting of the Society of Friends:

"23d of Fifth month, 1898.

"A report has been received from the Meeting for Sufferings in regard to the Doukhobortsi. This Meeting approves the action which has been taken by its Representative Meeting; and in strong and near sympathy with this suffering people we adopt the draft address which accompanies the Report, and we commend its circulation and the whole subject to the continued care and attention of the Meeting for Sufferings. We trust that our members generally may be able to raise funds to assist the speedy emigration from Russia of the Doukhobortsi.

"Signed on behalf of the Meeting,

"Caleb R. Kemp, Clerk.

"Devonshire House, 12 Bishopsgate Without, London, E. C."

"Address.

"To Members of the Society of Friends, and to those who unite with them in believing war to be incompatible with the teaching of our Lord and Saviour Jesus Christ.

"Dear Friends:—We desire to lay before you the case of the people who are known in Russia as the Doukhobortsi (a word signifying those who strive in the Spirit), who are at present under suffering in that country for their refusal to bear arms.

"They were originally drawn together in the last century by the conviction that it is unlawful for

Christians to shed the blood of their fellow men; and in acting on this conviction they came in conflict, on several occasions, with the law by which the conscription is enforced in Russia, until in the time of the Emperor Nicholas I. they were exiled from the Crimea, where they had been settled, to the western Transcaucasus.

"Gradually, however, they had declined from the measure of light and knowledge experienced by their predecessors, until they ceased to maintain their testimony against war, although they continued in the course of industry and probity which had made them outwardly prosperous.

"This was their general condition until some three years ago, when, through the instrumentality of one of their own number, their community was aroused from its lethargy with the solemn message, 'Remember from whence thou art fallen, and repent, and do the first works.' In the awakening which followed they were constrained again faithfully to witness to the truth committed to them. Humbly, but firmly, they refused any longer to perform military service, and thus exposed themselves to severe suffering at the hands of the authorities appointed to enforce it. Floggings, imprisonment, fines, exile of some to Siberia, and driving of others from their homes and farms into districts where they were left without food or shelter, followed in rapid succession, until many hundreds died of want, or of sickness resulting from their privations.

"Their condition being at length brought to the knowledge of the Empress-Mother, and of the Czar himself, by petitions entreating leave for them to emigrate from Russia, the Emperor, honorably discriminating between the disobedience to the law by evil doers, and a disobedience arising from conscientious endeavor to do right, granted this request, subject to some limitations.

"As the Society of Friends have, as a body, always maintained the incompatibility of war with that teaching of Christ which enjoins us to love even our enemies, we have felt deeply for the Doukhobortsi in the heavy trials through which they have been passing, for their witness to the same truth. We are humbled in the remembrance that the religious and civil freedom we ourselves enjoy has been gained through heavy suffering by those who have gone before us. Other men have labored, and we have entered into their labors; and we feel that the trials so patiently endured by these poor Russian peasants should not only recall to us the need of holding fast to our testimony to the truth so dear to them, but that their condition should awaken our active sympathy on their behalf.

"Gratefully recognizing, therefore, as we do, the desire of the Emperor of Russia to spare the Doukhobortsi from further suffering, in permitting them to emigrate, we feel we ought to give effect to it, as far as lies in our power, by contributing towards the cost of such emigration, as these poor people themselves are without the means of defraying it.

"We also desire to bring the circumstances to the notice of Friends everywhere, as well as to all others who hold the same conscientious conviction of the unlawfulness of war to the followers of Christ, as we believe they will gladly evince their sympathy for the Doukhobortsi by uniting in rendering them the monetary aid of which they are now in need.

"Signed, for the Committee of the Meeting for Sufferings,*

"JOHN BELLOWS.

"Subscriptions may be sent to Isaac Sharp, 12 Bishopsgate Without, London, E. C. The Funds will be administered under the care of the Society of Friends."

In the Ninth month, 1898, the arrangements were completed for bringing the colonists to Canada. One of the conditions which favored this settlement was an exemption clause in the Dominion Militia Act, section 21 of which reads as follows: "Every person bearing a certificate from the Society of Quakers, Mennonites or Tunkers, and every inhabitant of Canada of any religious denomination, otherwise subject to military duty, who from the doctrines of his re-

* The "Meeting for Sufferings" is the Standing Committee of the Society, and was so named from its having been originally appointed to aid members who were in prison, etc., etc., for conscience' sake.

ligion is averse to bearing arms and refuses personal military service, shall be exempt from such service when balloted in time of peace or war, upon such conditions and under such regulations as the Governor in Council from time to time prescribes."

From Quebec, where the prospecting party arrived on the 10th of Ninth month, Aylmer Maude wrote to V. Tchertkov in England that Prof. Mavor of Toronto had succeeded in interesting a number of government officials in the proposed exodus, and that the professor did not doubt the Doukhobortsi would be treated fairly upon their arrival, but that no money would be raised to bring them over the sea. He said: "The case seems to be that Canada is as free as any country in the world."

The interview with the Deputy Minister of the Interior was very satisfactory. The agreement on the part of the Dominion government, dated Tenth month 5th, 1898, reads thus: "(1) Those responsible for the organization of the emigration to receive the usual bonus of five dollars per adult, children counting half. (2) A further grant of one dollar and fifty cents for each man, woman and child settled, towards organization and transportation expenses. (3) The use of the Immigration Halls in Manitoba and the Northwest Territory granted during the winter months."

The Canadian Pacific Railway Company also showed a generous spirit, and allowed its alternate holdings of land in the Northwest Territory to be so exchanged as to aid the Doukhobortsi in getting their sections of land together.

At this juncture a cable message was sent to Tchertkov: "Let exiles come. Land ready. Arrangements progressing favorably." This was a most critical moment in the Exodus; the waters were parting, but how to insure the passage of the entire community was a problem still to be solved. The English Friends had done nobly, and under urgent circumstances had raised a guarantee fund of $80,000, demanded by their government in the island of Cyprus before the one thousand one hundred and twenty-nine Doukhobors first embarking from Batoum were allowed to land there, on the first of Ninth month, 1898. This was graphically set forth in *The British Friend* of Ninth month of that year: "While the Committee [of the Meeting for Sufferings] were diligently and carefully investigating the facilities which Cyprus afforded, they were suddenly startled and almost appalled by the information that three thousand five hundred of those who were in the greatest peril had resolved, without waiting for further advice and assistance from the Committee, to flee for their lives, and were already in movement for Batoum, their port of embarkation. Fifteen hundred acres of land having been offered them in Cyprus, under conditions which appeared equitable, the Committee at once concluded to accept the offer, as at least supplying a spot on which their weary limbs and heads might rest, and their sinking hearts possibly find courage. Already one thousand one hundred men, women and children had made their way to Batoum, and were chartering a vessel to carry them to a 'promised land,' when the committee was suddenly and unexpectedly confronted with the difficulty of furnishing the large financial guarantee (ultimately fixed at £15 per head) demanded by the British government before the refugees would be allowed to land in the island."

How liberally the Friends, touched by the supreme necessity of the movement, responded to the call, and how, within a few days—one might almost say within a few hours—the whole of the large guarantee of £16,500 was raised, has been touchingly told by the pen of a devoted member of the Committee (John Bellows), in a current issue of *The* (London) *Friend*: "Thus the way seemed cleared at last, and under a feeling of chastened relief and thankfulness the Committee breathed more freely. Meanwhile behind these one thousand one hundred stand the two thousand four hundred at Tiflis, who have sold the remnant of their belongings, and who telegraph that they have obtained their passports, and are ready to start. What is to become of them? Divine Providence only knows!

"The Committee's powers are exhausted, their means at an end, and they can only bid the exiles 'Wait!' Behind these also are four thousand more, now in the neighborhood of Kars, less impoverished by cruel persecution, but equally anxious to flee to a place of safety. What is to become of them? Probably since the persecution and slaughter of the Huguenots, two centuries ago, there has been no instance of such cruel, such relentless, persecution, as that directed against this harmless and industrious community. As France in that day drove out tens of thousands of the best of her sons and daughters, so does the Russian government of to-day cast off and trample under foot thousands of its worthiest peasant subjects. Whilst the former were victims of relentless and triumphant priestcraft, the latter are devoured by insatiable militarism. In conclusion, the Committee earnestly solicits the continued sympathy and support of all members of the Society."

This appeal, written by Edmund W. Brooks, and supplemented by that of another English Friend, to Friends of Philadelphia, Pa., were not made in vain. Wilson Sturge had already gone from England to help settle the first shipload of exiles in Cyprus, and Friends of Philadelphia Yearly Meeting appointed a Committee to solicit subscriptions, and in every way to assist those coming to America.

Prof. James Mavor, of the University of Toronto, wrote under date of Tenth month 24th, 1898: "The Doukhobors, to the number of at least two thousand two hundred, will sail in about a week from the port of Batoum direct to Quebec [Halifax]. The Canadian government has agreed to give them a free grant of land suitable and sufficient for the settlement of seven thousand five hundred Doukhobors. Of these four thousand have resources to bring them out and to establish them in the very minimum of comfort, with the aid the government gives.

"There are two thousand two hundred who need practically everything, the persecutions having resulted in their complete impoverishment. The circumstance that in a few months a number of their young men will fall to be drawn for military service, and the fear that the permission granted by the Czar to leave the country may be withdrawn, coupled with the dread of a return to active persecution, are the chief impulses which impel them to seek another country at all hazards of suffering from inadequate shelter in an inclement winter.

"The Doukhobors are communists in the sense that they have community of property within the group, comprising one hundred and fifty families. Some of the groups have larger accumulations than others, but they are all willing to help each other. Had this not been the case, the emigration of so large a number at this time of year would have been altogether impracticable. They seem, moreover, willing to encounter anything, rather than spend another winter in Russia."

There is an incident in connection with their departure from their Caucasian homes which is very characteristic of their consideration for others, not only for their brethren, but even for their oppressors. Prince Hilkov says: "When they abandoned their cottages and huts, scattered throughout the Georgian villages, these were left in a neat and tidy condition, and in each were arranged a table, two chairs, two loaves of bread, and a jug of water, so that any one who might come to them hungry would not go away unsatisfied."

The same writer says: "Drunkenness (a besetting Russian sin) and idleness are practically unknown among them, and they are always neat and tidy. They have no organization, no written regulations, no provisions for punishment. Instead of the latter, they merely remind one another, in a brotherly way, of their faults."

"They are possessed of an infinite patience under suffering and sorrow, and are essentially simple-hearted. They have, further, great vital energy, and quiet persistence of purpose, which are dominant traits of the Slavonic race."

Friends of Philadelphia now took up the emigration of the Doukhobors in good earnest. Several printed appeals were widely circulated, and near $30,000 was contributed toward their settlement in the Northwest Territory.

The second ship, with some two thousand of these Russian refugees, sailed from Batoum about the middle of Twelfth month, 1898. Before leaving Russia, the Doukhobors had to sign an agreement never to return within the borders of the Empire, or, in such event, to submit to Siberian exile.

While they were being driven away to the village

of Bogdanovka to present themselves before the Governor of Tiflis, before leaving forever their native land, they sang:

"For the sake of Thee, Lord,
I loved the narrow gate;
I left the material life;
I left father and mother,
I left brother and sister;
I left my whole race and tribe;
I bear hardness and persecution;
I bear scorn and slander;
I am hungry and thirsty;
I am walking naked,
For the sake of Thee, Lord."

This embarkation, and that of the previous one thousand one hundred who went to Cyprus, were effected by using the emigration fund of $23,000 which the Doukhobors had raised among themselves during the past three years, for just such an emergency, in conjunction with money contributed by Leo Tolstoi and others.

While these two thousand exiles were en route for Canada, Joseph S. Elkinton, a minister of the Society of Friends in Philadelphia, Pa., felt a religious concern to meet them on their arrival, which he did in company with Job S. Gidley, a fellow-minister, of North Dartmouth, Mass. The landing was an event long to be remembered by those who witnessed it.

As the *Lake Huron*, with its two thousand and seventy-three pilgrims, drew near the land of their adoption, they beheld a very different scene from that which they had left, some four weeks before, in

The First Shipload of Doukhobors Arriving at Halifax.

the Black Sea; and the welcome now awaiting them must have contrasted strangely with the treatment they had grown so familiar with at the hands of the Russian officials. The Canadian authorities almost vied with each other, during the suspense of a week's waiting, in making preparations for the comfort of these worthy colonists.

A Halifax paper (issued First month 20th, 1899) thus announced the safe arrival of this pioneer contingent: "Safe into port at 3 o'clock this afternoon came the steamship *Lake Huron*, Captain Evans, with her company of over two thousand Doukhobortsi,—the largest number of immigrants who ever crossed the Atlantic at one time, to an American port. For many days Deputy Minister Smart had been anxiously awaiting the coming of this curious people, who are turning their faces to the free and fertile lands of this Canadian domain; and when the Beaver Line flag was hoisted at the Citadel at 1.30 this afternoon there was rejoicing on all hands. From December 22d the *Lake Huron* has been battling with the gales which played high pranks with craft on the Western Ocean."

The same authority voices the impression made upon all who welcomed these sturdy sons and daughters of toil: "The Doukhobors are people of the purest Russian type, large and strong, men and women both being of magnificent physique. They are characterized by broad, square shoulders, heavy limbs, and a massive build generally. Their features are prominent, but refined, and bear the marks of a life that is free from vice of any kind. The most striking characteristic of all is the bright, kindly sparkle of their eyes, which gives a winning expression to the whole face, and quickly wins confidence in their character. All their habits demonstrate that they are possessed of keen minds."

The *Montreal Weekly Witness* of First month 17th, 1898, said: "They are a simple, kindly folk; a people of integrity and pure morals. . . . Clean and well-kept villages have always marked their habitations. Even in the Wet Mountains of the Caucasus they speedily earned the respect and good-will of their neighbors, the wild hillsmen. Prince Kropotkin, a keen observer, says that in the deserts of the Amoor region and that of Elizavetpol, in Georgia, the good qualities of this afflicted people have always secured friends for them."

The steamer was thronged from stem to stern by these at last happy exiles, and in most picturesque groups could be seen the children, with their bright faces and dresses of various colors. As the tug-boat from the shore approached within speaking distance, Job S. Gidley shouted, "Welcome, Doukhobors!" and almost immediately the whole company on deck burst forth in singing one of their low, melodious Russian hymns, which, rendered into its English equivalent by Prince Hilkov, reads:

HON. JAS. A. SMART.
Deputy Minister of the Interior.

"Know all men, God is with us. He has carried us through.
We lift up our voices, and sing His praises.
Let all people hear and join in our praises of the Almighty.
They that planned our ruin did not succeed.
We never feared them, for God was with us and gave us strength.
Our Lord had strength to save us; why should we fear?
They that put their trust in Him are never forsaken.
They that do not know Him now shall know Him hereafter.
The light shines in the darkness and will dispel it."

When this very touching expression of sincere thanksgiving was ended, Prince Hilkov, Deputy Minister Smart, and the two Friends, went on board the *Lake Huron*, and a most affecting scene followed. The joy on the part of those who knew the Prince was manifested by their thronging about and kissing him impetuously, until Joseph S. Elkinton knelt in prayer, when every head was uncovered, and a profound solemnity prevailed for a few minutes, in recognition of the many mercies which had been so conspicuously experienced by the exiles. The opportunity was brief, as the ship had not been "cleared" according to the quarantine regulations. The visitors soon retired, bidding the newcomers a "farewell" as sincere as their welcome had been.

The (Halifax) *Morning Chronicle* of that date said: "It was indeed a picturesque sight. There was not a ripple on the water, the sun was shining brightly, and, as the two thousand strangers crowded the decks, the steamer presented the appearance of a huge excursion boat. The immigrants were well clad; that is, warmly clad. The men and boys wore goatskin coats and caps, while the women wore skirts of bright red or blue, heavy black jackets, and colored shawls as headdress."

J. T. Bulmer was appointed by a committee of workingmen to address the immigrants, and he told them, before leaving the vessel (Prince Hilkov interpreting) that Canada welcomed them as "men who would stand by their principles, no matter how much suffering it cost them," adding, "Peace will have her victories, and the same gentle force which caused you to throw down your guns in Europe or Asia will dismantle even the forts of Halifax. . . . On behalf of the workingmen of Canada I welcome you to Canada, and bid you Godspeed."

Captain Evans gave the Doukhobors whom he brought to America the highest praise for order, cleanliness and industry, they having helped in the management of the vessel of their own accord. There were ten deaths on the voyage,—three very old persons, and seven very young children; also one birth and six marriages.

The strangers went to St. John in order to take the cars for Manitoba. Some impressive scenes were re-enacted as they landed. Just as the steamship was being made fast to the pier at St. John, Almanofsky, who was one of their countrymen, addressed those on board in behalf of the people of Canada. He told them that the people of the Dominion of Canada truly welcomed them, and would be as brothers and sisters to them, and he hoped that they would prove worthy of their adopted home. The Doukhobors were greatly pleased, listening to him most respectfully; and, when he concluded, they all knelt down on the deck of the vessel and bowed low their heads, giving thanks also vocally. The crowds on shore then cheered several times, to which the Russians responded by a low bow and taking off their caps.

Two old men were noticed by a reporter of the *Montreal Daily Star* to be deeply touched by this expression of good-will. He says: "I saw the large tears gather in their eyes and course down over their rugged countenances, furrowed with heavy lines, of the kind which bespoke little experience with human kindness. Quietly they uncovered their heads and bowed their gray hairs in solemn silence, to show they recognized the spirit of God working in the hearts of those who had so kindly welcomed them. So their religion taught them."

The women of St. John, and other cities of the Dominion, had made considerable provision for the comfort of the immigrants while *en route* for their Western homes. Five or six trains, of eight or ten coaches each, were in readiness, with ample supplies for the journey,—greatly to the credit of the Canadian Pacific Railway. An eye-witness says: "It was a pleasure to see the well-trained children, even from the tot of two years to the child of nine or ten, take off the cap and bow politely on receipt of the present of eatables to each child as it disembarked, supplied by the Women's Council." A valuable testimony is also given by the captain concerning these on shipboard: "They were ever on the alert for opportunities to be of assistance to their elders, and were frequently observed in the steamer giving up warm positions to the older people. . . . No people, whether older or younger, could show greater consideration for others than did these Spirit-Wrestlers on the way out. The larger and stronger men refused to allow the older and weaker ones to undertake their share of the work that had to be done, or that was voluntarily taken up." On this vessel the six hundred and twenty-nine men ranged in age from twenty to eighty-five years, but most of them were between twenty-five and thirty-five years; while the women (six hundred and seventy-three in number) were generally under forty. The seven hundred and eighty children were mostly over five years of age.

Prince Hilkov, Joseph S. Elkinton and Job S. Gidley went by boat from Halifax to St. John with the colonists, and during that short trip some ten of the Doukhobor men and women were united in marriage. The ceremony is thus described by one on board at the time. "It was the simplest thing imaginable. It took place on the spar deck. The young men approached the young women of their choice, who were attended by their parents, and asked the ladies to become their wives, having first shaken them by the hand. The wooed ones consented, the young gentlemen kissed them, and it was all over. But the brides' parents did not allow the newly-married couples to depart without a word of advice. The young couples had loved each other before they left Russia. Under the arrangements made for the distribution of the immigrants in the Northwest they would have been separated in every instance, but for their marriage, before their arrival here. It was a happy thought, and no happier young people ever entered St. John than these newly-wedded ones." Leopold Soulerjitzky, a friend of Count Tolstoi, had this company of Doukhobors in charge, and he had selected a number of the most capable young men to assist him during the voyage in relieving the captain and his crew. The five bridegrooms mentioned above were among these.

The first contingent had scarcely been landed in the immigration buildings at Winnipeg, and elsewhere along the Canadian Pacific Railway, when the second steamship, *Lake Superior*, brought another two thousand to Halifax, on the 27th of the same month. The son of Count Leo Tolstoi, Count Sergius Tolstoi, accompanied this party, and they were all detained some time in quarantine on account of one case of small-pox, which ended fatally during the passage from Batoum. On the 17th of Second month the embargo was raised, and the immigrants sent on to join their brethren on the prairies of the Northwest Territory. Joseph S. Elkinton also went with these colonists from Halifax to St. John, holding meetings with them on shipboard.

The Editor of *The* (Philadelphia) *Friend* wrote, under date of Second month 4th, 1899: "We are told that when the Pilgrims of Plymouth Colony, having escaped the persecutions of their native country on account of their religion, had reached the coast of Massachusetts in the winter season, and had formed their settlement, they were approached by a native with the cheering cry, 'Welcome, Englishmen!' Two hundred and seventy-nine years have now passed, when a migration of pilgrims of peace, on a far grander scale, and escaping a more murderous persecution, has reached our Atlantic coast from Russia, to be welcomed first by a native of the same Old Colony of Massachusetts, and member of a religious people, who in their turn were persecuted, some of them also unto death, on both sides of the Atlantic,—a people who, by the passive resistance made by their Gospel of Peace, wore out the sword of religious persecution for America.

"Who but a representative at once of the Quakers and of the old Pilgrim Colony, as his boat neared the two thousand Spirit-Wrestlers crowding the mighty ship, could more fittingly have sounded forth those living words, 'Welcome, Doukhobors!' And who but a representative of William Penn's colony of the 'Holy Experiment' of Peace, of his city founded in Brotherly Love, and of the very meeting-house lot left by Penn for the Gospel of Christ's Spirit, could with more historic appropriateness have been commissioned by the Spirit, as he felt he was, to meet the exiles in a Saviour's sympathy, and with bended knee, in that impressive scene on the ship's deck, to render devout thanksgiving and invoke upon the Pilgrims of the Universal Brotherhood the Divine Blessing, thus linking the religious Society of Friends with this historic advent and welcome?"

L. Soulerjitzky said that when he read from the Bible to the two thousand Doukhobors (in whom he was particularly interested), they said: "That is true; that is good; that is just what we believe; just like our religion." They also maintained that it was better to have the truths they had listened to in their hearts and heads, rather than in a book. And their expressions do impress one as coming from their hearts.

When groups of these sturdy champions of Peace were gathered about Joseph S. Elkinton on the vessel, as they sailed from Halifax to St. John, Prince Hilkov interpreted for him. The depth of their religious feeling and experience was very gratifying, and at times it was manifest that the gift of prophecy was possessed by some of them, the women in particular speaking with power and dignity. The equality of the sexes in religious matters is another point of resemblance between the Doukhobors and the Society of Friends.

Some forty Doukhobors who gathered in the cabin of the steamship spoke with appreciation of the visit to Russia of Stephen Grellet and William Allen, in 1818, and they also expressed great satisfaction in the interest shown for them by members of the same Society at the present time, saying, "We believe in Christ, who sent you to us."

The Canadian Government had provided some log buildings in the wilderness, but at this season it was difficult to reach them. Therefore, most of the four thousand immigrants were accommodated in the large immigration halls provided for colonists along the Canadian Pacific Railway. An eye-witness at one of these buildings in Winnipeg said: "The Doukhobors commenced to sing their psalms in that peculiarly plaintive manner which makes one feel like crying. The sensitive find it impossible to refrain from using a handkerchief, and during the closing ceremony many a hand was slipped into a pocket, and many a tear slyly wiped away." The hospitals of the Dominion received quite a number of those who were invalided from various causes, and provision was made, temporarily, for the support of all of the new settlers. One baker provided five thousand loaves of bread.

We can but contrast the fortunes of these members of the Universal Brotherhood with those of some forty-two of their brethren who were banished to the Siberian Province of Yakoutsk, in 1897-'98. After a year of great hardship, we learn that "their isolation from the civilized world, the wildness of the place, the severity of the climate, were not very much better than the situation of Nansen on an ice-bound stretch of Arctic land, without his health and modern appliances for coping with the severity of nature. And yet, owing to untiring energy and courage, that band of noble-minded, though simple-hearted, men, much exhausted by previous imprisonment and trials, torn from their families, contrived to establish a real outpost of civilization in a savage wilderness." These exiles are aware of the emigration of their brethren to Canada. Very naturally they manifest the greatest interest in emigration from Russia, and dream of being permitted to join their brethren. It is, however, very doubtful whether this permission will be granted soon, as they are all young or middle-aged men. The Czar's government seems to be firm in its efforts to enforce military service among them, or, if impossible to do that, to replace it by exile for the same term—eighteen years.

Besides these forty in Northern Siberia, there are sixty more in another province, for whom their families and friends in Canada continually mourn. *The Advocate of Peace* for Second month, 1899, commenting editorially upon this arrival on our shores, said: "It is a part of the great struggle now going on to rid the civilized world of the curse and tyranny of militarism; a tyranny more cruel and heartless has never afflicted humanity. The system of conscription has extended itself until only under the flags of Great Britain and the United States, of all the great powers, is there any liberty of conscience left, so far as military service is concerned. And there are many Americans and British subjects who so little understand and appreciate the real meaning of Anglo-Saxon civil and religious liberty, that they would set up forced military service in these countries also. There is a steady effort being made on both sides of the Atlantic to do this. But this contest with militarism must be carried on, not simply to save Anglo-Saxon civilization from its worst and most degrading form, but that it may be driven from every country in Europe, and all the peoples of the old world set free from its fetters. Anglo-Saxon freedom cannot be saved unless we can at the same time save the rest of the earth. It is a shame, for the description of which there is no sufficient adjective in the language, that, after nineteen centuries of Christianity, there should be any country on the globe calling itself Christian where an upright, industrious, God-fearing people like the Doukhobors cannot live in security of life and property. Russia is not the only military despotism. The Doukhobors could not live, without persecution, in Germany, or France, or Austria, or Italy."

The colony of exiles who went to Cyprus found the climate of that island poorly adapted to their habits, and, as about one hundred died within a few months, there was much discontent among the colonists, and a general desire to go to Canada. M. A. Marriage Allen, an English Friend, wrote under date of Third month 21st, 1899, that she had visited the settlements, and was very much pleased with their condition, or rather the ability of the people to adapt

PHOTOGRAPHED BY WILLIAM BELLOWS.

Deck scenes on the *Lake Superior*.

themselves to the circumstances under which they labored,—at considerable disadvantage. The children seemed anxious to learn English. Wilson Sturge was invaluable to the colonists, and, after they went to Canada, he settled up their affairs most creditably. He died on his voyage home.

Preparations were now set on foot to bring the one thousand survivors from Cyprus. The *Lake Superior* was again chartered, and William Bellows (son of John Bellows, of Gloucester, England) went to Larnaka, where he met with Arthur St. John, who had taken a very active interest in these emigrants from the inception of their emigration, visiting them in the Caucasus and following the fortunes of the first ship-load until they were settled in Canada. The re-embarkation of these exiles from Larnaka, Cyprus, was at once a most pathetic and a picturesque event. M. A. Marriage Allen describes the scene graphically under date of Fourth month 19th, 1898: "During the day some of the Pergamos Doukhobors arrived, and by the next evening over one thousand were camped in various groups. The nights were dry and mild, and for three days the authorities allowed them to stay there, make their fires and do their cooking on the quay, and all was so orderly.

"On Sunday Wilson Sturge and I went up to their sunrise service. One hundred and fifty in 'go-to-meeting' clothes were assembled in the center of the square. After their hymn-chanting, hand-shaking, kisses of peace (this is a national custom on Easter

Day, from Emperor to serf), and various bows, all performed in a most reverent way, their leaders came forward and tendered most hearty thanks to Wilson Sturge (their 'good grandfather,' as they call him) for his kind care and help during their stay in Cyprus. Then all prostrated themselves on the ground and dispersed.

"The people seemed much affected at this, their last religious service, in the island where they leave so many of their loved ones in the silent grave."

The voyage to Quebec was prosperous, and, with the exception of one who died on the way, all landed safely in that port. Leopold Soulerjitzky had this party also in charge. Joseph S. Elkinton was on hand, as before, to welcome them upon arrival, and Captain Taylor had him come upon the bridge to address the immigrants, who responded through an interpreter, expressing their appreciation of the sympathy and kindness manifested to them by the Society of Friends. The captain also said he had become very much attached to the Doukhobors, and spoke with a feeling of sincere sympathy with them in their trials, both before embarking from Cyprus and while on the ocean.

These colonists were promptly transported to Yorkton and Assiniboia, but the lateness of the season, retarded by unusually heavy rains, did not allow of their getting at once upon the land allotted to them, and many of them being sick with malarial fever (brought from the Caucasus and Cyprus), their condition was rather pitiable for some time, while they were temporarily encamped in tents near Yorkton.

We now turn to the 2,278 Doukhobors (1,540 adults and 738 children) who sailed from Batoum on the 12th of Fifth month, 1899, arriving at Quebec on the 6th of Sixth month following. This was the last of the "Larger Party" remaining in the Caucasus, and these came from the Province of Kars. They had sold out their belongings, and so raised some $42,000 (of which $33,000 was paid by them for the steamer), beside the provisions required for the passage. These pilgrims lost five of their number while *en route* to America, and there were two births on board during that time. They were detained in quarantine at Quebec for more than three weeks, because of a case of small-pox.

It was a disappointment both to Prince Hilkov and to Joseph S. Elkinton not to be allowed to speak with the newly-arrived colonists, but they accepted the situation, and journeyed westward, to see how those who had gone ahead were faring, in Manitoba and Assiniboia. They were accompanied by William Evans, a Friend from Philadelphia, who had taken a deep interest in the Doukhobors, and had acted as treasurer for the Doukhobor Committee of Philadelphia Friends. Prince Hilkov had previously gone to the Prince Albert district of Saskatchewan to secure land for this party of Kars Doukhobors, and he very much wished to explain to them the reason why the

Canadian Government preferred to give them sections situated some three hundred miles to the northwest from the other settlements in Assiniboia and Manitoba, where all of the previous arrivals had been located.

The soil of the prairie in these sections of the Northwest Territory is one or two feet deep, consisting of a black vegetable loam, resting upon clay of great depth; when wet it is particularly sticky. A missionary told the writer that when he was traveling through this district, some twenty-five years before, he overtook a Scotchman, who was wading through mud ankle deep. The first word addressed to the prospecting settler was one of commiseration for his lot. But it seemed very little appreciated, as the stranger forthwith plunged both hands into the liquid earth at his feet, and held up the dripping soil with evident satisfaction, protesting in his Gaelic dialect, "This is just the right kind of stuff to make bread out of." His would-be comforter, quickly adjusting his sympathy to the attitude of his newly-found parishioner, promptly responded, "Then *you* are just the right kind of a man to settle here."

The last contingent of the Universal Brotherhood were taken directly to their allotments, fifty miles south of the town of Prince Albert, early in the Seventh month, 1899, where more capacity and progress have been shown than at any of the other settlements.

William Evans described the colony of Cyprus

immigrants thus: "Upon awakening at Yorkton (where he, with Prince Hilkov and Joseph S. Elkinton, had arrived at midnight, the 13th of Sixth month), the first sight was the Cyprus conical tents, and others of various shapes, thickly dotting the prairie. In one roomy tent a sort of Russian stove had been constructed of stones and clay, with a circular aperture for the kettle, and a sheet-iron drum at the rear to radiate the heat. The women and girls were clad in vestments of bright colors, generally red and yellow, but sometimes in part blue, and there was no attempt at tight lacing. Skirts by no means dragged on the ground. The women's heads were invariably covered with kerchiefs, of lighter color than the dress material. We were told that it is considered unseemly for women to be seen by men with uncovered heads.

"Notwithstanding their total abstinence from flesh food, both men and women were of good stature and well developed muscularly, evidently able for work. The children seemed cheerful and lively, and wonderfully restrained, under parental care, from any display of selfishness or quarrelsomeness; but in no instance do I recall seeing a parent chide or correct a child. There seemed throughout the whole community no evidence of unhappiness or of impatience, but the indications all were of religious restraint and of apparent thankfulness for release from a country where they were unable to carry out their convictions unmolested, and of hopefulness for the future, in their newly-chosen land. In looking upon these people, I suppose I have never seen any who as a community have come so near realizing the advice of the apostle, 'Having food and raiment let us be therewith content.'"

On this day (the weather being very fine) Joseph S. Elkinton requested the opportunity of meeting with the colonists in a compact company for religious service. Their gathering was a novel and truly interesting scene, and very typical of their orderly way of assembling. William Evans describes the occasion thus: "As they approached, the women were stationed in rows of perhaps twenty feet in length, one behind the other, at the south end of a rectangle. The boys and girls were placed in rows of perhaps forty feet in length, at right angles to the women—the older children behind the lesser.

"The end of the rectangle opposite the women was left open, or unoccupied. Then the men stood in lines opposite the children, with the American strangers at the end next the women. After five or six hundred had thus assembled, and the chanting was ended, and after the visitors had addressed the company, they responded through Prince Hilkov. All knelt upon one knee and bowed their heads to the ground, and he explained that the bowing was not to man, but in acknowledgment of the blessing of the Divine Spirit, and to signify their entire assent to the spiritual truths that had been declared; and they also said that before they left Russia they had been told there was a people in this country, called Quakers, who held spiritual views like their own, and that they were glad to be acquainted with them; and that they were thankful to this people, not only for helping them pecuniarily, but also for giving them their sympathy in a strange land. Their demeanor and actions showed plainly the sincerity of their feeling and expression."

William Evans continues: "From the beginning to the end of our interview there was no indication of listlessness or inattention, but a serious and earnest entering into communion of feeling which was very remarkable. Finally, they asked through the Prince that our Society would intervene with the Czar for the release of their relatives who are banished to Siberia; and here one of the most interesting parts of the whole deeply-impressive occasion manifested itself. Six matronly women left the line in which they stood, and advanced in front of us. These were, the Prince said, the mothers or relatives of some of the banished ones." After they were told that such an appeal had been already made to the Czar, and that the Society of Friends would do all in its power to secure their release, "the women quietly wiped their tears, and one, with noble features, said that they were the mothers of sons who were in banishment, and they earnestly hoped that our people would do what they could for their help. By this time such was the intensity of feeling that the regular ranks of the rectangle were broken, and the people pressed in close, until there was only a small circle clear, with the women in the center. We asked them to give us a list of all their people who were in Siberia, with their post-office addresses, which they readily undertook to do, and by next morning some two hundred names were handed to the Prince."

Peter Jansen, of Jansen, Nebraska, whose father was driven out of Russia some thirty-five years ago, because of his conscientious objection to the Russian Church, visited the Cyprus Doukhobors soon after they arrived at Yorkton. He says: "I asked a pleasant-featured man, 'Do you think you will be able to get along in your new home?' He looked up, and the faith that was in him was depicted in his face when he answered, 'The God who has selected this land for us, where we can worship Him according to the dictates of our consciences, will certainly not let us starve!' The tears were hard to keep back when an old mother came and said, 'I have two sons who were deported to Siberia because they would not serve in the army, and I am here alone; and I will ask the blessings of God upon thee day and night if thou wilt bring them over to me.'" Peter Jansen adds: "I believe the Lord will take care of these His children, but we who believe in the Prince of Peace should be willing to act as His servants."

Dr. Mercer, of the *Lake Superior*, was so interested in the settlement of the Doukhobors in their new home that he obtained leave of the captain to accompany them to the Northwest Territory, and rendered them many valuable services.

Joseph S. Elkinton and William Evans received the following letter from the Kars Doukhobors, at that time detained at the quarantine station near Quebec, in reply to a letter written to them. It was translated by Prince Hilkov:

"13th of Sixth month, 1899.

"Dear Friends and Brothers:

"Deeply glad were our hearts that faith in Christ made you participators of the wisdom of God, and therefore you felt with us in our heavy trials.

"We believe that there are many kind people in the world, who, like shining lights, burn amidst the surrounding darkness. May the Lord save you, dear brothers, for the love which prompted you to come and meet us, as a people of the same faith in Christ, offering your life for your brethren and fellow-beings. May you reap a measure full of heavenly and earthly treasure from the almighty hand of our Heavenly Father.

"It is truly grievous that it was not permitted to you to meet us, but we must not be troubled at this. Let us place our faith in God and His mercy, for He is the Eternal and Living King, and will arrange all in accordance with His holy will.

"We pray the same Lord and all good people to forgive us our trespasses, by which we may have offended and grieved somebody; and we pray you, dear friends, to transmit our heartfelt greetings to all brothers and sisters who have faith in Christ, the Saviour of our souls, who live in Philadelphia and the United States. We remain your loving brothers of the Christian Brotherhood, now living in quarantine on Grosse Isle.

"SIMEON CHERNOV,
"PAUL PLANIDIN,
"SIMEON VERESCHAGIN."

About this time there was a lively debate in the Dominion House of Commons on the character of the immigrants coming in such numbers to Canada, and the Minister of the Interior felt called upon to defend the policy of the Government. After speaking of the testimony concerning their cleanliness, etc., given by the captains and conductors who had the Doukhobors in charge before reaching their Western home (where few had been willing to settle up to that time), he said: "In so far as the Doukhobors are concerned, I have only this to say: I am altogether at one with my right honorable friend the Prime Minister, when he suggests that it is not a reason why we should keep people out of Canada because they have conscientious objection to bearing arms. I think the House will not agree with the suggestion that because a man may have conscientious objections to bearing arms therefore he has not courage, therefore he has not those qualities which go to

make a good citizen. Sir, there is many a man who is ready to fight, and who has no courage at all; he has nothing in the sense of true courage. . . . I do not believe that I myself or my honorable friend would go through what these Doukhobors have gone through for the sake of their convictions. I doubt if there are five men in this house who would show the moral courage, who would show the tenacity, who would show the fortitude which these people have shown for the purpose of preserving the faith which they believe to be the true faith."

CHAPTER III.

THE CANADIAN SETTLEMENT.

The Dominion government set aside some two hundred and seventy thousand, four hundred and eighty acres of prairie land for the seven thousand three hundred and sixty-one Doukhobors (one thousand five hundred of these were men) who had taken refuge within its jurisdiction. The larger part of this tract was located near the junction of Manitoba and the Northwest Territories of Saskatchewan and Assiniboia, some seventy-five miles north of Yorkton. The most western settlement, on Duck Lake, is separated by three hundred miles from the former, and has about one-fifth of the entire number of villages.

The homestead laws, known as the "Three Years System," require every settler to reside six months of each year on his "quarter-section" of one hundred and sixty acres. Six months' "grace" is allowed those who "enter" their applications in the fall, while in the case of a foreigner, this is extended to a year. Fifteen acres must be under cultivation at the end of the third year, in order to "perfect" the title. If the homesteader fails to reside upon this quarter-section half of each year, or to "perfect" his entry by paying $10, he runs the risk of having another settler enter for the same, if the Land Department cancels the first entry. A settler cannot assign his prospective homestead, or any part of it, before receiving his patent, and the law provides that, even if he agrees to assign his homestead, or any part of it, before receiving his patent, the entry shall be forfeited, unless the Minister shall otherwise decide.

This is intended to protect the settler against persons who might otherwise acquire his rights for some worthless consideration. If an entry is thus canceled, the settler who has violated this law cannot obtain another homestead.

These regulations have been given in some detail, because the greatest difficulties in the Doukhobor Settlement have arisen in connection with these Immigration land laws, as we have already seen, because of the Doukhobors' communistic preference to hold their landed property together. The Canadian government therefore issued a notice to these colonists that they must apply in *severalty* for their homesteads by the first of Fifth month, 1902, or their lands will be open for occupancy by other settlers. This has not been permitted, as the time has been extended a year.

It is both reasonable and right that these colonists, in common with all who have received the benefits of such a liberal government, should be willing to submit to these legal requirements. As it is, however, a matter of conscience with many of them, education and time, as well as patience, will be required to adjust these difficulties, without doing injustice to either party.

The law permitting "Settlers' Effects" to be carried at greatly reduced rates, was, through the courtesy of the Dominion and railway officials, taken advantage of by the friends of the Doukhobors, who provided them with several carloads of food, clothing, etc., during the winter of 1899-1900.

Under the Customs Tariff of Canada, a bona fide settler may bring with him, free of duty, wearing apparel, household furniture, professional books, implements and tools of trade or occupation, which the settler has had in use for at least six months before removal to Canada. He can also take with him carts and vehicles and live stock, under certain limitations. Of course, these Russian Colonists had little to bring with them, after years of impoverishment, so purchases had to be made at once for the men, women and children.

The Montreal Women's Council interested themselves very much in the junior portion of these immigrants. One who had the pleasure of distributing some gifts among them, writes: "It would make your heart glad to see the joy of the children as I lifted article after article out of the bag, and to see the look of expectancy on their faces. The slates and books are very much needed. The readers are quite necessary, for the children are learning rapidly, and the older ones can read and write. . . .

"The Doukhobors themselves do not make their wants known. They are a gentle, kind people, grateful for any little kindnesses shown them, and they deeply appreciate what has been done for them here.

Some of their history is so sad. There is hardly a family but contains a father or a brother who has been in prison, and suffered frightful tortures. I have in mind several families whose fathers and mothers are exiled in Siberia, and a brave little fellow named Ivan Boynikov, one of the brightest pupils, who wishes me to thank you for his top and book, told me to-day that his mother died heart-broken just before he left Russia, because his father and brother could not come with him to Canada, for they are in confinement in mercury mines in Siberia. These people have been tried in the fire and not found wanting. These simple, unlettered peasants can teach us lessons of heroic sacrifice for the sake of the Truth.

"Unlettered as they are, for only about three in one hundred can read, they possess true spiritual wisdom, that puts many of us to shame. They have been much criticised here, owing to their peculiar religion. The fact is, they have hold of the very basis of Christianity, the true Christ religion without creed, forms or dogma, and they exemplify it in their lives. May their example enter the hearts of our Canadian people, and their light shine for all the world."

As an illustration of the practical way in which these exiles adapted themselves to the requirements of their new home, the picture shows a unique team of some twenty women drawing a plough through the prairie sod. This was done because the men of the colony went to work at once on the railroad, in order to get some money to defray the expenses of the community, and because they owned few, if any, oxen or horses at that time. Some one hundred acres were thus prepared for the wheat and other seeds, within a few weeks, without physical injury being sustained by those women, who were so serviceable in using their remarkable strength in this time of need. A matron would walk at the side of the plow to watch her younger sisters, lest they should over-exert themselves. There was some criticism expressed because of this noble effort on the part of the Doukhobor women, and, such is the perversity of human nature, that criticism was circulated from one side of the Continent to the other, so that Joseph S. Elkinton thought it necessary to deny some of the charges made about the Doukhobor men imposing upon their wives and sisters. *The* (Philadelphia) *Public Ledger* of Seventh month 12th, 1900, contained his rejoinder to its reprint of the (San Francisco) *Examiner's* false statements, viz.: "Having met the four arrivals of the steamships bringing seven thousand of the Doukhobors to America, and having sailed with the first two steamships from Halifax to St. John, and witnessed the work of the men on the discharge of the cargoes and loading of the trains, and afterwards at their work in Manitoba and Assiniboia, I saw nothing to justify the expressions in the clippings alluded to, as arbitrary, or domineering over the women; but what was

PHOTOGRAPHED BY WILLIAM BELLOWS.

carried on, was done with propriety and dignity, in a peaceable, quiet way, with no apparent want of affection, but decidedly to the contrary. The statement that they are quite willing to exchange a woman for an ox or a horse is a base slander.

"Where there is everything to do and very little means at command, men, women and children are compelled to do all they can to advance the general interest. . . . They had no horses or oxen upon arrival in Manitoba and Assiniboia, and very few of the villages, at this writing, have more than one or two teams; under these circumstances it was no disgrace for some of the plowing to be done by hand; as to their being yoked, the rope that drew the plow was knotted around the middle of a stick, which they could press forward as they walked, rather than pull by one hand on the rope. . . . Their situation appeals strongly to the humane, as not one-half of them arrived in time for spring planting, and a severe frost, coming on earlier than usual, has blighted much that was planted."

The superior abilities of the women were also demonstrated in the way they built their houses, even to plastering the walls with their own hands.

Upon arrival at their several allotments the Doukhobors at once constructed, in addition to those the Canadian government had previously built, log houses, with clay between the logs; some of these were half "dug-outs," while others were all above ground, and smoothly plastered on the inside. It was surprising to those who witnessed these women at work, to see how smoothly they finished the top coat of plaster with their bare hands, and what great deftness in manual labor of various kinds they exhibited.

Dr. William Saunders, of the Experimental Agricultural Department of Canada, made a visit to the North Colony settlement at Thunder Hill shortly after its villages were first laid out. He reported their houses "substantially built of logs, and roofed with poles, on which prairie sod about four inches thick is laid, and the interstices filled with fine earth. The sides of the houses are well plastered on the exterior, with clay mixed with cut straw, and sometimes on the inside with the same material. The furniture in the houses is all of their own make, and consists of a few rough stools to sit on, and higher benches which serve as tables. The beds are made of a series of poplar poles about six feet long and three or four inches in diameter, placed close together along the wall. On these some hay is placed, and over this a piece of thick felt. Most of the people recline on this structure with their heads to the wall, feet outwards, using such bed-clothes as they can command. A few have feather beds, and curtains to divide the sleeping places into compartments. Most of the houses consist of one large room for living, cooking, eating and sleeping. The aim is to have in all their villages a house for each family, and their

PHOTOGRAPHED BY WILLIAM BELLOWS.

PHOTOGRAPHED BY WILLIAM BELLOWS.

Interior view of one of the log houses erected by the Canadian government

houses are being erected at varying distances, in two rows, with a wide street between them. . . .

"In each house there is a Russian oven, which serves for the warming of the building and for cooking the food. Each village is provided with a steam bath house, in which steam is generated by pouring water on heated stones. In this way a profuse perspiration is brought out, and the body is whisked briskly with a bunch of small branches of the mossy cup oak, the large leaves of which still hold tightly to the branches." "Godliness and cleanliness" appears to be their living motto. The floors of their houses are made of earth beaten to a smooth, hard surface. Each room has a window or two and a door, although little provision was made for ventilation. Large iron kettles of the capacity of a barrel were used for laundry purposes, and a large bowl was the family dish, from which the vegetable soup was served. Wooden spoons are used.

Two blacksmith shops had been promptly erected by the Doukhobors, and some farm wagons and ox yokes made. Short sections of trees, hollowed out and closed at one end, were used as tubs and kegs. All their clothing was made by themselves, and the estimated cost of living was $2 a month per capita.

It was about this time that Eliza H. Varney, a minister of the Society of Friends in Canada, and Job S. Gidley, visited the Doukhobor Colonies. They were deeply impressed, not only with the cheerfulness under many privations, but also with their unusual powers to appropriate everything in their way for the purpose of improving their estate. Eliza H. Varney distributed medicines, which were much needed, and thus supplemented the self-sacrificing efforts of the Russian nurses, Vera Welistchkina, Sasha Satz, Marie Robitz and Anna de Carousa, who came over with the Doukhobors. She also ministered unto them spiritually. Under date of Seventh month 28th, 1899, she wrote: "Whilst we were at dinner, one of their women came to ask if it would disturb us if they sang in the large room. The interpreter said, 'No,' so they chanted all the time we were eating. After dinner we found that outside the doors they had collected a large number of children in a half circle, with the men and women at either end, and on stepping out all these children (one hundred and fifty or more) bowed down three times, in humble gratitude for what had been given for their benefit. Many of these children have the most open, kind-hearted faces I ever beheld."

Just before leaving Selkirk, Job S. Gidley addressed more than one thousand of the Doukhobors, who had not yet reached their prairie homes, and, Eliza Varney said, "he gave them excellent counsel, which they took very kindly, and they had their interpreter to thank us for our sympathy and words of comfort." As an instance of that spiritual communion which kindred souls can feel and enjoy together, even in the absence of a common language, she wrote to a

PHOTOGRAPHED BY WILLIAM BELLOWS.

Outside Bake-Ovens. The first structures erected by the Doukhobors upon their arrival at their settlements.

friend about this visit: "We visited both hospitals (in Winnipeg), one for infants and one for adults, and in both of these prayer was offered, believing our heavenly Father would understand the feeble petition of one of his little ones, even if there was no interpreter to enable them to understand. God so carried that petition home to their hearts that they were tendered to tears, and kissed our hands in token of love and respect."

Rose M. Osburn, who took a most active interest in these colonists from their first arrival in Canada, accompanied Eliza H. Varney and Job S. Gidley during this visit. She had taught some of the Doukhobor children who first came to Winnipeg, and considered them very apt scholars in learning the English language. This was also the experience of Nellie Baker, who went to the settlement in Assiniboia a year later, with Eliza H. Varney, for the purpose of starting a school for the children. The attention of Friends and others at this important period of their settlement in the Northwest Territory was fully appreciated by the Doukhobors.

It may be stated before passing from this timely visit of Eliza H. Varney and Job S. Gidley, that they visited thirty-eight out of the forty-two villages belonging to the North and South Colonies, eighty and fifty miles respectively, north of Yorkton, Assiniboia. They were accompanied by Ignace Almanovsky. He had come out to Canada twelve years before, having been repeatedly imprisoned in Russia for preaching the Gospel. His wife was an English woman, and both were good interpreters.

This trip over the broken prairie and along trails that were easily lost, involved a great deal of exertion, patience and fortitude, especially when fording the rivers. On one occasion Eliza H. Varney sat for an hour or more after nightfall, in the middle of the Assiniboine River, with the water pouring over the bed of the carriage, not knowing whether they would get to the farther side, as their horses had refused to pull, and the rope attached to their vehicle had repeatedly broken when those on the land attempted to pull them to the bank; yet she said she felt perfectly calm through it all.

The Western Sun (Brandon, Manitoba), of date Ninth month 14th, 1899, contained a very interesting report of Eliza H. Varney's experiences. It states that she found the dwellings of the Doukhobors to be of three kinds. "Where there is timber, logs are used, and good, substantial homes are the result. In places where no wood is available, sods make a wonderfully neat and compact little house, considering the material from which it is made. One village, where neither timber of any size nor sod was procurable, had houses made in a remarkably ingenious, but most laborious, way. Poplar sticks, five or six inches in diameter, were driven into the ground, one foot apart, to form an enclosure thirty by twenty feet, and in and out of these supports willow withes were tightly woven like baskets. The whole struc-

PHOTOGRAPHED BY WILLIAM BELLOWS.

Doukhobor ferries.

ture, when completed, was plastered inside and out with the clay mixture, and, though done entirely by hand, presented as smooth a surface as if the trowel of a first-class plasterer had been at work. The clay for the mortar was prepared by the women in this way: A trench was dug, into which the earth and water and chopped grass were placed; then half a dozen of these stalwart sisters, with their skirts kilted up, trod the mortar until it was as smooth as paste, while another company of women carried it to the houses; here six or eight more put it on the walls of the dwellings." "The great ovens and chimneys of sun-dried bricks are seen everywhere, as well as the smooth floors of trodden sand."

"At one of the many religious services held (by the Friends) with the Doukhobors, a letter from their exiled elder (Peter Verigin) was read, in which he exhorted his people to remain firm in their belief, to remember always their God and their fathers' God, to teach their children to learn the Commandments, and to read the glorious Psalms of David; but, above all, to remember to love their brethren. 'He that dwelleth in love, dwelleth in God and God in Him.' They must not only love one another, but must love their enemies, 'doing good to them that would despitefully use them and persecute them.'"

On another occasion a letter was read, stating that their elder, and other members of their Brotherhood, in Siberian exile, were to be sent to the sulphur mines in order to hasten their death. The mother and sister of Peter Verigin were present when this was read, and "the tearful pleadings of these women that their loved ones be not left to perish in prison were most pitiful to hear. Promises* were made that the Tsar would be approached, and the lives of these noble men saved if possible," and Eliza H. Varney prayed that the Most High would soften the Tsar's heart and release them.

Job S. Gidley describes another meeting out on the open prairie, where the Doukhobors had gathered to meet with him and Eliza H. Varney. He said: "One must be void of feeling not to be touched by such a scene. Here was a meeting for worship held upon the prairie, under the canopy of heaven, where the Dispenser of manifold blessings seemed near at hand. It brought to mind thoughts of the simple way in which the early Christians performed their worship."

The situation of the colonists at this time was critical, because early frosts had cut off the crops which they had planted, and without assistance they would have suffered greatly. Some villages had scarcely any food in hand or in prospect. Friends of Philadelphia took up the case in good earnest and held a public meeting, when a strong appeal was made by the Committee of their Meeting for Sufferings.

* These promises were kept subsequently, but no discharge obtained. It is not known certainly that these exiles were sent to the sulphur mines.

Thirty thousand dollars was raised in a few weeks, and three carloads of food and clothing collected.

The Friend of Tenth month 14th, issued about ten days after the above-named meeting was held, contained a stirring editorial, of which the following is a part:

"The Doukhobors having escaped from their Pharaoh, who had tardily heard the words, 'Let my people go,' witnessed the sea opened, by the ministration of Friends, for their passage to a strange shore, and have been left in the middle of a vast continent and of a short summer, that could scarcely yield the beginning of sustenance for so great a multitude.

"There they stand, remote from other populations, in a land already stiffening with its six months' freezing; and when presently two weeks' prospect of bread is exhausted, starvation is said to stare some of the villages in the face, unless manna descend upon them from heaven through our hands.

"Shall half of this modern Israel of Peace perish during the coming winter through indifference of the Friends of Peace? It is deemed by judicious minds that such must be the rate of their perishing, unless we of our superfluity 'cast in unto the offerings of God.' A living opportunity is now laid at our door, to prove before all coming history, how much our sincerity for the cause of peace is worth in dollars and cents. Inasmuch as we obediently do it for the willing martyrs and supporters of the cause, we do it unto the Prince of Peace Himself.

"Should but a pound of corn meal per day for each Doukhobor be furnished, to sustain life till another summer, it is estimated that $25,000 would be needed to cover the cost."

Friends responded nobly to this appeal, and provisions were promptly forwarded to the colonists, where they were distributed in time to prevent them from starving.

The Commissioner of Immigration, William F. McCreary, who had shown great interest in the Russian exiles, and sympathy for them, ever since their arrival on Canadian soil, now proved himself their true friend, and with marked ability dispensed the supplies placed at his disposal from every quarter. His agent, James S. Crerar, at Yorkton, also rendered very valuable assistance. Indeed, the attitude and services of all the Dominion officials were most helpful during this period of colonization. A carload of sugar, four cars of corn meal, and one of rolled oats, with some carloads of potatoes, and one or more of onions (the latter purchased in Canada), were distributed throughout the fifty-seven villages of the several colonies. Wool, yarn, leather and lamps were forwarded from Philadelphia, with tea and linseed oil, of which the Doukhobors are very fond. Three hundred spinning-wheels were also purchased, as well as forty-nine cows, and ten yoke of oxen. The gratitude expressed, both by men and women,

Sergius Tolstoi. Anna de Carousa. Leopold Soulerjitzky.
Sasha Satz. Prince D. A. Hilkov. Wm. F. McCreary. Maria Robitz.

Helpers of the Doukhobors

when the cows were allotted, was reported by Cornelius Jansen as "truly touching." A car of supplies, intended especially for the sick, aged and younger children, was particularly appreciated by the recipients.

May Fitz-Gibbon* ("Lally Bernard"), of *The* (Toronto) *Globe*, advocated very fully and sympathetically the cause of these suffering colonists, after she had visited them in their homes; and, as has been previously noted, the women of Eastern Canada came to their rescue, as also their neighbors on the prairie, among whom Alfred Hutchinson and his wife, with Robert and Elizabeth Buchanan, deserve special mention for their many services.

Joseph S. Elkinton and William B. Harvey visited throughout the settlements during the Eleventh month, 1899, to ascertain their condition and needs, and to oversee the distribution of the supplies forwarded. They also accompanied some of the last contingent of immigrants to their allotments on the prairie. After their return a very carefully-prepared inventory of the possessions and vital statistics of each village was printed and circulated.

John Ashworth, of Manchester, England, was making his first tour of the Doukhobor villages about this time, and these Friends compared notes with him. The problem of transportation was perhaps the most pressing at that time, as all the goods de-

* "The Canadian Doukhobor Settlements," a series of letters by "Lally Bernard."—William Briggs, Toronto.

livered at Yorkton had to be hauled from forty to eighty miles in wagons, of which there were comparatively few available. It required a team one week to make a trip to and from the North Colony. Most of the Doukhobor men were employed on railroads at this time, as they could save more money at this work than in any other way, at that season of the year.

The following letter was handed to Joseph S. Elkinton and William B. Harvey by representative Doukhobors:

"To the Friends, from their friends, the Doukhobors. God have mercy upon you for your care, love and generosity!

"Five years ago, the Spirit of God inspired our people, and we learned the way of Truth, the way which our ancestors followed, but we lost it. When we again tried to follow that way of Truth, the people of different opinions began to oppress and persecute us, and we were scattered like a flock of sheep that have lost their shepherd. The labor of our hands was destroyed, and the fruits of our efforts of many years were taken away from us and given to others.

"We were a small flock, and the persecutors a legion; and they laid their hands on us, and we did not defend ourselves.

"Privations and heavy labor exhausted us, and we died from sickness. Then God inspired you to help us, and you (being) used to attend to the voice of God, came to us.

"You clothed us, you dressed our wounds, comforted and encouraged us. Then, when you saw that our oppressors did not stop persecuting us, you protected us, and under your protection we found the way out of the land of oppression and slavery, to that of freedom and activity. And you continue to show us your brotherly love, seeing no end to the work that our Lord God inspired you with.

"You are constantly studying our needs, and your efforts to satisfy our needs are ceaseless. Now, what shall we do, not to seem ungrateful? How could we repay your generosity, care and love? The deeds of kindness cannot be repaid by men, but there is a Creator, who does not leave without reward a single cup offered to the thirsty, and He will never leave you unrewarded for all your goodness, which He Himself inspired you with.

"God have mercy upon you, for your care, love and generosity!

"For the Doukhobors' people, signed,

"Vassili Potapov,
"Ivan Krukov,
"Alexander Bodyansky."

The Dominion National Council of Women did their part nobly at this time of need. Early in 1900 two carloads of supplies were sent from Montreal, bearing some fifty spinning-wheels, fifteen pieces of heavy flannel, twelve hand-looms, with eighty box stoves, as also carving and metal-beating tools, to the colonists. The Friends of Philadelphia supplemented this shipment with two hundred spinning-wheels, $1,600 worth of wool, and $3,700 worth of garden and other seeds, all of which were much appreciated.

A Russian lady, Anna de Carousa, was so impressed with the religious and moral qualities of the Doukhobors while in Cyprus, where she resided, that she accompanied them to their Canadian home, and rendered invaluable services as interpreter, and distributor of the above gifts to these Russian immigrants. In this connection, a co-laborer (" Lally Bernard ") says: " The amount of work that this frail and gently-nurtured woman performs for her beloved Doukhobors, is simply astonishing. She is quite unaccustomed to a cold climate, and yet she resolutely remains in a tiny frame hotel at Yorkton, her pen and offices as interpreter being ceaselessly employed on their behalf." *

Frederick Leonhardt, a German, exiled from Russia ten years since, was also a very sympathetic helper in many ways. Coming from his home in Dakota to meet the newly-arrived immigrants, he assisted them in locating their villages and in planting their crops. His services as interpreter for the Friends and others have been mentioned elsewhere.

---

* *The* (Toronto) *Globe* of Second month 3d, 1900.

About the first of 1900 he was commissioned by the Canadian government to travel throughout the Doukhobor villages, to ascertain their condition and needs in all particulars.

It was only through the united effort of all interested in the Doukhobors that they escaped starvation at this time. The Duck Lake Settlement, in Saskatchewan, near Prince Albert, had expended their resources, although they had considerable more with which to leave Russia than was the case with most of their co-religionists. They have very seldom asked for aid, and only the greatest need would have compelled them now to say: "Last autumn we prepared ourselves with two bags of flour for each soul, but just now we have little left. It is very hard for us; we have no kruppà (meaning oats, barley, etc.), neither potatoes, oil nor butter. Our children are getting sick, but we have nothing to nourish them with. We have neither milk nor eggs, nor can we get them. We have received some sugar and wool from our dear brothers, the Quakers. May the Lord bless them and give them long life in this world for their goodness to our people. . . .

"There are some of us who have nothing at all. We have not even got our daily bread. We feel bad to ask from other people, but our great need compels us to stretch out our hand. So we turn to you with tears, if you have any means to help us, do it as quick as possible, for which we will continually bless you. This terrible persecution has made us so poor."

Several hundred of the Doukhobor men—in fact, all that were able-bodied—sought work upon the railroads that were then being built in Canada, and the testimony of one of the railroad contractors (Neil Keiths) by whom they were employed, is highly appreciative of their industry and economy and kindness to all, including their horses. They sent all their earnings to their families in the colonies.

The houses, for the most part built and plastered by the Doukhobor women, afforded ample protection against the cold, but the clay sides and sod roofs scarcely had opportunity to dry before the winter set in, and the hoar-frost could be seen standing out upon the inside of their walls. This was calculated to induce rheumatism, and many suffered therefrom, but the mortality was remarkably low considering all the circumstances.

Herbert Archer, who came from England to assist in settling these colonists, lived through this winter in the North Colony, and did what he could in finding employment on the railroad for the men, with some success, but he reported a decided difference between the progress of the North Colony and that of the South Colony, where there was less co-operation, economy and health among their several village communities. Some of the latter became so dissatisfied as to go to California—prospecting for a future home—but these came back in the course of a few months, much to the relief of their best friends. About this time (Second month of 1900) the Doukhobor Committee of Philadelphia Yearly Meeting sent an epistle of encouragement and counsel to all of their communities. This was met by a hearty response on their part, as the following letter shows. It was signed by the Secretary of the Committee of the North Colony, and reads: " We had the happiness to receive the dear letter to us, sent by you, of Second month 14th this year. We are very much pleased with your letter which we received; for which we are heartily and feelingly grateful to you for your instruction, as it is the truth. We are thankful to the good people who have delivered us from bondage, and brought us to this country. We are happy, not being in fear of oppression. Not a soul of the Northern Colonies desires leaving the free land of Canada. We are praying unto God our Lord that He may not deprive us of His heavenly mercy, and send us good crops this coming year, to enable us, a little, at least, to gain strength and energy, and cease to feed on the toil of others. Of course this depends on the will of God.

" We received through the Committees of the Southern Colonies forty-one spinning-wheels for our Northern District, as well as other articles.

" May the Lord bless you for all the kind deeds you have bestowed upon us. We greet you all, dear brothers and sisters, in the name of our Lord Jesus Christ.

" (From) the Committee of the Northern Colony

of the Christian Society of the Universal Brotherhood, as well as (from) all our brothers and sisters.

"SIMON RIBUN.

"*Village Vosnesenie.*"

Three or four carloads of dried fruit were sent by interested friends in California, and some cows were purchased and distributed where most needed, so a little variety was added to their too meagre vegetable diet. Thus the scurvy, which had appeared in several villages, because of insufficient nourishment, abated, as also the prevalence of sore eyes and bad sores from the same cause.

These gifts brought out much expression on the part of the recipients. One poor man who had been in exile for two years, and had lost all his property, "and there," as he says, "got cold and took severe malaria," and through that lost his health, writes to Joseph S. Elkinton:

"Kirilofka, April 15th.

"May the Lord bless your great work to us, your brethren in the Lord Jesus Christ. Peace and grace be unto the workers and followers of our Lord Jesus Christ, remembering the commandment of our Lord before His crucifixion. Our dear and never-to-be-forgotten friends and brethren and sisters and your small children (some of whom had contributed to Doukhobor needs), we greet you all with a loving heart, and with best wishes for eternal happiness in the Heavenly Kingdom, seeing the Lord face to face. May the Lord bless a hundred-fold your great benevolence to us, poor, worn-out strangers. Our love and thankfulness to all kind benefactors." Then (after reporting the several articles of diet and clothing and seeds which had come to their village) he continues: "All this we have divided to each soul in our village alike. For all this we heartily thank you, and may the Lord save you, because you do not leave us without assistance in our need, and count us as your brethren.

"We pray and ask our Lord to keep you in health, and our little children, with tears, send up praise to God. God hear our prayer and that of our children, and may He provide for your kind people in His heavenly kingdom. Dear friends, we wish you all grace from our Lord. To all our brothers and sisters from the community of Kirilovka.

"Your brother,

"IVAN NIMANICHIN."

The dear old grandmother, Anastasia Verigin, some eighty-five years of age, after expressing her gratitude for the favors received, says: "From my loved son, Peter Verigin, I have lately received a letter which was very dear to us, the first letter (from our exiled brethren) we received in Canada. He is alive and waiting the time when the Lord will grant them liberty." Naming five other sons in exile, she adds: "They tell us they are very lonesome for us, and pray the Lord we may see one another again face to face."

In the Sixth month of 1900, Jonathan E. Rhoads, of Philadelphia, a minister of the Society of Friends, felt a religious concern to visit the Doukhobors in all their communities, and he was accompanied by his friend, Joseph S. Elkinton.

The Doukhobors in Russia.

CHAPTER I.

NATIONAL RELIGIOUS CHARACTER.

Before entering upon the early history of the Doukhobors it will be helpful to take a glance at the national religious character, as this both affords an interesting field for study and furnishes an explanation of much of the superstition, fanaticism and lovable simplicity of the race.

From the beginning of the Christian era the Russian Slav has been known to be decidedly religious, by whatever form he may have expressed his feeling. For centuries before the introduction of Christianity he professed highly developed nature-worship. His supreme deity was represented by the sky. The sun, the thunderbolt and fire were also regarded with awe, and many minor deities had a place in his system. Without any temples or ritual, these sons of the forest and of the steppe worshiped in the open, upon some hill or at a shrine made sacred to Perún, who hurled the thunderbolt. No priest deluded or robbed them, while the chief performed the ecclesiastical functions. Life after death was provided for by placing food and weapons in the graves of their departed friends.

The patriarchal custom of the father having absolute control of the household, which continues to this day, did not destroy a kind-hearted hospitality or an intense individualism.

In those early days, as now, they were mostly engaged in agricultural pursuits, although skilled in making iron tools and weapons. The migratory instinct was strong among them, and soon brought them into contact with the Finns on the north and the Tartars on the south and east of their country, and this fusion with their neighbors gave them a solidity of character, a power of endurance and perseverance, which they did not originally possess.

Prince Vladimir (980-1015) introduced Christianity, of the Greek form, to these pioneers of the Greater Russia of to-day, and forbade pagan worship among his people. The sudden transition was not accomplished, however, without opposition, and, as has always happened when a belief has been forced upon an unwilling people, compromise became necessary, and the attributes of some of the pagan deities were attached to the Christian saints.

Tradition says that men, women and children were assembled on the cliffs at Kiev and compelled to witness the humiliation of their gods, which were cast into the Dnieper. After this the multitudes were commanded to descend into the river, where they were baptized, and transformed by the words of the priest and the force of Greek ritual into Christians.

The blending of pagan and Greek conceptions is illustrated in its simplicity and crudeness, by a Turanian prayer, such as the following: "Look here, O Nicholas, god! Perhaps my neighbor, little Michael, has been slandering me to you, or perhaps he will do so. If he does, don't believe him. I have done him no harm and wish him none. He is a worthless boaster and a babbler. He does not really honor you, and merely plays the hypocrite. But I honor you from my heart, and, behold! I place a taper before you."

By thus obtaining their religious and secular ideas from Constantinople, the Russians cut off those opportunities of reform and enlightenment which the western culture would have brought them during the period of the Renaissance. While this was particularly unfortunate, it accounts for some of their most peculiar and interesting characteristics.

There was something in the Greek ceremonial that was fascinating alike to the Slav, the Finn and the Tartar, and even in its perverted presentation this form of Christianity was some improvement over the paganism it supplanted. It brought a higher social order, and elevated the domestic condition by increasing the respect shown to women. The rights of children were also recognized, and slaves received rather more generous treatment at the hands of their masters.

One can find in the Russian character, from the earliest period, much that might have developed into the highest type of enlightened Christianity, and the ever-reviving protest against formality, to be found in every age and among every class of that nation, is one of the most promising evidences of the possibility of casting off the yoke of priestly domination.

CHAPTER II.

TRADITION AND EARLY HISTORY.

William Allen, of London, when visiting Russia with Stephen Grellet, in 1818, said the Minister of the Interior, General Djunkolesky, gave them good reason for supposing that originally the Doukhobors came from the followers of John Huss. But there is so little certainty in the very scant records concerning their rise, that we prefer to believe, according to their own tradition, that they sprang from three brothers, Cossacks of the Don, who, through the teaching of the Spirit, and a careful perusal of the New Testament, were led away from the ceremonies of the Russian Church to worship God in spirit and in truth. "It is quite useless, however," as one of their own countrymen, T. Abramov, truly observes, "to discuss the question as to whether such and such a religious idea comes from within a nation or from without, from the Quakers or from some one else; as when once an idea begins to spread it must undergo a long and imperceptible assimilation and reproduction in the minds of the people at large, and will therefore undoubtedly be looked upon as quite an original idea, incorporating all the characteristic features of the people among whom it has spread."

It would be too distressing, as well as difficult, to narrate the many persecutions of this people, yet their endurance and heroic fortitude under all the adverse conditions which the Russian Government has imposed upon them for more than a century, can best be appreciated by citing some particular instances on record.

In 1797, Andrei Tolstaev and his wife were tried because of their adherence to the Doukhobor principles, and after being punished with the knout, and having their nostrils cut off—(this inhuman punishment was frequently inflicted on dissenters)—they were sentenced to hard labor in the Government of Irkutsk. This was about twenty years after the Cossacks of the Don, who had first embraced the same faith, fell under the ban of the ecclesiastical law as heretics. The renowned Senator Lapukhin wrote, in 1806: "No sect has, up to this time, been so cruelly persecuted as the Doukhobortsi, and this is certainly not because they are the most harmful. They have been tortured in various ways, and whole families have been sentenced to hard labor and confinement in the most cruel prisons.

"Some were confined in cells in which one could not stand upright, nor lie down at full length. This was boastingly told me by one of the officers at a place where they were confined.

"Every procurator and general, on the recommendation of the governor of a province, promulgated a *ukase* for banishing whole families to various places for settlement, or for hard labor; and many families were thus expelled."

As a sample of such an edict, issued at the end of

the eighteenth century, some thirty-four Doukhobors, after prolonged sufferings during the investigation made by their accusers, received their sentence in these words: "As the same prisoners remain inflexible to suggestion and persuasion, in order to guard men from like superstition in the future, and also to retaliate upon them for their renunciation of the Church, her sacraments and saints, they shall receive, each man, thirty strokes of the knout, and each woman forty strokes of the lash publicly. The Doukhobor, Jacob Laktev's daughter, Katrina, and Ivan Shalayev's daughter, Nastasia, as minors, are, in accordance with the *ukase* of May 2d, 1765, to be whipped with rods. After all these criminals have been thus punished they are to be banished to Siberia, their goods are to be confiscated and sold by public auction, and the money sent to the treasury office in Perekop, to be entered to the account of public revenue; the carrying out of which sentence is to devolve upon the police court of Perekop."

The higher criminal court, to which this case came up from the district court, altered the sentence as follows: "The prisoners convicted of Doukhobortsi heresy are to be put in irons without punishment, and sent to work perpetually in the mines, at Ekaterinburg, Siberia, excepting the younger children. The bringing up of the children under ten years of age in the faith of the Greek Orthodox Church is to devolve upon the mayor of the town or of the parish, together with the priests."

Some thirty-one Doukhobors from another district were similarly sentenced in 1799, and in 1800 a *ukase* reads: "Everybody who shall be convicted of belonging to the sect of Doukhobortsi shall be condemned to life-long hard labor."

Alexander I. was, however, graciously disposed to restore to them their rights, after his minister, Lapukhin, had investigated the civil and other disabilities of this sorely persecuted sect, and some of them came back from the places of their banishment.

They conversed with Lapukhin on friendly terms, and he petitioned the Emperor on their behalf for a place of settlement apart from the Greek Orthodox Russians. This was granted, with permission to emigrate to "The Milky Waters" in the Melitopol district of the Tauris government (near the Crimea), where each emigrant received about forty-five acres of land. Other privileges were also granted, such as exemption from taxation, for Alexander seemed genuinely interested in their welfare. Thus some thousands eventually congregated just north of the Crimea and remained there until 1840. The authorities were recommended to leave the Doukhobors in peace unless they displayed "an open disobedience to the legal authority." They were not to be convicted as criminals on account of their opinions, and the clergy were ordered to stay away from them.

In 1807, the Doukhobors still in Siberia were accused of "seditious acts by openly declaring their beliefs," so the Governor-General was ordered to place the able-bodied men in military service. It is interesting to note about this time (1807) the first instance of refusal to bear arms on the part of the Doukhobors engaged in the first Turkish War. These men threw away their arms in the midst of the fighting, while two Cossacks, who refused to obey the military authorities, were sentenced to death. This sentence was afterwards commuted to imprisonment for life.

In 1809 the privates of the Kiev regiment, who were Doukhobors, refused to receive ammunition and provisions, or to perform military service, and they were sent to work in the Siberian factories. A peasant, Simeon Matrossov, given up by his landlord to military service, refused to take the oath, and would not serve in the ranks. This was in 1817, and because of his refusal to take the oath, the ministerial committee ordered that "Doukhobortsi should be taken into military service without being compelled to swear," which order was confirmed by the Council of State in 1820.

In 1811 a petition was made to the Czar by four thousand Doukhobors, who declared that because they were "oppressed everywhere, and in every way," they would be glad to settle on the right side of the Danube, or on the left, in territory "recently acquired from the Ottoman Porte"; but this was not allowed.

THE MILKY WATERS COLONY.

Some details of this colony may be of interest. There were nine villages in this settlement, situated along the River Molotchna and its estuary. The central village was called Terpenie (patience). In it sat the parish assembly. In it too was the orphan house. It was a large wooden building, surrounded by a park, containing fruit and forest trees, a brook and two fountains. This house was called "Zion" by the Doukhobors. A few men and women lived in it. Some girls who had become church singers, after having learned their psalms by heart, also lodged there.

The households generally were in a flourishing condition, thanks to the abundance of land, communal husbandry, and the enterprising spirit of the Doukhobors with regard to agricultural improvements. There were 13,500 acres of arable land in this tract, so that each man had rather more than forty-five acres. Their farming was all done in common, and the produce divided into equal parts. They also erected storehouses for food in case of famine.

Several industries were successfully introduced, such as the manufacture of sashes and woolen hats. Improvements in agriculture were adopted from their Mennonite neighbors, while the other Russians remained quite indifferent to such improvements. Many of their houses were built in German fashion, and even the dress of the German colonists was adopted to some extent, while their Greek Orthodox neighbors continued to wear their former worn-out "zeepoon" (a peasant's coat) and "lapti" (bast shoes).

As to the moral side of the life of the Doukhobors in this community, there is strong testimony from the Governor of the district that drunkenness and idleness were rigidly prohibited. "State taxes and commercial obligations were punctually discharged. They were active, indefatigable in labor and industrious in agriculture, and, being sober and well-living men, they were more independent than others" of their countrymen.

Physically, the men were mostly tall and the women pretty. In this connection it may be in place to comment upon the splendid physique of both men and women, who for a century have been able, without doctors or medicine, to keep healthier and stronger than most other races, even while under the most unfavorable circumstances for living comfortably.

In 1808 the Chamberlain Zherebtzov visited the Crimea to examine into their condition, and he found them "well settled on their land, with sufficient live stock, and leading a sober and industrious life, and so far from complaining, they only expressed their gratitude to the government for the quietness they enjoyed."

The Emperor Alexander I. himself passed through this settlement in 1818, and was so pleased with their prosperity that he "ordered the prompt return to their native land of all the banished Doukhobortsi, for whom their co-religionists had petitioned." "But," continues the same historian, "even the personal patronage of Alexander I. could not alter the behavior of the second and lower class members of the administration and clergy, who, partly from selfishness, partly from ignorance, have always oppressed by every means in their power, these peaceable and industrious sectarians."

Their pretext for these persecutions was the fact that the "Doukhobortsi converted Greek Orthodox men to their sect." It is uncertain whether the Doukhobortsi "converted" or the Greek Orthodox were carried away by the *example* of their moral life, and by an appreciation of the value of community life as developed in their villages. The latter supposition is the more probable, because, as is generally known, the great mass of the proselytes of any new teaching always adopt it without propaganda, solely in consequence of the moral influence and purer life of the followers of the new teaching. And besides, as we shall see later on, upon investigations being instituted, no Doukhobor propaganda was discovered. Be this as it may, the officials and clergy, taking advantage of the fact that the beliefs of the Doukhobors were spreading among the Greek Orthodox in the neighborhood of Milky Waters, committed the most cruel acts of violence with impunity. Nor were these so-called zealots of Greek Orthodoxy particular as to the means they employed, making use of the men who had been expelled from the Doukhobor community for theft, drunkenness and profligacy. This practice is now common in relation to other sects also, as the Stundists, Molokans and others. In consequence of the evidence of these notoriously immoral men, they made "incursions into the villages of the Doukhobortsi, arrested the first men they met, and kept them imprisoned for years."

There is a chapter of considerable interest, explaining the friendship between Alexander I. and the Society of Friends, pleasantly told by Jane Benson, in her "Quaker Pioneers in Russia." We may perhaps discern strong indications of Quaker influence in this emperor's enlightened treatment of his Doukhobor subjects.

In the spring of 1814 the Emperor visited London, and attended a Friends' meeting for worship. William Allen, as a representative of that Society, had been summoned to meet the Royal party on a First-day morning, and was informed that the Emperor wished to see a Quaker meeting. As the hour was already past when they usually assembled, William Allen said, "Then it is quite plain we must go to the nearest, which is Westminster, and lose no time, otherwise it may be broken up."

The Emperor, the young duke of Oldenburg, the Ambassador, the King of Wurtemburg, and Count Lieven, were seated facing the assembly, "and the whole party conducted themselves with the greatest seriousness."

They sat in silence for fifteen minutes, and then three "testimonies" were delivered by the Friends, one of which made such an impression upon the Emperor that he desired to see John Wilkinson, one of the speakers, and William Allen, in a private interview next day. Stephen Grellet, a Philadelphia Friend, was also present, and reported a very pleasant hour's informal conversation, which he "thought had been appreciated by them all."

The questions the Emperor asked referred generally to the realities of every-day life. He liked our principles, he said, so far as he had heard them, but he had the wisdom to recognize the great distance that often exists between preaching and practice. He liked the meeting he had attended, and now he wanted to visit a Friend's house.

Subsequently, as he was about to leave England, two Friends, Nathaniel Rickman and his wife, were seen standing at the door of their home at a little distance from the road. The Emperor stopped his carriage, got out, and courteously inquired of them if they belonged to the people commonly called Quakers.

On receiving a reply in the affirmative he next asked leave for himself and sister to enter the house, which, of course, was granted. They stayed some time, looking over it, taking refreshment, and telling their host and hostess, to whom it was news, of their attending a meeting, and of their interviews with members of the Society, in London. Here his favorable opinion of Friends was confirmed. The farm and house were well cared for and orderly, and he did not forget his impressions when the time came for making use of them.

Three years later (1817) Alexander I. sent to England for a member of the Society of Friends to come to Russia to cultivate certain bog lands in the neighborhood of St. Petersburg.

The information was spread throughout the meetings of the Society, and a prompt response came from Sheffield. Daniel Wheeler, a convinced Friend and acceptable minister among them, told his fellow-members that he had felt for some time previously that it would be right for him to go to Russia.

His friends could only regretfully confess that he was especially qualified for the position to be filled, and pass on his offer, which was gladly accepted by the Emperor.

He had had considerable experience in farming, and had remarkable success in the difficult task which he now undertook of redeeming for agricultural purposes the spongy morass, "covered with a white moss to the depth, on an average, of about sixteen inches, with cowberry and other bog plants, small shrubs and young fir trees," with the roots and trunks of a primeval forest underneath all.

There he labored for fifteen years, preaching by the example of a holy and industrious life, and occasionally visited by the Emperor, with whom he had the most cordial relations.

The visit of Stephen Grellet and William Allen, in 1819, to the Doukhobors, then residing in or near the Crimean colony, was a notable event, still remembered by Ivan Mahortov (the patriarch of the Canadian colonists), and related by him to recent visitors, after the lapse of eighty years, and after much of the following prophecy had been fulfilled. Stephen Grellet told them that if they were faithful to their religious convictions they would be exiled and finally banished from their native land after they had been robbed, imprisoned and sorely persecuted, in some instances even unto death, and that when they were settled in that foreign country, among a people of a different language, they would be visited by members of his Society, and then they would prosper.

As Stephen Grellet's Journal contains an important passage in reference to these dissenters from the Orthodox Greek Church, which has led some to query whether they were Orthodox Christians, it might be well to say once for all, that they revolted against the icon-worship of the Russian Church so radically as to place the emphasis of their belief upon the Spirit, as their infallible guide. An infallible Church, an infallible Book, or an infallible Spirit, represent the bases of Christian belief, and professing Christendom still gives abundant evidence of the untenable positions which the first two assume.

It is indeed strange that so good and spiritual a man as Stephen Grellet did not perceive that the Doukhobors were only stating their *foundation* principle, when they gave the pre-eminence to the *Spirit* of *Truth*, rather than to the outward authority of the Scriptures (invaluable as these are). In like manner they put the emphasis upon the indwelling Spirit of Christ rather than upon His historical appearance, important as this was and is to our salvation. They do believe in Jesus Christ as the Saviour of men. This was the confession of their elders since coming to America, and so far as they are able to read they value the Bible. How otherwise can we account for their memorizing so much of the Scriptures, which has gone on for generations? Stephen Grellet himself says: "They said they met together to sing the Psalms of David." He also gives a graphic account of their mode of worship, which is retained to this day: "On a spacious spot of ground out of doors, they all stood, forming a large circle; all the men on the left hand of the old man (about ninety years of age and 'a chief' among them), and the women on his right. The children of both sexes formed the opposite side of the circle. They were all cleanly dressed. An old woman was next to the old man. She began by singing what they called a Psalm (these are partly from the Scriptures of the Old and New Testaments and partly their own composition). The other women joined in it. Then the man next to the old man, taking his hand, stepped in front of him; each bowed down very low to the other three times, and then twice to the woman, who returned the salute. That man resuming his place, the one next to him performed the same ceremony to the old man and to the woman. Then by turns all the others, even the boys, came and kissed three times, the one in the circle above him, instead of bowing. When the men and boys had accomplished this, the women did the same to each other; then the girls, the singing continuing the whole time. It took them nearly an hour to perform this round of bowing and kissing. Then the old woman, in a fluent manner, uttered what they called a prayer, and their worship ended."

All this ceremony evidently did not appeal to Stephen Grellet, for he says: "No seriousness appeared over them at any time"; whereas the solemnity and sincerity of their worship, as witnessed by those Friends who have visited them in Canada, has been very impressive, although the ceremony is somewhat tedious. We may hope that if they leave off some of their ceremoniousness they will lose nothing of their fervency of spirit. Their custom of bowing is an expression of reverence for the Divine Nature or Spirit in man. However much this sect—in common with most others one hundred and fifty years old—has lapsed at times from its primitive spirituality, the fires of persecution have eventually in good measure purified its membership. That a people with so few outward advantages should retain so large a portion of their original simplicity of character and beautiful devotion to high spiritual conceptions, based upon the love of God, is a most hopeful sign of the possibilities of the coming of His kingdom of peace and righteousness on the earth.

THE CAUCASIAN EXILE.

The story of Evangeline and her exiled countrymen was re-enacted in the removal of this thrifty and devout people from their homes on the "Milky Waters" to the Caucasus.

In 1819 the Ministerial Committee decided that "Doukhobortsi and Molokani should not be elected to public offices, while those already elected should be dismissed"; with a heavy tax imposed upon the whole community for their release from such service. Two years later we find a Caucasian chief, who had some 2,500 Doukhobors in his district, advising the Central Government that all their families be dispersed among the Russian villages, and that children be separated from their parents, "that thus the exhortations and example of the clergymen might influence them to embrace the Orthodox religion." This was literally carried out in that very locality seventy-five years afterward, and even Prince Hilkov's children were violently taken from him within the last decade and placed with members of the Russian Church. The Stundists also suffered from the same cruel separations at this time.

There was evidently a determination on the part of those in authority to dispossess the Crimean Colony, and transplant them with all their co-religionists to the Caucasus, for the chairman of the law department of the State Council (Pashkov) complained in 1824 that "the Doukhobortsi are striving to destroy everything on earth that is dear to a true son of the Church, the throne and the fatherland," and he suggested dispersing all of the "obnoxious sect" throughout the Caucasus. This ministerial decision was confirmed by Nicholas I., in 1826, and literally carried out fifteen years later. The Cossacks of the Don who had embraced the faith were the first to be transported to that inhospitable region, where they were brought into close contact with the fiercest hillsmen, for the avowed purpose of compelling them to defend themselves, their property and families, by force, and so voluntarily to deny their own teaching. Besides this they were obliged to bear the name and duties of *Cossacks*, and to live along the line of the frontier fortresses.

While these followers of the Prince of Peace were being put to the test under such trying conditions, their brethren in and near the Crimea were forbidden to leave their villages under any pretense, without the knowledge of the police, and hence they could not market their produce as had previously been their custom. Thus they became wholly dependent upon the Greek Orthodox middlemen, who took every advantage of them.

In 1826 the Minister Lanskoi proposed that these and similar sectarians should be sent to Western Siberia, while the propagators of heresy should be exiled to the eastern side of that vast domain. This was inflicted, however, upon only such men as were unable for active military service in the Caucasian corps, and these soldiers were to remain in the army until death. They got neither furlough nor leave to retire, unless they embraced Orthodoxy, in which case they received many privileges. These severe measures only strengthened the resolution of the faithful, and the Government was practically defeated in its own purpose.

In the course of a decade another move was made to extinguish this ever-increasing sect. They were forbidden to profess their religion publicly. Their assemblies were then prohibited, and, until they left their fatherland, they continued to be dispersed violently at any time, either by the police or clergy, while those arrested at such times were confined in "places of the bug" (untidy rooms where prisoners are kept), or in cold village cells that are never heated.

How similar these actions seem to those we read of in England during the seventeenth century, when Friends, with other dissenters, were carried off to prison, where many of them died, for no other offense than having declared "the Truth," as it appeared to them.

To those who have studied the history of persecution in the Christian Church, whether inflicted by non-Christians or by their fellow believers, one of two results has invariably followed, from the days of Nero to the present time: either men welcome martyrdom or regard heresy as a virtue, while yielding passive submission to their oppressors. Thus we find many of these Russian sectarians irritated until they had an almost fanatical desire to "suffer for the faith," while others so far complied with the requisitions of the State Church as to be registered "Orthodox," though secretly adhering to their heretical opinions. Happy will be the day and the people when true toleration shall prevail in any community, as William Penn designed it should, in that settlement which he so aptly called his "holy experiment," on the banks of the Delaware. Count Tolstoi has been writing for years, and in every way endeavoring to inculcate liberty of conscience and toleration alike in State and Church. His work thus far has apparently resulted only in his own excommunication. The Russian Government still endeavors to coerce its subjects into adopting the unscientific and un-Christian conceptions of a semi-barbarous civilization and mediæval theology.

In 1835 passports were forbidden to the wives of those Doukhobors and other dissenters who were taken for military service in the Caucasus, the object being to prevent them from communicating with their Orthodox neighbors, and so propagating their errors. The same year all such "specially pernicious" sects as the Spirit Wrestlers were prohibited from joining any town community in Russia, except in Transcaucasia. This was a great deprivation, as citizens registered in towns or cities have many more privileges in that country than those who are registered only as peasants or village residents.

However, these restrictive and oppressive measures were insignificant in comparison with a *ukase* issued about the same time, whereby those sectarians who had been transported to Transcaucasia were forbidden to return to Central Russia. This *ukase* also confined the Doukhobors to seven Caucasian towns, without the opportunity of visiting their fellow exiles elsewhere, even in the same territory, unless they carried a passport defining minutely the object of their visit. But all these hindrances did not prevent them from prospering in a material way, so they literally turned the wilderness into a garden, and in the course of a few years became again comparatively comfortable.

An imperial decree went forth in 1836 that all "the Doukhobortsi settled in Siberia were, in the event of their spreading their beliefs, to be removed to a remote part of that country, and those condemned to hard labor were to be sent to the mines at Nerchinsk," having their terms lengthened. A year later their brethren who were sentenced to military service in the Caucasus were ordered to be sent to the regiments quartered in Siberia, and those unfit for service to be settled there.

In 1839 a new measure, specially designed to impoverish the Doukhobors and Molokans, was passed, by which it was illegal for them to acquire property in land, situated more than thirty versts from their place of residence. But this was a slight affliction compared to the decision by the Government to transport the whole population settled on the Milky Waters in the Melitopol district, just north of the Crimea, to the cold and inhospitable mountains of the Caucasus.

Whatever could have induced Nicholas I. to authorize so heartless a treatment of ten or twelve thousand of his most inoffensive, moral and industrious subjects, is beyond conception, or at least beyond satisfactory explanation. But the facts are these, as related by Madame Filiberte,* who obtained her information from old inhabitants of Melitopol. A police officer, whose extortions became intolerable to the Doukhobors, was objected to at last by them, and he forthwith brought to the Central Government a charge against the whole community. "The irritated official used every means in his power to blacken the character of his victims in the eyes of the Governor-General, Prince Vorontzov, accusing them of various crimes of which they were, according to the evidence of reliable men, quite inno-

* This was written in 1870, when this deportation and devastation of 1843-'45 was still fresh in the memory of those who witnessed it, twenty-five or thirty years before.

cent. The result was the expulsion of the entire population from their homes to a far-away land."

The Imperial order, signed in 1839, reads: "All the Doukhobortsi shall be removed from Molotchna Voda (The Milky Waters) to the Transcaucasian Provinces." This edict was announced to them by the Governor-General, and the deportation began at once, and lasted through four years. The account of their removal is thus vividly portrayed by T. Abramov: "It was a depressing picture—the expulsion of the Doukhobortsi from their homes. The whole property, acquired by long years of toil, was sold for almost nothing, the houses abandoned, the fields given up.

"On parting from the land, which for so many years had fed them, the Doukhobortsi women kneeled and pressed to her their breasts; they kissed her, and, sobbing, stretched their hands to heaven and sang mournful psalms. But the earth, to which they pressed their breasts, and the men, who should have heard them, all remained deaf to their sorrow."

This people, who but a year ago were wealthy, were now removed to the Persian frontier, where they were continually subjected to robbery at the hands of the Tartars.

The Government tried to win over the emigrants by allowing all who were ready to join the Orthodox Church to remain in their old homes. Only twenty-seven out of twelve thousand agreed to these conditions. "Banished to a strange land, where the soil, climate and conditions of life were quite new and unknown to them, surrounded by hostile mountain tribes, and precluded, by their religious principles, from using arms even in self-defense, the Doukhobortsi seemed condemned to perish without leaving a remnant. But such is the strength of their communal principle, which forms the basis of the life of this community, that in spite of continual suffering from invasion, change of climate and fevers, they at last succeeded, not only in adapting themselves to local conditions, but even in reviving the trade of the province and becoming the most prosperous section of the Transcaucasian population."

The moral influence of the Doukhobors was so generally recognized throughout the Caucasus, that their absence came to be regretted by the Government itself. After the last Russo-Turkish war the Government actually solicited them to move into the newly-acquired district of Kars, to civilize the Mohammedans. These new Mohammedan neighbors soon made friends with them, concluding that they were *not* Christians, for, said they, "the Christians always fight."

"Such is," says Abramov, "the bitter irony of history upon the oppressive measures directed against the Doukhobortsi." "And these persecutions," says Count Tolstoi, "as is always the case, when they are endured with the Christian meekness shown by the Doukhobortsi, produce a result the very opposite of that intended by the persecutors.

"People wish to hide the fire which has appeared in the forest, and to extinguish it; they press it to the earth with whatever comes to hand—leaves, grass and wood—but the flame burns more and more fiercely, and its light spreads farther and farther."

CHAPTER III.

THE FAITH OF THE DOUKHOBORS.

Aylmer Maude, in his interesting chapter (in "Tolstoi and His Problems") on this long-persecuted people, says, very truly, " A turning-point in the history of the Doukhobors was reached in the early years of the nineteenth century, when the members of the sect, scattered over the length and breadth of Russia, were allowed to come together and form one community [on the Milky Waters of the Crimea]. From being a religious sect, held together by unity of opinions and beliefs, anxious to propagate those views among their neighbors, and obliged to adjust their lives and occupations to a diversity of circumstances and local conditions, the Doukhobors became an industrial and economic community, no longer persecuted for their theoretical beliefs.

" When a sect thus becomes a community, the interest shifts to a considerable extent from the question, What did they believe? to the question, How did they live? They cease to be propagandists, and become engaged in the welfare of their own community and the maintenance of their own religion. Their opinions seem to have undergone little change during the remainder of the century, so that a statement of what they believed a hundred years ago may pass, almost unmodified, for a statement of what most of them believe to-day.

"Then, as now, different individuals and different groups would express themselves variously, yet almost all would show a united front on matters on which they differed from the Orthodox Russian Church.

"The difficulty of describing the faith of a sect composed of illiterate peasants, who produced no books, and whose propaganda was carried on by word of mouth, and for the most part secretly, would be very great but for Orést Novitsky's book (first published in 1832), and certain State documents on file at St. Petersburg, to which we have had access. As these papers, found among the archives of the empire, contain some clear typical statements of belief, at first hand, they are introduced here as the oldest and most reliable known to the present writer. It is gratifying also to find the appreciation which the Doukhobors express in their letter to the British and Foreign Bible Society for the Bibles supplied to them in 1815, and to know that the opinion formed by the Society's worthy agent, Robert Pinkerton, who visited some of them in that year, agrees so well with their character seventy-five years later."

The account of his visit is here subjoined:

"We went forty miles to the north of Wiborg to see a famous waterfall, and then fell in with a colony of Doukhobortsi, from the Cossack country, consisting of about ninety persons. From all we could learn concerning them they are truly a pious, intelligent people, well reported by all around them. We had a long conversation with one of them, who himself could not read, but who has a more intimate acquaintance with the Scriptures than many I have met with. He answered all our questions in the language of Scripture, and explained some texts to us in a manner which would have done honor to an Oxford or Cambridge divine. These poor, forgotten people had not a Bible among them—(their persecutors had taken these away from them)—nor indeed a book of any kind, although some of them could read. We furnished them with some [Bibles]. I most heartily wish you had seen how his countenance brightened when we told him of the Bible Society and what has been done for the extended promotion of the Redeemer's kingdom. He could not believe for joy and wonder. 'No person,' said he, 'has ever told us of these things before.'"

After Robert Pinkerton's visit, the following letter from some of the Doukhobors was addressed to the Bible Society:

"We, the undernamed, make known that we have received the most precious and divine gift of seven copies of the Holy Scriptures from the Bible Society, according to our desire. We account it our duty to return thanks to God for His unsearchable mercy and condescension to us in having put it into the hearts of the members of the Society thus to strengthen mankind against sin. We present our ardent petition to the Society, that they would unite with us in thanksgiving to the Almighty God, who has bestowed upon them the spirit of Light and Wisdom and Grace, to lead us by the right knowledge of Himself, from the path of ignorance into the way of truth and salvation. We offer up our prayers in union with you for the life of our great monarch, Alexander, and for his brethren and the allies. May they who love his life live as pillars of the world, and may their days be as the days of heaven, because they are called to do the work of God. May the Lord of Hosts help them, and preserve them from all their enemies, that righteousness and peace may abound in their days, and may the Lord number them among His elect forever and ever. Along with this we send each of us, the undernamed, according to our promise, two roubles in aid of the Bible Society,—in all twenty roubles from nine peasants."

The following official reports, taken from State papers in St. Petersburg, are valuable, as representing the principles of the Doukhobors from the point of view of an opponent:

"To his Excellency the General Governor of Karkov:—

"Sir: Michael Stchirov, Ainkie and Timothy Suharev, sent by your Excellency from the vicinity of Karkov, have been admonished by Innokenty, Rector of the Nevsky Seminary and the Archimandrite.

The conversation which took place between them I forward to you along with this letter.

"This sect has been known to me since 1768. Then I admonished them, and succeeded in turning several of them to the Church, but on their returning home they again fell into their former errors. Since I became Archbishop of St. Petersburgh I have also admonished some of the Don Kossacks, but they remained obstinate. Their obstinacy is founded on enthusiasm. All demonstration that is presented to them they despise, saying that God is present in their souls, and He instructs them; how then shall they hearken to a man?

"They have such exalted ideas of their own holiness that they respect that man only in whom they see the image of God; that is, perfect holiness. They say that every one of them may be a prophet or an apostle, and therefore they are zealous promoters of their own sect. They make the sacraments consist only in a spiritual acceptance of them, and therefore reject infant baptism. The opinions held by them not only establish equality, but also exclude the distinction of ruler and subject. Such opinions are on that account the more dangerous, that they may become attractive to the peasantry; the truth of this Germany has experienced.

"Their origin is to be sought for among the Anabaptists or Quakers. I know the course of their opinion, and we cannot rest assured that they will desist from spreading abroad this evil.

"These are my thoughts, which I have conceived it my duty to communicate to your Excellency.

"With sincere respects, I am, etc.,

"GABRIEL,

"Metropolitan of Novgorod and St. Petersburgh.

"*May* 12, 1792."

A DIALOGUE BETWEEN THE RECTOR OF THE NEVSKY SEMINARY OF ST. PETERSBURG, ARCHIMANDRITE INNOKENTY, AND ONE OF THREE OF THE SECT CALLED DOUKHOBORTSI: MICHAEL STCHIROV, AINKIE AND TIMOTHY SUHAREV, IN MAY, 1792.

Archimandrite.—By what way did you come into this state that people confine you, as one dangerous to society?

Doukhobortsi.—By the malice of persecutors.

A.—What is the reason of their persecuting you?

D.—Because it is said that all who desire to live godly in Christ Jesus shall suffer persecution.

A.—Who is it that you call your persecutors?

D.—Those who threw me into prison and bound me in fetters.

A.—How dare you in this way speak evil of the established government, founded and acting on principles of Christian piety, which deprives none of their liberty except such as are disturbers of the public peace and prosperity?

D.—There is no other government but God's, who rules over the hearts of kings and men; but God does not bind in fetters, neither does He command those to be persecuted who will not give His glory unto any other, and who dwell in peace and in perfect love, and in the service of each other.

A.—What does that signify, "who will not give His glory unto any other"; whom other?

D.—Read the second commandment and you will know.

A.—By this I observe you mean to reflect censure on those who worship before the images of the Saviour and His saints?

D.—He hath placed His image in our souls. Again it is said that those who worship Him must worship Him in spirit and in truth.

A.—From this it is evident that you have brought yourself into your present condition by falling into error, ill understanding piety, and entertaining opinions hurtful to the faith and to your country.

D.—It is not true.

A.—How? Do you not err when you think that there are powers that be which exist in opposition to the will of God?—for "there is no power but of God";—or that that government persecutes piety which is appointed to restrain and correct the disobedient and unruly?—for "he is the minister of God, a revenger to execute wrath upon him that doeth evil."

D.—What evil do we do? None.

A.—Do you not hurt the faith by your false reasonings concerning the holy ordinances, and by your blind zeal against God, like the Jews of old, whose zeal was not according to knowledge?

D.—Let knowledge remain with you, only do not touch us who live in peace, pay the taxes, do harm to no one, and respect and obey earthly government.

A.—But perhaps your paying the taxes, harming no one, and obeying earthly government are only the effect of necessity, and the weakness of your power; while your peace and love respect those only who are of your opinion?

D.—Construe as you choose.

A.—At least it is far from being disagreeable to you, I suppose, to behold your society increasing?

D.—We desire good unto all men, and that all may be saved and come to the knowledge of the truth.

A.—Leave off your studied secrecy and evasive and dubious answers. Explain and reveal to me your opinions candidly, as unto a man who has nothing in view but to find out Truth.

D.—I understand you, because that same spirit of truth which enlightens us in things respecting faith and life assists us also in discovering affectation and deceit in every man; but, in order to get free of your importunity, and with boldness to preach the true faith, I shall answer your questions as I am able.

A.—By what way,—by the assistance of others, or

by the use of your own powers only,—did you obtain this spirit of truth?

D.—He is near our hearts, and therefore no assistance is necessary. A sincere desire and ardent prayer only are required.

A.—At least you ground yourself on the Word of God?

D.—I do ground myself on it.

A.—But the Word of God teaches us that God has committed the true faith and the dispensing of her ordinance and instruction in piety to certain persons, chosen and ordained to this purpose;—"according to the grace of God given unto me, as a wise master-builder, I have laid the foundation."

D.—True. Such were our deputies who were sent here in 1767 and 1769. But what did the spirit of persecution and of wrath do to them? Some were consigned to be soldiers, and others were sent into exile.

A.—You doubtless understand by those deputies well-meaning people like yourself?

D.—Yes.

A.—But you and people like you, though good people, cannot be either ministers or teachers of the Holy Faith.

D.—Why?

A.—Because a church cannot be established by one's own power, as is manifest from 1 Corinthians 3: 5. Secondly, because thereto particular talents and gifts, bestowed from above, are requisite, by which we are made able ministers of the New Covenant (2 Corinthians 3: 6). Thirdly, it is therefore absolutely necessary to this lawful and gracious calling to have that ordination which remained in the Holy Church from the time of the apostles, as it is said, "And He gave some apostles and some prophets and some evangelists, and some pastors and teachers for the perfecting of the saints, for the work of the ministry, for the edifying of the body of Christ (Ephesians 4: 2)."

D.—There is no calling to this office but that which crieth in our hearts; neither does our learning consist in the words which men's wisdom teacheth, but in the manifestation of the Spirit and of power. Are the gifts which you require such as the being able to gabble Latin?

A.—You do not understand the Holy Scriptures, and this is the source of all your errors. The Apostle in the words quoted by you does not reject the talents and gifts of acquired knowledge, but contrasts the doctrine of Jesus Christ with the wisdom of the heathen, which latter prevailed at that time. And that the calling of pastors and teachers always depended on the Church, by which they were chosen, is manifest from the very history of those pastors and teachers of the Church, who are eternally glorified.

D.—What Holy Scriptures? What Church? What do you mean by Holy Scriptures?

A.—Did not you yourself say that you founded

your opinions on the Word of God? That is what I mean by Holy Scriptures.

D.—The Word of God is spiritual, immaterial, and can be written on nothing except on the heart and spirit.

A.—But when the Saviour saith, "*Search the Scriptures*," and gives us the reason of this command, because "in them ye think ye have eternal life," can we really understand anything else than the written Word of God? This is the treasure He Himself has entrusted to His Holy Church as the unalterable rule of faith and life.

D.—And what do you call a church?

A.—An assembly of believers in Jesus Christ, governed by pastors according to regulations founded on the Word of God, and partakers of the ordinances of Faith.

D.—Not so. There is but one Pastor, Jesus Christ, who laid down His life for the sheep, and one church, holy, apostolical, spiritual, invisible, of which it is said: "Where two or three are gathered together in my name, there am I in the midst of them"; in which no worship is paid to any material object, where those only are teachers who live virtuous lives, where the Word of God is obeyed in their hearts, on which it descends like dew upon the fleece, and out of which it flows as from a spring in the midst of the mountains; where there are no such noisy, ostentatious, offensive and idolatrous meetings and vain ceremonies as with you, neither drunken and insulting pastors and teachers like yours, nor such a degree of evil disposition and corruption as among you.

A.—Well, do you render becoming respect and thankfulness to those men who were distinguished for holiness, and, after death, glorified by God, as having been observers of faith and virtue?

D.—Where and whom has God thus glorified?

A.—Are the names of Chrysostom and Gregory the Great, and such like, known to you?

D.—I know them.

A.—What do you think of them?

D.—What do I think? They were men.

A.—But holy men; that is, their faith and lives were agreeable to God, and on this account they were miraculously glorified from above.

D.—Let us suppose so.

A.—But for all those offices and ceremonies which you denominate idolatrous and vain, the Church is indebted to them, and the worship of images has been declared not to be sinful by the Council of the Holy Fathers. How, then, will you make this agree?

D.—I know not. I only know that hell will be filled with priests and deacons and unjust judges. As for me, I will worship God as He instructs me.

A.—But can you without danger depend upon yourself,—that sometimes you do not take your own opinion, and even foolish imagination, for divine inspiration?

D.—How? For this purpose reason is given to us. I see what is good and what is bad.

A.—A poor dependence. With the best reason sometimes good appears to be bad, and bad to be good.

D.—I will pray to God that He will send His Word, and God never deceives.

A.—True, God never deceives, but you deceive yourself, assuming yourself of that on His part which never took place.

D.—God does not reject the prayers of believers.

A.—True. Those requests which are agreeable to the law of faith Divine wisdom will not reject, but you ask and receive not because you ask amiss. For this purpose hath He given us the Book, His Divine Word, that we might behold in it His will, and that our petitions may be directed according to it. But miracles and immediate inspirations from Him without a cause it is vain to expect in the present day, particularly such as are improper and unworthy of Him. And to pretend to such inspirations and revelations is very hurtful to society, and therefore ought to be checked.

D.—But to me they appear to be very useful, salutary and worthy of acceptation.

A.—What? To break off from the society of your countrymen, united with you by the same laws and the same articles of faith, and to introduce strange doctrines and laws of your own making? To begin to expound the doctrines of the Gospel without the aid of an enlightened education, disregarding the advice of those men who are most versed and experienced in those things; and out of your own head to found a separate society upon all this? Is not this to rise against your country, to refuse to serve it when the sanctity of an oath is required? And will the simple command of the higher powers be sufficient to unite you with others to defend your country, your fellow citizens and your faith?

D.— . . .

A.—Why do you make no answer to this?

D.—There is nothing to say. I am not so loquacious as you are; neither have I need of it.

A.—That is true. But do you not see at least whither your blind zeal is leading you, and that you have deserved to suffer much more than has yet befallen you, because your repentance and amendment is expected?

D.—Do what you choose with us. We are happy to suffer for the faith. This is not a new thing. Did you never hear an old story?

A.—Tell me, I pray you, what one?

D.—A certain man planted a vineyard, and set a hedge about it, and digged the place for the wine vat, and built a tower, and let it out to husbandmen, and went into a far country. And at the season he sent to the husbandmen a servant, that he might receive from the husbandmen of the fruit of the vineyard. And they caught him and beat him, and sent him away, shamefully handled. And again he sent another, and him they killed; and many others, beating some and killing some. Having, therefore, one son, his well-beloved, he sent him also last unto them, saying, They will reverence my son; but those husbandmen said among themselves: This is the heir; come, let us kill him, and the inheritance shall be ours. And they took him and killed him, and cast him out of the vineyard. What shall therefore the Lord of the vineyard do? He will come and destroy these husbandmen, and will give the vineyard unto others. More with you I will not speak.

A.—At least tell me this: How can this be reconciled, that you reject the Holy Scriptures, and at once endeavor to support yourself upon them?

D.—Reason as you will; I have spoken what was necessary, and shall not say another word.

FINIS.

The foregoing partial statements of their belief, made, no doubt, at some disadvantage, may be supplemented by other of their own explanations, collected by Novitsky and recently published by Aylmer Maude. As to their belief in the Eternal Deity, they say:

"There is *one* God. The Holy Trinity is a being beyond comprehension: The Father is light, the Son life, and the Holy Spirit is peace; it is affirmed in man, the Father by memory, the Son by reason, the Holy Spirit by will: the one God in Trinity."

Aylmer Maude tersely and pertinently remarks, in this connection: "We continually find in the Doukhobor statements of belief two different notes. The one is calm, moderate, persuasive, couched almost in the orthodox phraseology of the Eastern Church, but importing a philosophic truth into the conventional phrases, and, at dangerous points, taking refuge in mysticism. The other is clear, resolute, radical; there is no mysticism or secrecy about it, but it is often harshly contemptuous and inimical, not merely to all authority in church and state, but towards all who do not agree at once and absolutely. It answers to the harshest note sounded by the first generation of Quakers, in their scorn of 'steeple-houses' and 'hireling priests.'"

With regard to the outward knowledge of the historical Christ they say,—

"For our salvation it is not essential to have an external knowledge of Jesus Christ; for there is the inward Word which reveals Him in the depths of our souls. It existed in all ages, and enlightens all who are ready to receive it, whether they be nominally Christians or not."

In this statement we see a full recognition of the inshining Light of Christ, and His inspeaking Word, upon which George Fox and his co-laborers laid particular emphasis.

Touching the Resurrection, they believe,—

"Those enlightened by the Spirit of God will after death rise again;—what will become of other people is uncertain. It is the soul, and not the body, that will rise.

"Sensual desires sow the seeds of future torment. The craving for honors now torments the ambitious man, and the craving for drink the drunkard, but much more will those who have sown the seeds of such desire be tormented in the future life, when they will not be able to gratify the passions.

"If this is the result of sowing evil passions in this life, on the other hand the result of sowing good seed will be continued growth towards perfection, till the purified souls become like God Himself."

Novitsky says, "Luxury in food or dress is condemned, because luxury, indulging the flesh, strengthens it to stifle the inward light coming from above."

Concerning military service, they say, "To go to war, to carry arms and to take oaths are forbidden." Regarding war as a forbidden thing, they say they have set themselves a rule not to carry arms.

The Church is a society selected by God himself. It is invisible and is scattered over the whole world; it is not marked externally by any common creed. Not Christians only, but Jews, Mohammedans and others may be members of it, if only they hearken to the inward Word: and therefore—

The Holy Scriptures, or the outer Word, are not essential for the sons of God. It is, however, of use to them, because in the Scriptures, as in nature and in ourselves, they read the decrees and the acts of the Lord. But the Scriptures must be understood symbolically, to represent things that are inward and spiritual. It must all be understood to relate in a mystical manner to the Christ within.

The Christ within is the only true Hierarch and Priest. Therefore no external priest is necessary. In whomever Christ lives, he is Christ's heir, and is himself a priest unto himself. The priests of temples made with hands are appointed externally, and can perform only what is external; they are not what they are usually esteemed to be.

The sons of God should worship God in spirit and in truth, and, therefore, need no external worship of God. The external sacraments have no efficacy; they should be understood in a spiritual sense. To baptize a child with water is unbecoming for a Christian; an adult baptizes himself with the Word of truth, and is then baptized, indeed, by the true priest, Christ, with spirit and with fire.

True confession is heartfelt contrition before God, though we may also confess our sins one to another when occasion presents itself.

The external sacraments of the Church are offensive to God, for Christ desires not signs, but realities; the real communion comes by the Word, by thought, and by faith.

Marriage should be accomplished without any ceremonies; it needs only the will of those who have come of age and who are united in love to one another, the consent of the parents, and an inward oath and vow, before all-seeing God, in the souls of those who are marrying, that they will, to the end of their days, remain faithful and inseparable. An external marriage ceremony, apart from the inward marriage, has no meaning; it has at most this effect, that being performed before witnesses, it maintains the bond between the spouses by the fear of shame, should they break the promise of fidelity they have given.

The priesthood is not an office reserved for specially selected people: each real Christian, enlightened by the Word, may and should pray to God for himself, and should spread the truth that has been entrusted to him.

"What am I then? A temple to the Lord most high.
The altar and the priest, the sacrifice am I.
Our hearts the altars are; our wills the offering;
Our souls they are the priest, our sacrifice to bring."

The forms of worship of all the external churches in the world, their various institutions, all the ranks and orders of their servants, their costumes and movements, were invented after the time of the Apostles,—those men of holy wisdom,—and are in themselves naught but dead signs, mere figures and letters, externally representing that sacred, invisible, living and wise power of God, which (like the sun's rays) enlightens and pervades the souls of the elect, and lives and acts in them, purifying them, and uniting them to God.

To pray in temples made with hands is contrary to the injunction of the Saviour: "When thou prayest, enter into thine inner chamber, and having shut the door, pray to thy Father which is in secret." (Matt. 6 : 6.)

Yet a son of God need not fear to enter any temples,—Papal, Greek, Lutheran, Calvinist, or other: to him they are all indifferent. All the ceremonies of the churches, being useless, were much better left alone.

Icons they do not respect or worship, but consider as idols.

The saints may be respected for their virtues, but should not be prayed to.

Fasting should consist in fleeing from lusts and refraining from superfluities.

The decrees of the Churches and the Councils should not be accepted.

The Church has no right to judge or to sentence anyone; for it cannot know all man's inward, secret motives.

The Doukhobors take nothing from travelers who stop at their houses either for lodging or food, and they have been accustomed to erect a special lodging house for visitors.

Respect from children to parents is strictly observed, and, in general, from younger men to those older, though the latter, and even parents, do not appropriate to themselves any ascendency over the younger ones, but regard these as spiritually their equals.

There exists no punishment among the brethren. As soon as a brother thinks another has behaved improperly, he, according to the precise Gospel instruction, reminds him that he is acting wrongly; if the one at fault will not take this counsel kindly, he is admonished in the presence of two or three of the brethren; if he does not take heed of them, he is invited to appear before the general assembly. There have been cases, though very seldom, in which some of the offenders have left the Brotherhood in order to live at liberty according to their own unrestricted desire.

The men elect to learn various handicrafts, while agriculture has generally employed the majority.

They have no written or printed regulations for their communities, a fact which might be supposed to lead to disagreements and disorder; but this is quite the exception. Parents watch over and correct the faults of their children, far more effectually than is apparent in most Christian countries. The system of education among the Doukhobors is simple and uniform. As soon as the child begins to speak and understand, his parents begin verbally to teach him prayers and psalms, and to tell him something out of the Scriptures; and they thus continue to instruct their children in Christian doctrine. These little Doukhobors very early accompany their elders to the gatherings for religious expression, where they take their part in reciting such prayers and psalms as they have learned. Owing to such education, which also embraces teaching some useful way of working with their hands, the spirit of the parents passes by degrees into their children; their ways of thinking take deep root, and the tendency towards good is most strongly encouraged by good examples.

CHAPTER IV.

THE RASKÓLNIKS AND OTHER DISSENTERS.

The history of religious dissent in Russia dates back to the latter part of the seventeenth century. Some peasants, and others more favored with educational opportunities, who thought they could explain the meaning of the figures in the Apocalypse, had decided that the mysterious number of the beast was 1666,— and there doubtless was enough falling away from the faith in that year of our Lord to afford the evidence they wanted to support their interpretation.

It was also about this time that Tsar Alexei Michailovich ordered a revision of the Russian Bible and other church books, for it was well known that many errors had crept into the text. This was finally accomplished by the Patriarch Nikon, who compared his revision with the original Greek manuscripts, and, as this work obtained the approval of the Tsar and two ecclesiastical councils, it was made obligatory upon the people. Many of them, however, would have none of "Nikonian novelties," as they dubbed the revision, and thus began the *Raskol*,— the schism, or "split," in the church.

Great objection was made to the most trivial changes in spelling, or in the number of times the sign of the cross should be made and the position of the fingers while making it. "What have you done with the Son of God? Give Him back to us! You have changed Issus [the old Russian form of Jesus] into Iissus! It is fearful not only to commit such a sin, but even to think of it!":—these are fair examples of the attitude of many toward the altered text of the Scriptures.

It might be well, before entering further into this account of religious persecution, to understand the motives of the Russian Government in its hostility to these dissenters; for at one time the "Old Believers," as they called themselves, "waged an unrelenting war upon the whole body of European reforms, and, having reached the conclusion that every feature of the machinery of government, from the taking of a census to the keeping of a registry of births and deaths, was essentially evil in its purpose and nature, they carried their antagonism to the extreme of attributing the miserable condition of the country to the machinations of an Antichrist Tsar." ("Russia and the Russians.")

One naturally wonders, however, why such peace-loving, industrious and honest people as the Doukhobors, Molokans and Stundists should be persecuted, while their German or Mohammedan neighbors, also living under Russian rule, go unmolested, so far as religion is concerned. Evidently nationality plays an important part in this distinction. Wallace says: "Tartars, Germans and Poles are all, in a sense, heretics, but in the very nature of the case a Tartar should be a Mohammedan, the German a Protestant and the Pole a Roman Catholic, while the Russian must needs be a member of the Orthodox Russian Church, and an inclination on his part to change his religion, no matter how pure and elevated his motives may be, brings down upon him the criminal law and popular opinion as if he had been a traitor." The Russian Church has long paid inordinate attention to an elaborated ritual, no doubt gaining thereby many converts from peoples who were accustomed to pagan rites and magical incantations, but gaining also at the expense of a moral and spiritual life.

In this connection it is pre-eminently true that "The weakness inseparable from all ceremonialism is that it curses and blesses according to some prescribed ritual, and thus divorces itself from human nature. The doctrine of 'apostolic succession' is a case in point. Its upholders are forced by the logic of facts to admit that some through whom they believed it to have descended have been wicked men; and so, to save their theory, they claim that the official (pretended) possession of the Holy Ghost has no connection with personal morality. It thus blesses what God has cursed. In Christianity there are no essential—and can be no essential—ceremonies, for genuine Christianity has to do only with the attitude and the development of the character, and with acts naturally flowing therefrom. A dogmatic creed is really an intellectual sacramentalism. It tends to substitute ideas and formulas in the place of life."*

* Dr. R. H. Thomas, in "Present-Day Papers."

Simple traditional custom and religious convictions have often been confounded, until it became difficult to distinguish between a social habit and a doctrine of faith. An old Russian would have resisted the attempt to deprive him of his beard as stoutly as a Calvinist of the present time would resist the suggestion for him to abjure predestination, and both for the same reason,—because they believed it essential to their salvation. "Where," asked one of the patriarchs of Moscow, "will those who shave their chins stand at the Last Day,—among the righteous adorned with beards, or among the beardless heretics?"

Thus we recognize an honest purpose on the part of both the persecuted and their persecutors, but with this difference,—the latter missed the benefit Jesus said would rest upon those who were cast out for His sake.

The decree of excommunication pronounced by the Ecclesiastical Council placed the nonconformist beyond the pale of the Church, and since 1680 the civil power has undertaken the part of persecuting him,—an endless and gruesome task. The immediate effect was to confirm the victims in their belief that the Church and the Tsar had become heretical, and to drive thousands across the frontier into Poland, Prussia, Sweden, Austria, Turkey, the Caucasus and Siberia, while still others fled to the northern forests, where they worshiped according to their consciences and sent out missionaries to sow what they called "the living seed." Thousands perished by self-immolation when pursued by the agents of the government. To them the "revision" of Peter the Great was a profane "numbering of the people," and an attempt to enroll in the service of Antichrist those whose names were written in the Lamb's Book of Life. They said, "The world could not have been created, according to the corrected calendar, in the month called January, because apples were not ripe at that season, and consequently Eve could not have been tempted in the way described in Genesis."

At first these "Old Ritualists" had no organization, but, as time went on and the world did not come to an end, as they had predicted, nor did the Tsar return to the true faith, they found themselves in a dilemma, created by their notions about "apostolic succession,"—for to them the historic continuity of the Church could only be preserved through its priesthood, and of this official order they had none properly "ordained." The result was another schism among these zealous advocates of orthodoxy. The "Old Ritualists" held to the sacraments and ceremonial observances on the old form, while the *Bezpopoftsi*, or "priestless people," have tried to find some other way to Heaven.

It would be amusing, if the subject were not so serious, to follow the account of expedients resorted to by these excommunicated conservatives in order to secure a "consecrated" bishop. Suffice it to say that in the course of a century they finally succeeded.

The priestless section went into all sorts of fantastical notions, but as Wallace pertinently says, " Extreme fanaticism, like all other abnormal states, cannot long exist in a mass of human beings without some constant exciting cause.

" The vulgar necessities of everyday life, especially among people who have to live by the labor of their hands, have a wonderfully sobering effect on the excited brain, and must always, sooner or later, prove fatal to inordinate excitement." Thus most of these poor people gave up their unnatural ideas. However, they split up into divers sects, such as the "Theodosians," "Philippians," and "Pilgrims." The total number of dissenters is about 11,000,000: this includes Protestants and all who do not accept the Græco-Russian form of belief, such as the Molokans, or "Milk Drinkers," and "Flagellants."

Time and interest would both fail in trying to name and define the distinguishing characteristics of all the various sects which have become more or less noted for their protest against the Orthodox Church. We may not, however, pass by the Stundists without some mention of their character and sufferings.

Mysticism, rationalism and evangelism are all represented in many phases by the general body of dissenters. The Doukhobors might be classed with the first and second of these divisions, while the Stundists belong more properly to the evangelicals.

THE STUNDISTS.

This sect has been so closely associated with the Doukhobors during the past forty years that their rise and sufferings are almost a counterpart of those of the older sect.

The Germans who settled in the government of Cherson during the reign of Catherine II. maintained their Lutheran and Mennonite faith, and it was through their faithfulness that certain Russian peasants embraced similar religious views.

The first man who spread the gospel among his fellow-countrymen was one Onishenko. He declared himself " converted " in 1858, and so successful were his efforts in arousing those among whom he lived and labored, that meetings for reading the Bible and aiding propaganda interests were held throughout Southern Russia. Masses of people crowded the meeting houses; they sang and prayed and read the Gospels and multiplied exceedingly. The police were nonplused and the priests stood aghast;—it was a tide the force of which they could not stem, and the depth of which they could not fathom. " We must worship God in spirit," said the Stundists,* " and the spirit being free, our worship should likewise be free "—from the fetters of ceremonies and priestly rule. " My Saviour is my only priest! O God, enlighten me! and make me a changed man! " Onishenko had prayed; and his prayer was heard, for he says, " A

* From the German *Stunde,* or hour, as these secretaries were in the habit of meeting together for an appointed hour.

marvelous sense of freedom, a feeling of intense joy, came over me, and I knew God henceforth." His co-religionists declared the ceremonies of the Greek Church to be mummeries. They boldly asserted the service of God to be living for others and dying to ourselves. "God is love, and what He asks of us is love for each other, who are His images, and not reverence for temples and wax-lights and icons." "The whole monstrous fabric of Russian orthodoxy, with its debasing image-worship and sacerdotalism, was put away," says Charles Lowe. "Old and young set themselves to learn to read and write, and it came to pass that in a land otherwise sunk into brutish ignorance and superstition, the tiller chanted scraps of the Gospel as he walked after his plough, the weaver sang chapters of it to the noisy accompaniment of the shuttle, and the traveler beguiled the tedium of his journey with the thrilling stories of the Book." Within three years no less than three hundred thousand had joined the Stundist movement, and, like Quakerism in the seventeenth century, it threatened to proselytize the nation.

The testimony of Russian officials and of those not in sympathy with them, affords strong evidence in favor of their character. An Orthodox Russian journal says of them: "Force and violence are foreign to their character; guile and double-dealing are banished from their lives; and such is their natural kind-heartedness that the insults and injustice which they suffer, instead of kindling their anger, evoke their compassion. They set such store by honest labor that they eschew every kind of pleasure, even the most innocent of all,—the squandering of their time in idleness. They neither drink, nor steal, nor swear, and in the ups and down of life they bear themselves like genuine Christians. Crime amongst them is almost unheard of. One of their cherished virtues consists in feeding the hungry, clothing the naked, caring for the sick, and sheltering the wanderer;—in a word, in helping in every possible way their necessitous neighbors. An upright, sober, compassionate people."

Such a light could not be hid, and its rays only illuminated the national and religious gloom enough to reveal the cruelty that lurked within its embrace. The Church and State combined in 1878, by the old-time tortures of confiscation, banishment and exile, to crush out that life which is ever the light of men. "My predecessors knouted the Stundists with whips, but I will beat them with scorpions," said the newly-consecrated Bishop Sergius under Alexander III., and the Procurator of the Holy Synod,—known throughout the empire as "Terror" and "Keeper of the Imperial Conscience,"—C. Pobiedonostzev,—willingly assisted in endeavoring to root out "the accursed sect." Scandalous fines were levied on the poor people. Misery and ruin to many a family, with banishment of their leaders to Siberia or to the Caucasus, were the common experience. "Walking with ordinary criminals in chains, with shaven beards and clad in ordinary prison-garb, they were pushed and hustled along, at the point of the bayonet."

The anonymous author of "The Stundists" says: "The fabric of Russian power is an autocracy based on ignorance and superstition, and therefore it is the interest of self-preservation that has always prompted the Tsar's government to crush everything that would bring enlightenment in its train.

"Thousands of Stundists and Baptists, of Molokans and Doukhobors, are banished to the remotest corners of the vast empire, and are imprisoned and tortured in a variety of ways,—only a degree less inhuman than the scourgings of the Middle Ages. Russia works in secret, her methods are underground, and her victims are voiceless. She has no press to denounce each case of persecution as it occurs. The trials of heretics are conducted with closed doors, the public being carefully excluded. Russians themselves do not know a tenth of what is being done."

Thus were the faithful disciples of a crucified Lord banished, bankrupted, and deprived of all civil rights,—torn from the bosom of their families, and treated as most dangerous criminals. Surely, if the blessing of the Saviour rests upon those who are persecuted for His "name's sake," a rich reward is in store for these sufferers—in common with many others of their dissenting brethren.

This chapter would hardly be complete without some account of a visit to the Stundists by Joseph J. Neave, of Sydney, Australia, and John Bellows, of

Gloucester, England, in 1892. The former had a distinct call to go to Russia, while visiting Friends in Australia.

He was in Hobart, Tasmania, at the time, and his experience is thus related by himself: "One morning (early in 1890), in reading the 47th Psalm, before leaving my room, my mind held to the last verse as I turned in quiet toward the Lord: 'The shields of the earth belong unto God. He is greatly exalted.' With this came a sense wherein I seemed able to see every individual believer in the Lord Jesus the world over, and His protecting power about them as a shield, preserving them from evil.

"While meditating on this wonderful revelation, it seemed as if a voice in my ear said, 'Thou shalt go to Russia.' I had not been thinking of Russia, and I never expected to go to a people who could not understand my speech. I said, 'I cannot; it is impossible.' Very soon, however, I was able to say, as I felt my *utter* unfitness for such a work. 'If thou wilt go with me and go before me—(this the Lord fulfilled in a marvelous manner all through our Russian service),—I will go to the ends of the earth, if it be Thy will.'" In the course of a year the way very unexpectedly opened for him to go to Europe,—by a woman Friend in England leaving him $1,000. "So here I was, with the money in my hands, from a quarter I never looked for anything to come from. I did not have it more than two or three days when I saw I must go off to England at once." As a vessel

Joseph James Neave.

Hermann Fast.
(Interpreter.)

John Bellows.

was about to sail direct for London, he took passage in it from Lyttleton, New Zealand, in the Fourth month of 1892, arriving in time to attend the Yearly Meeting held in London.

His prospect was duly presented to the proper meetings and his concern approved by Friends. One of these wrote to John Bellows, who was not present: "I have just returned from the morning meeting, where Friends have liberated Joseph J. Neave for religious service in Russia, of which prospect no doubt thou hast heard." John Bellows, however, had not heard of it previously, but, upon reading the letter, he did hear the query inwardly addressed to himself, "If thou shouldst be called to go with Joseph J. Neave to Russia, wouldst thou be willing to obey?" The suggestion, which struck him with surprise and pain, remained with him; but, after conferring with his wife, and being fully approved by the three Friends who had charge of carrying out the arrangements for Joseph J. Neave's journey, he gave himself up for the service. "And here we see the wonderful care and wisdom of God who brought me," says Joseph J. Neave, "from Australia to open a gate for the right man to go through:—all in that perfect order and wisdom which reveals the faithfulness of Him who is ever ready to guide a church or an individual whose hope and trust is in Him. Dear John Bellows was admirably fitted for the delicate and difficult service that lay before us, and so we worked together in much harmony throughout the whole of our journeyings."

After these preliminary arrangements were perfected, Joseph J. Neave and John Bellows went to St. Petersburg, and obtained the necessary liberty to visit the persecuted dissenters in Southern Russia. In the course of six months they reached the Caucasus, and found Prince D. A. Hilkov among the Doukhobors, as he had been exiled to that province a few years before their visit. As previously stated, the Prince had given up his sword in 1877, as the result of a deep conviction that the profession of a soldier was contrary to the teachings of the New Testament. His interest in the Universal Brotherhood opened the acquaintance of the Society of Friends in England with the Doukhobors.

CHAPTER V.

THE MIR (MEER).

Many of the peculiarities of the Doukhobors become clearer to us if we understand some of their national institutions. From time immemorial the Village Commune, or *Mir*, has been a unique Slavonic institution. This form of government includes five-sixths of the entire population in European Russia, and is one of the most democratic in the world. Without any written law, its authority is recognized as equally binding upon every member of the community. The methods of different communities vary much, and yet some salient features are common to them all.

The rural population of Russia is scattered over an immense territory, and the arable land is in excess of the needs of the people.

The peasants all live in villages and farm the adjacent land. The *Mir* was primarily instituted in order to secure the payment of taxes due to the Imperial Government, and each village is held responsible for a certain sum, so large as in many cases to impoverish it. The taxation is based upon the number of "revision souls," or men registered on a census list made up at regular intervals, averaging about once in fifteen years.

The Village Assembly is composed of heads of households, who meet frequently (preferably on the first day of the week) to discuss the affairs, civil and domestic, of the Community. No nobleman is admitted into membership. An Elder, or "Stárosta," is selected from the peasants assembled, whose duties correspond somewhat to those of a Chairman or Speaker in an English-speaking gathering for similar purposes, with this difference,—the lowest *State* official may at any moment supersede or suspend the elder's functions. His only mark of distinction is a bronze medal hung about his neck, as the insignia of his office,—a trifling compensation for the onerous duties of his position. The most important of these is the distribution of the communal lands among the families of each village.

In order to understand this allotment, it may be well to explain that each rural district has three divisions of its property, viz.: the land on which the village is built, the portion to be cultivated, and that which is reserved for pasturage or hay-making. The sites of the buildings and the surrounding gardens are the hereditary property of the family occupying the same, and are not affected by the periodical redistributions of the other land. The arable and meadow lands are apportioned somewhat differently.

The whole of the land to be plowed is first divided into three fields, to suit the triennial rotation of crops, and these again into sections, until every household can have at least one strip in each field, so as to insure some equality of soil. This is done by the peasants with measuring rods, and with remarkable accuracy. The ground to be used for hay-making is divided in like manner, except that the division is made annually.

Every year, on the day fixed by the Assembly, the whole community of men proceed to the harvest field, where, by casting lots, they determine what each man shall cut. Each family can sow any seed, according to choice, but none may cut hay independently. One of the most interesting and picturesque scenes is that of the villagers, both men and women, chanting as they work together or return from the field.

The *Mir* supplies conscripts to the standing army, and has power to banish its members to Siberia or to call them home from any place where they have settled. This power has sometimes been abused in order to extort money from its absent members, who would rather pay a considerable sum than undergo the inconvenience of travel.

One curious feature of this institution is the unreserved obedience its members yield to its decisions. D. M. Wallace says: "I know of many instances where peasants have set at defiance the power of the police, of the provincial government and of the central government itself, but I have never heard of any instance where the will of the Mir was opposed by one of its members." The money is paid to the proprietor of the land on the instalment plan; and the burden of this, in addition to the government tax, falls pretty heavily upon the sons of the soil, and frequently a peasant's cow or horse is seized by the tax-gatherer because some deficit appears in the accounts of the Headman.

Every married man and every widow must hold land, and if any wish to migrate, some satisfactory arrangement must be made with the Community in order that his share of the taxes shall be paid.

Courts for the trial of persons guilty of minor offences can be held by the *Mir*, but the government police keep a surveillance over its action.

As the domestic affairs of the Community may be interfered with by the Stárosta, much annoyance may come to the presiding officer; and, as a matter of fact, the responsibility of the position renders it quite unpopular.

One of these meetings is a most entertaining spectacle. It is thus graphically described by Wallace: "The peasants, male and female, have turned out in Sunday attire, the bright costumes of the women helping the sunshine to put a little rich color into the scene, which is at ordinary times monotonously gray. Slowly the crowd collects in the open space at the side of the church. There are women present who, on account of the absence or the death of their husbands, happen to be heads of households: as such, their right to take part in the deliberations is never called in question. In matters affecting the general welfare of the Commune they seldom speak, remembering the Russian adage applied to their sex, 'Woman's hair is long, but her mind is short.' Yet as the head of a household they may speak freely on any subject directly affecting their homes. For instance, when it is proposed to increase or diminish her household's share of the land and the burdens the woman may speak. A typical scene is that of three peasants and a woman standing a little apart from the crowd; the woman explaining with tears in her eyes that her 'old man,' who is Elder for the time being, is very ill and cannot fulfil his duties. 'But he has not served a year yet, and he'll get better.' 'Who knows?' replies the woman, sobbing. 'It is the will of God, but I don't believe that he'll ever put his foot to the ground again.' 'Very well; that's enough; hold thy tongue,' says the graybeard of the little group to the woman; and then, turning to the other peasants, remarks, 'There's nothing to be done. The Stanovoi (officer of the rural police) will be here one of these days and will make a row again if we don't select a new Elder; there is Alexei Ivanov; he has not served yet!' 'Yes, yes; Alexei Ivanov,' shout half a dozen voices, while he protests in the strongest terms, giving half a dozen reasons why he should not be chosen. But his protestations are not listened to, and the proceedings terminate. A new village Elder has been duly elected."

In the main, the decisions of these assemblies are marked by plain, practical common sense, the most disturbing influence being that of alcohol, and even under its stimulation the members seldom come to blows, for there is no class of men in the world more good-natured and pacific than are these Russian Moujiks.

There are certain disadvantages connected with the communal system, which arise from the redistribution of land; those who have improved their shares by cultivation and manuring losing the benefit of their labor, unless the land apportioned to them has been equally well tilled.

The members of a family all farm together year by year when at home, and when earning money elsewhere are expected to put their money into a common purse. The households composing the village commune farm independently, and pay into the common treasury a fixed sum.

Notwithstanding the restrictions put upon individual ownership, this system of land tenure has secured a *home* to the Russian peasant when he has gone into neighboring communities, or has sought employment in towns. In this way he became, in many instances, half peasant, half artisan.

The peasant might work most of his life in towns, but he never severed his connection with his native village; he remained, whether he desired it or not, a member of the Commune, possessing a share of the communal land, and liable for a share of the communal burdens. Manufacturers in Russia have sometimes allowed their employees to go home to mow their strip of grass or to sow a few acres of wheat.

CHAPTER VI.

THE GOVERNMENT OFFICIALS.

There are ten ministers and five assistant ministers in the Russian Cabinet. These are not servants of the public, but of the Tsar; their duty being to carry out his personal will in their several departments. When a law is to be made, custom and the statute-book require that it should be submitted to a committee of ministers; if approved by them, or by a majority of them, it is passed on to the Imperial Council; and if it there secures approval, it is laid before the Tsar, who signs it or not as it meets his views. These formalities, however, are sometimes dispensed with, especially when the enactment in question is one not likely to secure the approval of a majority of the ministers. Such, for instance, was the edict expelling the Jews from Moscow, which was decreed without asking the advice of the ministers or of the Imperial Council. It was promulgated after a report handed in to the Minister of Foreign Affairs, who had been encouraged to take this step by the Grand Duke Sergius Alexandrovitch, brother of the Emperor, and in some respects a reproduction of the Grand Duke Constantine Paulovitch of a preceding generation.

Another illustration of this Imperial action—one that has done the most to undo the reform set on foot after the emancipation of the serfs—was the edict which practically effaced the Zemstvos, or Provincial Assemblies, and in their place set over the village communities what are called district commanders. This measure, which has produced a radical transformation in the entire internal organization of the empire, was made law by Alexander III., in opposition to the votes of his ministers and council.

The district commander must be an hereditary noble. He is appointed by the Government, and need not be in any way connected with the district which he is to govern. His functions are those of both administrator and judge. His duty is to see that no *Mir* goes contrary to the Emperor's policy.

The agents of the district governor are the police. It is the reintroduction of centralized bureaucracy into the rural districts—setting over the emancipated serf the *Mir* and the commander of the district, in place of his hereditary master and the headman of his village.

Ministers need not agree with each other's views, but, happily, since the late students' troubles, when the Tsar vindictively ordered some of them to be sent to Port Arthur as soldiers—from which service students had long been exempt—his ministers have discussed and disapproved this edict. They have compelled him to withdraw his *ukase* committing students to the army, and have prevented him from declaring a state of siege at St. Petersburg. They also demanded of him the dismissal and practical exile of the *prefect de police*, General Cleighills, of St. Petersburg, who directed the Cossacks to use their murderous *nagaikis*, or lead-weighted horsewhips, upon the heads of the students, so that nineteen of them were killed, and six hundred of the *literati* were taken from their homes and committed to prison because of their sympathy with the students. Prince Kropotkin says in this connection: "The importance of these three steps cannot be overrated. For the first time in the history of Russia, for the last one hundred years, the Committee of the Ministers *has discussed* the orders of the Tsar, and disapproved them, acquiring thus a power which it never had before, and taking a responsibility before the country and not before the Tsar.

"These are evidently the first germs of constitutional rule which will necessarily bring about further ones."—(*The Outlook,* April 6th, 1901, p. 764.)

"Russia must be for the Russians" has been the imperial maxim for two decades, and this means that in all that vast empire, embracing many races, nations and religions, there shall be only one faith,—that of the Græco-Russian Church, of which the Emperor is the appointed head. It also means that the Tsar's will, as set forth in his *ukases* and carried out by the one hundred thousand officials of his kingdom—through whom it percolates to the people—must be absolute and paramount. And that which proves a yet more galling yoke to his subjects is his effort to Russify all the national institutions which they have inherited from their ancestors.

Thus the *Mir*—the Slavonic village system—has been forced upon the Poles, the Finns, and the inhabitants of the Baltic Provinces; while the Jews are to be wiped out of the empire as speedily as may be, and Lutherans, Catholics and orthodox dissenters are to realize that they cannot live comfortably in Holy Russia. None of these can hold any governmental position, because of their dissent from the state religion. As near as possible it is to be an empire for *Slavs* only—a crusade against modern progress. The person whose indirect influence has been most powerful with the present Tsar and his father is Constantine Pobiedonostzev, the Procurator* of the Holy Synod, and a man whose ideals of statesmanship are worthy of a Torquemada.

Half the ministers of Alexander III. owed their nominations to his influence, and he is scarcely less influential with Nicholas II. Without being a religious enthusiast, he has conceived the sacred duty of coercing men's consciences in order to conserve the interests of the state. He holds that Russia was once saved by the Church, in a critical national period, and so his duty is now to safeguard that Church against anything which will menace its security and unity. Thus the name of this omnipotent ecclesiastical statesman is whispered with mysterious awe, throughout that land of religious and political intolerance.

* Now happily retired from his procuratorship.

CHAPTER VII.

RUSSIAN POLITICAL HISTORY—862-1901.

Rightly to understand the present autocratic rule in Russia we must go back to the ninth century, when the Slavs who were settled about Novgorod concluded to invite certain Scandinavian Princes to come over and govern them. In A.D. 862, they sent over the sea to the Varyags, saying: "Our land is rich and large, but there is no order in it. Come and be our princes and rule over us."

This was a unique invitation, but accepted in good faith on the part of Princes and people. Three brothers responded. Rurik (Rörikr in Scandinavian), the oldest of them, soon became sole ruler of the Russian country. It was under his administration that the Slav tribes came to be known as *Russi*, or Russians. His brother Oleg (879-913) attacked the southern Slavs by force and chose Kiev for the capital of Russia.

The centralizing effect was soon apparent and continuous. The quarrels between Commune and Commune,—*Volost* and *Volost*,—which made the old order unendurable, subsided. Apart, however, from administrative benefits which it has conferred—including social and juridical ideas—the Varyag princes did not greatly impress their subjects. They did not attempt to modify the language, as the Normans did the English, nor introduce the Norse tongue among the Slavs, but left them a military system which has lasted a thousand years, and has been the bane of the nation.

From the tenth to the twelfth century, inclusive, Russia was largely made up of federated republics in the form of trade guilds. The most important of these was that of Novgorod, claiming one hundred thousand inhabitants, with three hundred thousand more of subject populations. This republic had a democratic form of government, and compelled the ruling Premier to respect the popular assembly.

In all these republics the assembly could call and dismiss the Premier at will, and they gave the final word in war and peace. This, then, was a larger degree of independence than was possible under the old régime.

Under this system of sharing the land among the princes there were three distinct ideas struggling for the mastery,—the Slavonic custom, which prevailed before the arrival of the Varyags, that of bestowing the highest dignity in the gift of the *gens* or family on the oldest member; the Scandinavian custom of dividing out the land to the successor of the prince, and the western idea of primogeniture, introduced by way of Byzantium. This conflict would have proved fatal to the national authority had not a new capital been founded, as well as a new dynasty, and that is just what came about when Andrei Bogolubsky marched against the beautiful city of Kiev ("Mother of Russian cities") in 1169, took it by assault and gave it over to pillage. Thenceforth the power of a single monarch was to be recognized, whether under Tartar or Romanov rule.

Moscow, in the forest to the northeast, was built for the purpose of changing the old régime.

The Tartars, under Ghengis Khan, sacked Kiev in 1240, and from that time until this "galling yoke" was broken by Ivan the Terrible, in 1480, the Khan, whose residence was at Sarai, assumed the right to dispense the Russian principalities, or "shares," to persons of his own choice—as often to a Tartar-Mongol as to a prince of the Rurik family.

The poor of the land, who have always been in the vast majority, suffered greatly under the Tartar domination, as a capitation tax was imposed and collected from house to house with immediate enslavement in default of its payment. Many debtors were mercilessly beaten before being sold into slavery, and it was a great relief to Russia when the princes, instead of the *baskakis* (Tartar tax collectors) were ordered to collect the tribute themselves and hand it over to their oriental masters at Sarai.

The Tartar invasion considerably affected the historical development and national character of the Russian people, but the Tartars did not attempt to Tartarize the Russians, but allowed them to retain their land, their language, their courts of justice, and all their other institutions, as long as they were willing to acknowledge the Mongol authority and pay their specified tribute.

Had the Khans of the Golden Horde been prudent, far-seeing statesmen, they might have long retained their supremacy over Russia, by keeping its princes on the same level. But by favoring some more more than others the entering wedge of jealousy finally proved able to secure independence. Meanwhile the Tartar rule interrupted that normal development of democracy, which has been the crown of the Anglo-Saxon race, by extinguishing all free political life. "The Grand Princes of Moscovy" were the political descendants, not of the old independent Princes, but of the Tartar Khans, their autocratic power being, in a sense, created by the Tartar domination.

"The position of the Christians under the Khan of the Golden Horde was analogous to that now held by Christians in Turkey."—(Wallace.)

From the founding of Moscow, about the middle of the twelfth century, to Ivan the Terrible (1533-4), there was a constant tendency to disregard individual rights and those of the Popular Assembly. Ivan, most appropriately called "The Terrible," was the first to assume the title of Tsar. He was the very culmination of despotism—a typical madman on the throne.

We would not wish to follow the details of his inhuman acts, but only to point out that the trend of his autocratic régime gradually brought under one central authority all the free republics of Russia, and substituted for the Slav custom of possession by the *gens*, the present system of a personal right, on the part of the Tsar, to all the land, and a paternal feeling toward his subjects not at all consistent with their freedom.

"Besides being merely the holder during his lifetime of possessions which belonged to the whole family of Princes, he had become the absolute owner of those possessions. Meanwhile the people once his *subjects* were now literally the slaves of a monarch invested with absolute power over their lives."—(E. Noble.)

In the century between the death of Ivan the Terrible (1584) and Peter the Great (1689) the Romanovs displaced the Rurik dynasty.

The first Romanov Tsar was elected by a council of Princes in 1613. His grandson, Peter the Great, sought to introduce the western idea of civilization among his subjects, but the time was not ripe, and his efforts at reform, while successful in creating a marvelous city in a swamp, did not permeate the masses of the people. He cared little for their religious opinions so long as they replenished his exchequer. Thus those who were more devout regarded him as the incarnate spirit of evil.

In 1705 new regulations in regard to dress were enforced without exception. The luxuriant Russian beard had to give way to the reforming razor of a monarch to whom all memorials of ancient Russia were odious. People who regarded the beard as sacred, such as the sectarians, were allowed to compound for its retention by paying one hundred roubles annually, and by wearing a receipt for the money in the form of a medal, on one side of which was inscribed, "The beard is a useless embarrassment."

He also tried to abolish the old practice of falling on the knees as the imperial carriage passed, as well as of beating the head against the ground, remarking, "The honor due to me consists in people crawling before me less and in serving me and the state with more zeal and fidelity."

Peter made complete the subjection of the Church to the State (1691), abolishing the patriarchate and founding the Holy Synod at St. Petersburg. The fortunes of the peasantry suffered between his death (1725) and the accession of Catharine II., in 1762.

This gifted woman did much to lift the disabilities of the dissenters from the Orthodox Church, and she invited foreigners to reside within her realm. She gave up the German Protestant faith to identify herself more fully with the Russians, and was wont to say, "Freedom, thou soul of all things, without thee everything is dead." "I want the laws obeyed, but I don't want to have slaves." "If you have truth and reason as allies, you can give them to the people." "Her tolerance toward the sectarians not only protected them from the fanaticism of the ecclesiastics, but secured for them certain rights."—(Noble.)

Passing over the short reign of Paul, sometimes called The Mad, who was strangled by his courtiers, to his son Alexander I. (known as "The Blessed"), we find he followed up this humane policy of Catharine. He abolished torture, put an end to confiscation of property, restricted the application of corporal punishment, reduced taxation, reformed the criminal code, and founded schools and universities.

This unified empire was doubtless an improvement on the divided federal arrangements of the Rurik family; the autocracy of the Tsars was better than the incessant civil war in which the country was held by the Varyag princes. "Yet the amelioration thus secured was purchased at an enormous price, and its burden fell, not on the high and mighty, in whose interest the state was magnified and embellished, but upon the humbled and yet withal the largest class in the empire—the peasantry."

"It is the contrast between the degradation of this class and the luxurious magnificence which it fed through centuries of serfdom that makes the story of the common people—originally called the Smerdi, 'ill-smelling,' the 'black' people—one of the most tragic chapters in Russian history."—(Noble.)

Just such a chapter was inaugurated by the accession of Nicholas I., upon the death of his brother Alexander I., in 1825, his elder brother Constantine having relinquished his right to the throne in order to marry the woman of his choice. Nicholas proposed to carry out the plans of Peter the Great, to make Russia the greatest military power in Europe, and to extend his dominions into Asia.

Everything in his vast empire was made subservient to this imperial end. The Caucasus lay in his way, and he bent his energies to reduce it to subjection.

As this country has recently been brought to our notice as a former home of the Doukhobors, it may be in place to say that Georgia, Circassia, Mingrelia, Daghestan, Russian Armenia, Ehristan and Karaback are all included within its boundaries, and that the Caucasian Mountains run through it diagonally from the shores of the Caspian to those of the Black Sea. Since 1802 disaffected troops and political prisoners, to say nothing of thousands of dissenters from the Russian Church, have found their graves in its frontiers. One of the bravest defenders of that country was the Caucasian Prophet-chief Schamyl, who held the Russians at bay for twenty-five years; and when he surrendered, in 1859, he was pensioned by the Russian government. He afterwards lived at Kalooga on the Oka as an intimate friend of the imperial family, because of his personal attachment to the Tsar, who treated him so humanely.

The inhabitants are a mixture of many races, no less than seventy languages being spoken in Tiflis alone. Some of these tribes have been there from time immemorial, while others are thought to be the descendants of the crusaders. Their complexion and features are European, their dress and military equipments are mediæval rather than Asiatic, and though Russia nominally owns the country, with its

Schamyl,

The Circassian Chief and Prophet, 1797–1871.

mountain fastnesses and pastures and fruitful valleys, its inhabitants are only partially subdued, and they have long successfully resisted the invasion of their Slavonic neighbors.

Queen Victoria's estimate of Tsar Nicholas I., after his visit to her in 1844, is interesting and doubtless correct, viz.: "There is much about him that I cannot help liking, and I think his character is one that should be understood and looked upon for once as it is. He is stern, reserved, with strict principles, which nothing on earth can make him change. Very clever I do not think him, and his mind is not a cultivated one; his education has been neglected. He is not, I am sure, aware of the dreadful cases of individual misery that he often causes, for I can see by various instances that he is kept in ignorance of many things, although he thinks he is very just. His feelings are strong. He feels kindness deeply, and his love for his children, indeed for all children, is very great."

Alexander II. did not resemble his father in disposition, and it is said that his mildness was a great disappointment and annoyance to the Emperor Nicholas. He is described as a kind-hearted, liberal-minded man, although a despot. There was a great contrast between him and the stern, stiff, sergeant-major-like bearing of his father. Every inch of him bespoke the well-bred nobleman; very rich, very good-tempered, affectionate to his children, a man fond of a good dinner, of shooting, of hunting, and of making everybody comfortable—himself included.

During his reign a marvelous amount of reform was set on foot. The emancipation act of 1861 liberated fifty million serfs, at a cost to the government of $500,000,000. One expression in a manifesto that he issued to the people has a very different note from that characterizing the usual imperial *ukase*. "By the combined efforts of the government and the *people*, I hope," said he, "the public administration will be improved, and that justice and mercy will reign in the courts of law."

When Alexander II. came to his throne (1856), Russia had not recovered from the Crimean war—that most inexcusable international blunder and crime. The methods in vogue throughout the agricultural districts were primitive. There were only six hundred miles of railroad, and hardly any other roads worthy of the name over an enormous territory. "The Emperor applied himself at once to the peaceful work of reform, and carried it out with skill, tact, and, above all, with an ease which a foreign people is hardly able, at present, to appreciate." In twenty-five years a work was done in Russia which it has taken a century to accomplish in England. Every town of any size has now its railroad connections, and steamers ply upon the rivers, even of Siberia. Gladstone says of this monarch, after his assassination: "The sole labor of a devoted life was with the deceased sovereign to improve his inheritance for the benefit of his subjects and of mankind." He recognized the herculean task he had undertaken, for, in 1879, he said, in a speech: "We have great tasks yet before us. There is much more to be done which must wait until the existing passions are appeased. If I must die before such reforms are accomplished, I trust they will be carried out by my successor."

Had Alexander III. used the supreme moment which Providence placed in his hands, to promulgate the Constitution his father had signed and ordered to be published on the morrow;* if he had kept his first resolution to change nothing in this beneficent instrument of reform, saying to his minister, Loris-Melikov, "This shall be my father's bequest to his people," his name would have gone down to posterity with praise, and the cause of religious and civil freedom would have been advanced among his one hundred million subjects." How often in human history has the action of a moment seemed to decide the destiny of a nation! If one were disposed to be fatalistic such an event as this might tend to confirm the thought, but the law of human progress can-

* "I have just signed a paper, which I hope will produce a good impression upon Russia and show that I am ready to give her all that it is possible to give. To-morrow it will be published. I have given the order," were the words of Alexander II. to his new consort a few minutes before leaving the Winter Palace on the morning he was assassinated (Third month 13th, 1881).

not be violated forever or the demands of justice eternally ignored.

The Liberator was succeeded by the Persecutor. The Procurator of the Holy Synod, C. P. Pobiedonostzev, who had been tutor to the new Tsar, brought his influence to bear, and the Minister of the Interior received an order in the middle of the night countermanding the publication of the imperial document (Manifesto), upon which the new Tsar had previously written, "Very well done."

The condition of the Tsar's mind at this time is graphically set forth by a writer of the period: "He was as bewildered and helpless as a man suddenly aroused from a profound slumber by a murderous onslaught of robbers. His advisers could offer him no help. They hopelessly contradicted each other and themselves. The one asked for a constitution, another advocated *status quo;* his own brother pleaded for a speedy return to the iron rule of his grandfather Nicholas.

"The air was saturated with treason; the very palace was believed to harbor an imperial protector of assassins.

"The Emperor found himself face to face with an invisible power of darkness, with no one to stand between him and it, or to stretch out a helping hand. To crown all, he had no motive power within himself, no stimulus to action, no goal and no ideal.

"No one of his advisers rose to the level of the occasion, not one had faith in him, much less in his methods. It was under these conditions that his teacher, Pobiedonostzev, on being called to the Imperial presence, came prepared with a complete system of policy, a soothing religion, an inspiring faith and a glorious ideal.

"He played to perfection the part of Samuel to the Russian monarch. He proclaimed that everything had taken place in accordance with the inscrutable will of God, who had chosen the Tsar as His anointed servant to lead His favorite people out of the wilderness of sin and misery.

"The halcyon days of Nicholas I. were to be brought back under infinitely more favorable conditions. Religion was to be reinstated in her place, and the Lord was to be ruler in the land; in a word, God was God and the Tsar was His Prophet."

Count Ignatiev, otherwise called the "Father of Lies," became Minister of the Interior upon the accession of Alexander III., and such a chapter of Russianization began as was scarcely ever attempted before by any Tsar.

The Emperor never attended the council of his ministers, who were obliged to submit to him personally every measure they wished to enact.

He is not to be held entirely responsible for the persecutions permitted in Russia, as they generally originate with the Holy Synod.

"The people repose implicit confidence in the Tsar's wisdom and justice. He is absolute master of the life and property of every man within his dominions, and no exception may be taken to his orders. The occasional blunders he makes, however heavy they may be, must be borne with patience, as they can only be temporary. The Tsar will redress the evil as soon as he is informed on the matter."

"Russia for the Russians" became the imperial policy under Alexander III., and so he attempted to root out every foreign custom. The Finns first fell under this ban. These loyal, prosperous and contented subjects were subjected to the most humiliating denationalization.

"Their postal system, far superior to that of the Russian, was completely remodeled; Parliamentary privileges were rescinded, although the latter had been solemnly guaranteed to them by himself; the press in the principality was curtailed, and autonomy in the matter pertaining to customs duties abolished; indeed, the whole nation was treated as if they were rebels on the eve of an unsuccessful rising."

The Germans inhabiting the Baltic Provinces, Esthonia, Livonia and Courland, next received attention, because of the "most affectionate solicitude of the ruler of all the Russians." Their schools were limited, and the Russian language made obligatory in all of them; in short, liberalism and sectarianism were stamped out. The Poles were, perhaps, the chief victims of this pan-Slavism. Under the reigns of the Emperors Nicholas I. and Alexander II. they had been practically dispossessed of their property, and in many cases reduced to beggary. They were hanged by thousands, because of their faithfulness to their convictions.

A modern writer * sums up the domestic policy of Alexander III. thus: "Naturally a man of conservative instincts, and driven partly by circumstances, partly by irresponsibility, into illiberal and reactionary extremes, Alexander III. has for some time devoted himself to stamping out of Russia all non-Russian elements and setting up an image, before which all must fall down and worship, of a Russia, single, homogeneous, exclusive, self-sufficing, self-contained. Foreign names, foreign tongues, a foreign faith, particularly if the former are Teuton, and the latter is Lutheran, are vexed, or prohibited, or assailed. Foreign competition, commercial or otherwise, is crushed by heavy dead weights hung around its neck."

One of the most unwise acts of this sovereign was the suppression of education, that bulwark of progress. The common people were debarred the privilege of universities and gymnasia, and in many instances even of parish schools. "The Government," says E. B. Lanin, "is resolved to reduce the people to a condition of abject unreasoning slavishness, which will permit them to be dealt with like cattle. If the nation were as ready to dispose of its soul, or the remnant of its soul, at the beck of its one hundred thousand tsar-lets, the ideal of the Russian government might be considered realized. But be-

* George Curzon, in his work, "Russia in Central Asia."

tween them and this goal stand a few million *Raskolniks*, on whose victory or defeat depends the future of the Russian government."

The press was suppressed with even more virulence by this Tsar pan-Slavist, who considered the tendering of journalistic advice a menace to his imperial rights.

"There was silence in all languages from the Ural to the Prut," could as truly be said in his reign as in the reign of his grandfather, Nicholas I.

"The nation was virtually dumb, for it had no sort of parliamentary representation, and no press worth the name."—(Lowe.)

It is almost inconceivable that in the last decade of the nineteenth century such a benighted policy could be carried on by the most powerful monarch in Europe. "No epoch or country has ever yet offered so disgraceful a spectacle of systematic demoralization," is the testimony of one who knew whereof he wrote. Yet there were minds who could not be silenced, and there is scarcely a more heroic instance of true patriotism than that of Mary Tzebrikova, "after she resolved to address the Tsar on behalf of her fellow countrymen, in spite of every custom or law, which made such an act penal in the highest degree."

She was an accomplished lady in her fifty-fourth year, when she wrote to "his Majesty" as follows: "And after all, what is the use of all this oppression and persecution? Why should free speech be suppressed and public justice abolished?

"Is it for the sake of peaceful development, or is it for the sake of autocracy; that is, really for the advantage of the officials?

"Your Majesty's self is proved powerless to struggle against abuses, even if the court for judging of ministers should be really instituted. You are inevitably powerless, because all the imperial measures are founded upon the same slavery and enforced silence of society.

"Freedom of speech, personal security, freedom of meetings, full publicity of justice, education easy of access to all talents, suppression of administrative despotism, the convoking of a national assembly, for which all classes can choose their delegates—in these alone is our salvation."

She subscribed herself, after saying: "You are one of the most powerful monarchs in the world; and I am a working unit in the one hundred millions whose fate you hold in your hands; but none the less, I, in my conscience, fully recognize my moral right and duty as a Russian woman to say what I have said."

And what effect did such an appeal have upon Alexander III. After reading it, he simply exclaimed: "That is all very well, but what on the earth does all this matter to *her*?"

The letter was printed, however, and of course she

was duly exiled for two years to "a remote corner of the empire."

I have gone into some details concerning this period in order to place before the reader an adequate picture of the present conditions, both civil and social, which confront the dissenters, whether peace-loving or otherwise disposed, in this unhappy land.

The awful famine of 1890-'91 had brought twenty millions of the inhabitants to death's door, throughout a district three thousand miles long and from five hundred to one thousand miles wide. The general distress, added to the effort to root out all races and religions other than pure ones "of ancient and holy Russia," was enough to bring grief to the strongest and most hopeful.

We will not pass away, however, from this sad condition without first expressing a word of sympathy for this ill-advised ruler, who must have had a most unenviable life, haunted continually with fear of meeting the same horrible fate as that of his own father. Think of him standing out on the desolate steppe, surrounded by those who had been killed at his side; the car he and his family occupied being terribly wrecked, his wife trembling as she moved among the dead and dying, and his little girl with her arms about his neck, exclaiming, "Oh, papa, now they'll come and murder us all!" And surely the situation would not fail to draw from the most stolid a sigh of pity.

The Emperor died at Livadia on the first of Eleventh month, 1894, and was succeeded by his son, Nicholas II., as autocrat of all the Russias, whose name will go down to posterity inseparably connected with the greatest international event of the nineteenth century—the convening of the Peace Conference, at The Hague, during the summer of 1899.

This young ruler of one hundred million subjects seemed to give promise of a more enlightened policy than his father pursued, although he has been sadly handicapped by his ministers and his devotion to his father's memory. "As a child he was thoroughly conscientious, possessed of a wonderfully receptive mind, an excellent memory, sound judgment and great common sense."

His mother has much influence with him, and she took a great interest in his education. It was she who prevailed with him to grant the liberation of the Doukhobors.

He is most amiable in manner and generous in spirit, and if it were not for such advisers as Pobiedonostzev, doubtless his sorely persecuted subjects would receive greater evidence of these qualities.

He traveled around the world in 1890-'91, and narrowly escaped assassination in Japan. His marriage to Princess Alix, granddaughter of Queen Victoria, took place shortly after his father's death.

From these chapters we can see there is a dual system of government existing in Russia. The *Mir*, instituted for the exclusive benefit of the peasants, is founded upon custom, while the district and provincial assemblies, to which the volosts appoint delegates, represent written law and the higher classes.

The democratic instincts of the peasants continually come into conflict with the autocratic rule of these elective assemblies—to say nothing of the Executive Commission appointed by the Tsar to exercise an over-lordship—so we can easily account for the perpetual unrest which has perennially threatened the empire with revolution, apart from any religious dissent. And when we add to this the independent attitude of Christian faith, assumed by the Doukhobors, we can clearly see how nothing but persecution awaited them.

INDEX.

CPSIA information can be obtained
at www.ICGtesting.com
Printed in the USA
LVHW081425250319
611739LV00022B/751/P

9 781361 952962